THE PROBLEM OF JUSTICE

BRUCE G. MILLER

The Problem of Justice

Tradition and Law in the Coast Salish World

University of Nebraska Press

Lincoln and London

Acknowledgments for the use
of previously published material
appear on page xiv. Manufactured
in the United States of America ♾

LIBRARY OF CONGRESS CATALOGING IN PUBLICATION DATA
Miller, Bruce G., 1951–
The problem of justice : tradition and law in the Coast Salish world / Bruce G. Miller.
p. cm. – (Fourth world rising) Includes bibliographical references and index.
ISBN 0-8032-3221-7 (cl.: alk. paper) – ISBN 0-8032-8275-3 (pbk.: alk. paper)
1. Coast Salish Indians – Legal status, laws, etc. – Washington (State) 2. Coast Salish Indians – Legal status, law, etc. – British Columbia. 3. Indians of North America – Legal status, laws, etc. – Northwest, Pacific I. Titla. II. Series.
KFW505.5.C63 M55 2001 305.897′90795–dc21 2001027347

For Laraine, Cameron, and Alastair

CONTENTS

ILLUSTRATIONS

Series Editors' Introduction

The Problem of Justice is the second volume in Fourth World Rising, a new series of contemporary ethnographies from the University of Nebraska Press. The series focuses on contemporary issues, including class, gender, religion, and politics: in sum, it addresses social and cultural differentiation among and between native peoples as they confront those around them and each other in struggles for better lives, better futures, and better visions of their own pasts. This focus thus represents a departure from many of the monographs produced by anthropologists about native peoples, which often have sought to reproduce either visions of ways of life now long past or else pasts refracted through current idealization. In the process, traditional anthropology has helped enshrine a backward-looking focus to native culture that has, at times, been influential in the way laws are framed and even in how native peoples come to see their own identity.

Ideas, especially when enshrined in law and lent the authority of governments, have power. And the idea that native cultures and societies are historical artifacts rather than ongoing projects has served to narrow the politics of native identity or indigenism worldwide. One purpose of this series is to change this focus and broaden the conception of native struggle to match its current complexity.

This is especially important now, for the last two decades have provided prominent examples of native peoples seeking to recast the public—ultimately political—basis of their native identity in ways other than the reproduction of often fanciful, even fictional pasts. Our hope is that by offering a variety of texts focused on these and other contemporary issues, structured for classroom use and a general audience, we can help change the public perception of native struggle—allowing people to see that native cultures and societies are very much ongoing (and to a surprising extent on their own terms) and that the issues they confront carry important practical and theoretical implications for a more general understanding of cultural and political processes.

Series Editors' Introduction

The primary geographical and topical emphasis of the Fourth World Rising series is the native peoples of the Americas, but the series will also include comparative cases from Australia, Africa, Asia, the circumpolar Arctic and sub-Arctic, and the Pacific Islands. Yet beyond its unique topical and contemporary focus, four critical theoretical and political features distinguish the series as well:

1. A focus on the struggles native peoples must fight, with the dominant society and with each other, whether they wish to or not, in order to survive as peoples, as communities, and as individuals, as well as the struggles they choose to fight.

2. A consideration of how the intensifying inequalities within and between native communities—emerging from social, cultural, and economic differences among native peoples—create unavoidable antagonisms, so that there cannot be any simple lines of cleavage between a dominant, oppressive, and exploitative state on the one side and its long-suffering victims on the other. Thus the series pays particular attention to gender, identity, religion, age, and class divisions among native peoples, along with differences in the goals and strategies that emerge from these struggles.

An emphasis on internal differences and tensions among native peoples is not at all intended to let the dominant states and societies off the hook for their policies and practices. Rather, this perspective calls to the foreground how internal complexities and divisions among native peoples and communities shape their struggles within and against the larger societies in which they find themselves. Indeed, it is precisely these internal differences among and between native peoples (and how these differences unfold over time and through native peoples' complex relations to one another) that give native people their own history and their own social processes that are, ultimately, partly separate from the history imposed upon them by the dominant society.

3. An emphasis on the praxis of native struggles: what works, and why, and with what intended and unintended effects; who benefits within native communities and who loses what, and why. The series monographs are thus not advocacy tracts in the conventional sense of that term, though they are undeniably political constructs. Rather, the emphasis on contemporary social processes and the political praxis of participants, advocates, and anthropologists serves as a stimulus for dialogue and debate about the changing pressures and possibilities for

particular native societies and the political situations confronting native peoples more generally.

4. An attempt to clarify the situation facing those whose concerns and fundamentally decent impulses lead them to want to help the victims of domination and exploitation. Such honorable commitments need to be developed in the midst of realizing that the radiant innocence of an earlier applied anthropology, and of many aid programs, along with the social world that sustained this innocence, has crumbled. It is no longer possible to say or to think "*we* will help *them*." Now we must ask who is helped and who is hurt both by the success and by the frequent failure of aid programs, and why, and how.

The primary audience for this series is students in college courses in anthropology, political science, native and ethnic studies, economics, and sociology. Yet the series achieves its importance among a college and popular audience by being developed for a second audience as well. One of the major purposes of this series is to present case studies of native peoples' current struggles that have broader strategic relevance to those engaged in similar or complementary struggles, and to advocates whose concerns lie more directly along the lines of what has worked in the past or in other areas, what has not, and with what consequences.

Hence this volume becomes part of a new way of both doing and teaching anthropology and native studies. On one level, the case studies seek to bring together activists, native peoples, and academics, not simply by dramatizing the immediacy of native struggles, but also by dispelling the notion that native societies derive their nativeness from being internally homogeneous and externally timeless. On a second level, the series as a whole helps those currently teaching native studies to pursue an engaged, contemporary perspective and a broad geographic approach—allowing for and in fact encouraging a global, contemporary native studies that is deeply rooted both in a fundamental caring for native peoples' well-being and in the realities of internal differentiation among native peoples.

Gerald Sider
Kirk Dombrowski

Acknowledgments

Many people, members of American Indian communities and Canadian First Nations as well as academics and lay people, have provided their help, support, and ideas for this book. My sincere thanks go to all of these people, in particular those elders and community culture experts who shared their knowledge. I wish to give special thanks to several people whose contributions have been invaluable over several years. Thanks to Chief Frank Malloway (S'íyemches) of Yakweakwioose for his kind nature, his gift of wisdom and knowledge, and his support of all of the University of British Columbia graduate students who have had the wonderful fortune to live for a while in his winter ceremonial house. To Mary Malloway (Qwe'tosel'wet), my thanks for her hospitality and warmth. I wish to acknowledge and thank Sonny McHalsie (Naxetsi), Stó:lō culture adviser and my traveling companion to Papua New Guinea, whose respect for his own people's teachings caused him, literally, to give the last of his clothing to the Maisin people. Thanks to Doreen Maloney, Upper Skagit, for her thoroughgoing knowledge of contemporary tribal politics and law and her clear vision for the future. I thank Clarence "Kat" Pennier (X̲a:yslem tel) for his consistent support for establishing and building a reciprocal relationship between the Stó:lō Nation and University of British Columbia students and faculty. My thanks to Stó:lō Nation historian Keith Carlson for his tremendous energy, new thoughts about indigenous history, and willingness to share ideas. Cindy McMullen and Jane McMillen, University of British Columbia graduate students, helped in the process of interviewing and provided wonderful insights in talking through what we were learning. My colleagues at the University of British Columbia and at other universities, among them Julie Cruikshank, John Barker, Michael Kew, Charles Menzies, the late Marjorie Halpin, Blanca Muratorio, Dan Boxberger, Crisca Bierwert, Jo-Anne Fiske, and Dara Culhane, have all shared stimulating ideas. In addition, I thank series editors Gerald Sider and Kirk Dombrowski for their helpful comments. I must add that all errors in fact and interpretation are my own.

Portions of chapter 3 have appeared in slightly different form as "The Individual, the Collective and Tribal Code" and "Contemporary Tribal Codes and Gender Issues." The articles are reprinted from the *American Indian Culture and Research Journal*, volume 21, number 1, and volume 18, number 2, respectively, by permission of the American Indian Studies Center, UCLA, copyright (c) Regents of the University of California. I wish to thank the editor, Duane Champagne, for his help with those earlier publications and the journal for permission to reprint here. Brian Thom is the cartographer for the three maps. The photographs of Chief Frank Malloway and the Coqualeetza Longhouse are by Laraine Michalson; Michelle Robbins photographed the Upper Skagit Tribal Court; and Ann Mohs took the photograph of the Stó:lō tribal officials. Thanks to Stó:lō Nation archivist David Smith for the Stó:lō photos. The University of British Columbia provided UBC-HSS research funding to help carry out portions of this work, as did the Melville Jacobs Fund of the Whatcom Museum, Bellingham, Washington.

THE PROBLEM OF JUSTICE

Introduction

The coastal and riverine areas of Puget Sound in Washington State, southern Vancouver Island in British Columbia, and the adjacent Fraser River valley are spectacularly beautiful and abundant in resources. Snow-capped mountains, including the majestic 14,400-foot-high Mt. Rainier, tower over river valleys that are home to deer, elk, bear, and many other species. Salmon return annually in the millions to spawn in the rivers of their origin, attracting predators such as seals in the saltwater and bald eagles and coyotes along the rivers. Migratory birds in great numbers pass through these lands, eating the various species of berries that grow seemingly everywhere. There are other foods readily available as well: shellfish such as clams, oysters, and geoducks and vegetation such as tiger lily and camas, a root crop once harvested in great amounts. Huge cedar and Douglas fir trees over two hundred feet high still exist here and once dominated the landscape, making overland travel difficult and canoe travel the preferred mode in the nineteenth century for indigenous people and settlers alike. After massive mile-high glaciers receded to the mountaintops more than ten millennia ago, indigenous peoples occupied the area. Over the last nine thousand years, they gradually learned to make intensive use of these resources, building large houses in favored, protected locations along the rivers and ocean front. They moved seasonally through the varied, complex landscape to harvest diverse resources in the alpine meadows of the mountains, on the saltwater, in the forests, and on the islands. Through a pattern of marriage beyond the kin group, individuals and families developed a wide network of relatives and friends, giving access to resources in several ecological zones. People in one now vanished Coast Salish village, Sosotia, near present-day Mount Vernon, Washington, for example, could harvest migratory birds with nets, catch fish gathering along a naturally occurring logjam in the Skagit River, harvest shellfish on the nearby saltwater, and hunt deer in the foothills and mountain goats in the adjacent Cascade Mountains. They could trade with neighboring communities for items they could not obtain locally or simply for the sake of variety and maintaining good relationships.

However, rich resources attract attention from outsiders and, potentially, create problems internally, and the Coast Salish people in the period before contact with white traders and colonizers faced the problem of controlling access to their resources while ensuring that all community members were provisioned. Unlike many areas of indigenous North America, important productive resource stations in this region were not open to all comers; in common with other peoples of the Northwest Coast, only those who could establish kin ties were given access. In addition, high-status members of communities exercised control over access even among kin, restricting lower-ranked people (commoners and slaves) in some instances to the use of fishing weirs in times when higher-ranked people were not using them. These elite, the upper class, acted to ensure the viability and sustainability of the resource stations, such as shellfishing beaches, and could close the stations to all use. Non-kin were kept away from the resource stations, with the exception of less valuable resources available to those passing through. Food was stored in wood boxes and in the rafters of houses and was stockpiled for distribution at large intervillage giveaways, known today as *potlatches*. These accumulated items, together with manufactured prestige goods, such as canoes, boxes, masks, and blankets, helped community elite fulfill their ceremonial and ritual obligations to kin and permitted them to gain stature and significance among the larger community of Coast Salish people, even beyond their kinfolk.

In the period before contact, all of this production, maintenance, defense, and distribution of valuables was carried out without the presence of armies, police, jails, judges, or even formal political positions. Disputes and conflicts between family members, between families, between communities of Coast Salish, and between people from more than one indigenous nation were resolved, or in some cases failed to be resolved, within a Coast Salish set of practices and concepts. Not all people viewed these practices and concepts the same way, however, and teachings about how to behave varied between families, as they do today. Nor did all people have access to all of the content of Coast Salish culture; there was, and is, differentiation between people along the dimensions of social class, personal status, the nature and power of one's spirit helper, private knowledge of spiritual practice and magic, and, simply, personal experience and capacity. The resolution of conflict and of disputes required that these differences be negotiated.

Although the first sustained contacts with white explorers occurred in the late eighteenth century, and with traders in the early nineteenth century, it was not until the middle and late nineteenth century that non-indigenous settlement in Coast Salish areas began in earnest. Agricultural settlement and logging, milling, and mining brought efforts to dispossess indigenous people from the land and to enclose them on small reserved parcels of land, where they could be effectively monitored by agents of the federal government, regulated, and, in theory, missionized and eventually assimilated. Cut off from access to many of the resources that would have enabled them to continue in their previous economic patterns and restrained from equal participation in the emerging economy, they were likewise gradually cut off from administering their own practices of justice and self-regulation of community life. Coast Salish communities were introduced to new institutions of regulation, including police (initially, appointed members of the communities themselves), judges, courts, and other trappings of Western politics and jurisprudence. Over time, significant social changes arose in the communities, with new sources of wage labor and, consequently, wealth and influence available to some, but not others. New religious practices were introduced or arose locally, particularly Catholicism, several sects of Protestantism, and the Indian Shaker Church, a merger of indigenous concepts with Christianity. All of these changes in wealth, income, and religion produced new sorts of differentiation, and fractures arose among community members. Rapid oscillations in federal policy and practice further exacerbated differences while older, precontact disputes and problems in social relations remained.

In the late twentieth and early twenty-first centuries opportunities rose to once again self-administer justice, although in diverse forms. In British Columbia, Canada, impetus for tentative experiments in diverting a limited portion of the administration of justice to tribes has arisen as a result of three factors: a widespread recognition of the failure of mainstream courts to appropriately administer justice to indigenous people, the press by British Columbian tribes without treaties, which are eager to enhance self-government, and a society-wide interest in restorative justice, which allows the offender to acknowledge the harm done and to repair relations with the victim and be reintegrated into the community (see Galaway and Hudson 1996; Hazelhurst 1995). In the United States, the development follows from a political and legal recognition of tribal sovereignty and from the practical necessity for Puget Sound tribes to manage and adjudicate their share of the salmon fishery. A tribal councilor from a Washington State tribe, Upper Skagit, described the development in her community this way during a meeting between representatives of the Upper Skagit Council and the Stó:lō Nation:

> In 1976 after the Boldt decision [court decision upholding tribal rights to salmon harvests] the government had an obligation to have all of the components—we needed a forum for adjudication. First we set up the misdemeanor/criminal system under the enabling documents. It's different than the federal system. . . . The tribe's constitution [provides for] a General Council and Tribal Council—there's no executive branch to set up the court. It's adopted by ordinance—the trial court and appeals mechanisms. It gave power to review—total review authority—to the court. It's outside of the U.S. constitution. There are boundaries to our jurisdiction, but federal law [concerning this] changes regularly.
>
> Criminal jurisdiction is determined by who are the victims, the criminals, the crime and the location—an easy sort. For non-natives there is no jurisdiction. For natives, the council has determined to prosecute natives, even Canadian. We prosecute U.S. Indians if the crime is here. For off-reservation crime, the County has jurisdiction. Major crimes go to the federal system, but if there is a failure of the Feds to act, we can jump in and grab the crime. The limits are $5,000 [fine] and one year [incarceration]. We can pick up jurisdiction if the Feds don't prosecute. We have safeguards in code—we can process cases within the spirit of tribal law as long as due process exists. Courts can make up court rules as they go—and can use state law (Doreen Maloney, notes taken by author, 16 September 1998).

Today, tribal court is held at the Upper Skagit community building on their small, rural reservation. The two-story building is the first thing visible from the winding road leading to the reservation, standing next to a tribal health clinic, education building, and small industrial building. Inside is a general-purpose room—for elders' lunches, informal gatherings, and tribal annual general meetings. The tribal business office is upstairs, and several administrative offices are downstairs. The downstairs common space is furnished with a dozen tables and surrounding chairs and with tokens of tribal culture, including a two-hundred-pound spirit rock petrogylph with a carving of a human-like face and a small totem pole. A display case contains gambling sticks, photographs, and copies of publications about the tribe. Announcements are arrayed on a bulletin board, telling of jobs, the opening of the fisheries, tribal meetings, pow-wows, and health concerns. The tribal court itself is at one end of the first floor, inside tribal council chambers. On the door to this room is a sign informing viewers not to enter council chambers. This small room, about twenty feet square, contains somewhat more expensive and formal tables and chairs than in the common space, and a microphone. Historic photographs depict military veterans, racing canoes, large gatherings from the beginning of the twentieth century, and families poling their canoes up the Skagit River. Here, a tribally appointed prosecutor and judge hold monthly court, joined by defendants, witnesses, police, and onlookers.

The Coast Salish commuities of Washington State and the province of British Columbia have undertaken several justice initiatives over the last twenty-five years. Although all employ concepts and practices that derive from the past and that are held to be traditional, they are remarkably dissimilar. What is most notable is the variation in the aspirations for these justice systems, in their fundamental claims about the nature and primacy of "traditional life," and in the role of elders. All the communities face significant difficulties in reestablishing internal control over the practices of justice and in thereby regulating their own membership. There are significant problems concerning the degree to which what is called *traditional practice* can be brought into the present and, perhaps more fundamentally, concerning what traditional law and practice might have been. Additionally, the "problem of justice," referenced in the title, is also one of resolving the pressures and difficulties imposed on indigenous communities by the dominant American and Canadian societies. Indigenous communities in some cases have responded by a conscious rejection of mainstream values and practices and by framing the discussion of their own indigenous practices in reaction to the mainstream, thereby distorting their own legacy by emphasizing harmony and deemphasizing problems. In particular, I argue, claims to the sacred nature of justice practices and to primordialist discourses that uncritically incorporate concepts of healing, restoration, and el-

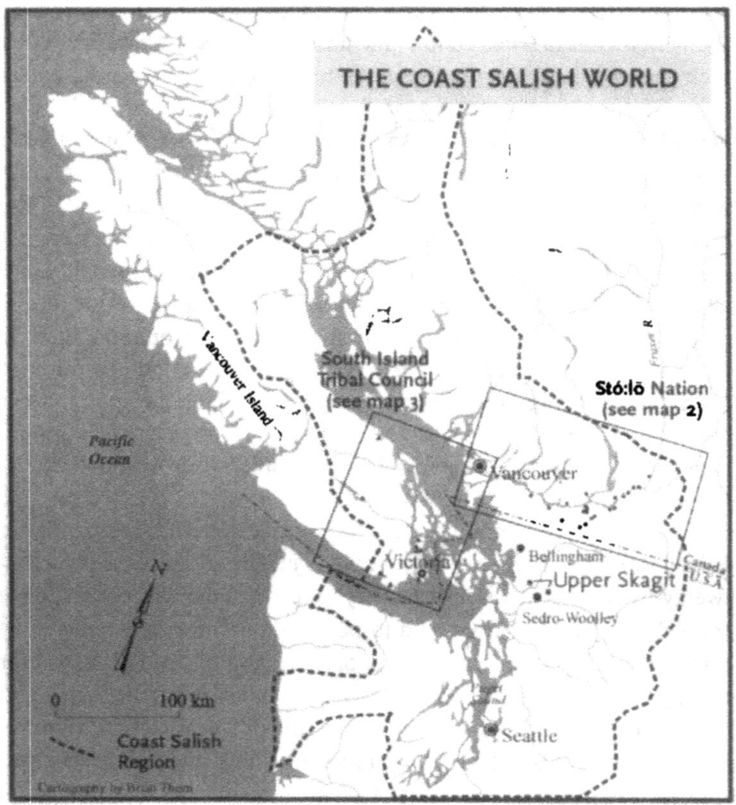

derhood without due regard for the relations of power between the various segments of the community potentially undermine the capacity of tribal governance to recognize diversity and community members' sense of fair, just participation in their own governance. Coast Salish communities have historically used measures to restore community order that included sanctioned violent recriminations in addition to more pacifistic methods of feasting together with others to end disputes and difficulties. Today, in common with other communities, the Coast Salish communities face difficult problems in treating the contemporary issues of violent crime and interfamily conflict. These issues are not easily resolved by reference to reconciliation and restoration or by emphasis on community harmony.

In the broadest terms, this book is a look at the circumstances indigenous communities face in the process of reinvigorating their own local justice. To do this, I consider the intellectual and practical problems in understanding prior justice practices and the historical transformations in communities and the approaches to justice that have led to the present. I examine three of these community projects and contrast the ways in which they have developed in order to explore how justice and tradition are understood and how narratives about them are employed. These three programs are the tribal court system of the Upper Skagit of western Washington State, the justice initiatives of the Stó:lō Nation of the lower mainland of British Columbia, and the now discontinued South Island Justice Project (SIJP) of the bands of Vancouver Island, British Columbia.

The three communities are not merely linked by an abstract participation in a language community; they are members of a broader network of social relations with considerable time depth (Suttles 1963, 1990:473). People from each of the three communities marry and have relatives in the other locations. Ritual relations such as Winter Spirit Dancing (Syowen) and Shaker services include members of each community, and there is mutual participation in summer Coast Salish festivals built around war canoe racing, sports, princess contests, and gambling (Dewhirst 1976; but see Bierwert 1999:184 for a consideration of differences between communities). These intimate connections predate the formation of "tribes," which arose as a consequence of colonial domination, and although I refer here to distinct tribal and band entities, the immediate precontact and postcontact reality was of a dense network of complex relations (Miller and Boxberger 1994; Harmon 1998). Each settlement, longhouse, and family had its own distinct set of relations, which was somewhat different from those of the other villages that now compose their present-day tribe or band (see Sider 1993 for a discussion of similar processes of change in the Southeast).

The oldest of the three justice programs, the Upper Skagit Court, was established following a landmark legal decision, *U.S. v. Washington*, 1974, in which the tribe, and other tribes in western Washington, regained access to the salmon harvest as specified under the terms of western Washington treaties signed in 1854–56. The ruling created the need for a venue in which to try fishing violations in order that the tribe could manage its own fishing interests along with the state and the federal government. The tribe has acted on their legal jurisdiction under U.S. law by gradually expanding the repertoire beyond resource regulation, and now its jurisdiction includes zoning, felony, and other legal issues within the system. The activities of the tribal justice system, including the court session, are today carried out almost exclusively on the reservation. The tribe employs its own judge and court officials, a circumstance that has arisen after several years of sharing resources with other local tribes within a legal services consortium. Tribal members and tribal employees have developed and fine-tuned tribal codes in order to both manage their relations with the outside and regulate activities within their own territories.

A defining feature of the administration of justice is the process of "sorting out" in which court officials examine community problems brought to them and provide a range of options to resolve the conflicts. This process appears to diminish the problem of the translation of disputes into legally definable cases that plagues local-level courts in the mainstream society and that appears to deny justice. This process has the effect, optimally, of providing a timely resolution to resolvable problems and allowing disputants to employ processes and seek remedies from within the repertoire of culturally sanctioned traditions, or, alternatively, it provides the structure for disputants who seek to redefine themselves and their adversaries as litigants within a formal, adversarial system (Doreen Maloney, interview). The Upper Skagit justice program emerged at the level of tribal government within the overview of the tribal membership as a whole.

The South [Vancouver] Island Justice Project emerged out of an effort in the 1980s to educate mainstream legal personnel about Coast Salish practices and concepts and became, in addition, a diversionary justice project in which cases could be treated by Coast Salish peoples themselves. The limitations to the program were several: cases had to come through the mainstream court, which maintained jurisdiction; all parties had to agree to the diversion; and penalties and sanctions were limited. The defining characteristics were the separation between band elective government and the band elders who drove the program and the highly ideological effort to generate normative "tribal law" as a collaborative effort between elders. This attempt dehistoricized Coast Salish oral traditions by presenting a collection of cultural teachings that did not easily allow shaping into practical application in the current world. Warry draws a distinction between "customary processes, rules or penalties" and "traditional law which is a system of values embedded in social relationships, rather than a domain separate and discrete unto itself" (1998:176). The codification effort of these elders fell awkwardly somewhere in between customary process and traditional law, as Warry defined them. The unworkable system collapsed, in part, under the weight of critique from those living in urban settings who found the interpretation of tradition to be self-serving and self-protective and, consequently, found women and children without protection.

The Stó:lō Nation justice initiatives arose in the 1990s out of three primary motivations: to create a justice program that could be put into place following treaty negotiations with the province and federal governments and thereby assert Stó:lō rights and title, to implement Stó:lō cultural practices as they pertain to justice, and to begin a process of restoring communities to a state of health, viewed holistically. Initial efforts included a study of Stó:lō people in incarceration, the creation of a House of Elders and a House of Justice to serve as advisers in the process, and a search for appropriate, interim, diversionary practices that could benefit members and families. This involved a small-scale application of a widely popularized and diffused New Zealand Maori family counseling model (Warry 1998). In addition, as the Stó:lō Nation took over service delivery, including educational, child welfare, and health services, efforts were made to incorporate current Stó:lō concepts of justice. In 1999, an effort was made to consider how to create codes for a tribal system that would integrate Stó:lō cultural concepts.

From an analytic perspective, an advantage to examining these cases lies in the fact that the three communities have somewhat different contact histories and have been subject to different regimes of public policy. In general, there are important comparisons to be made between the indigenous peoples of Canada, known as First Nations, a name which emphasizes claims to first inhabitation and the status as nations equal to federal and provincial governments, and American Indian tribes. Many indigenous nations are divided artificially by the international border, as the Coast Salish are, and American and Canadian public policies are both linked and divergent at the provincial/state levels and at the national levels. Early civil and criminal law in the colony of British Columbia, for example, relied on imported code from Washington State, and Canadian public policy frequently borrows from American developments. Nonetheless, there are significant differences. The international border divides the Coast Salish world, and the most significant specific outcome for this study is that the Upper Skagit (Washington State) tribal justice system has significant civil and criminal jurisdiction (see B. Miller 1996–97 for a more detailed treatment of the implications of the boundary). The two Canadian justice initiatives have arisen without similar jurisdiction and are simply efforts at diversionary programs closely tied to the federal ministry of justice. The justice systems, of necessity, address a variety of approaches and issues, but this variation in jurisdiction helps focus the issues. These comparisons, then, reveal conditions under which particular responses emerge.

In addition, the extant literatures concerning the indigenous peoples of the Americas north of Mexico have long been divided, for intellectual as well as practical reasons, into "culture areas," contiguous regions comprised of various peoples thought to have more in common with each other than with the others neighboring them (see Suttles 1990 for a discussion of this approach). In this scheme, the Coast Salish peoples, mutual speakers of a set of related languages, are described as members of the "Northwest Coast," which is generally defined as the long, narrow region bounded in the south by Mt. Shasta in northern California, in the west by the Pacific Ocean, in the north by the Aleutian Islands, and in the east by the Cascade and Coastal Mountains. But here, too, an unfortunate fissure occurs, and the academic and popular literatures concerning both the Northwest Coast and the constituent subunit, the Coast Salish, are ordinarily divided by the international boundary, with insufficient overlap between both the literatures and the authors producing them. This work, then, is an effort to pull together, on one dimension, the discussion of both American and Canadian sides of the Coast Salish world.

More significantly, much of the literature on indigenous justice in the English-speaking world is in the form of case studies that are largely ungeneralizable, or are summarized into culturally and historically generic form, or promote untenable and misleading dichotomous analyses of evil Western systems and their opposite, holistic, spiritual, indigenous ones. In one such binary analysis, for example, indigenous law is characterized as "horizontal," a spiritual, holistic, harmonious way of life aimed toward community restoration, while Western justice is "vertical" and hierarchical (Melton 1995:126–28; see Griffiths and

Belleau 1995:172–73 for a Canadian example of such binary analyses, and Victor 1999 for a consideration of these issues among the Stó:lō). Such analyses misrepresent the Western legal traditions in omitting the various processes of reconciliation, adjudication, and restoration that have always been part of mainstream justice in focusing on the punitive feature and omit the punitive features of indigenous justice, including the sanctioning of death sentences, violent reprisal, and ostracism, in favor of more benevolent features. In addition, indigenous cultures are reduced to a list of traits that oversimplify, infantilize, and promote rigid and doctrinaire solutions to complex issues (see LaRocque 1997:77).

My argument, in brief, is this: the processes of internal differentiation that existed prior to contact have long been exploited by colonial authorities and have since become explosively divisive within indigenous communities. These differences have spawned a great variety of views concerning justice and reflect a new set of power relations within the communities themselves (see McDonell 1995; Fitzpatrick 1992; Monture-Angus 1995; Clairmont 1998 concerning internal differentiation). Despite this, contemporary justice narratives from within the communities are largely outward looking in that they are primarily directed to managing relations with the dominant society and focus conservatively on a purported period of harmony prior to contact and the establishment of treaties and reservations. As a consequence, they fail to adequately describe and analyze historical or contemporary issues of power, a step that appears necessary for the establishment of meaningful, localized, community-based justice practices. Politically progressive movements aiming at removing indigenous communities from the domination of the state rely on radically conservative representations of their own society and culture, representations themselves built on misleading binary oppositions with white society. I argue, further, that unless justice is practiced within a freestanding system associated with real civil and criminal control over community residents and over real tribal assets and resources, one can expect the discourses to continue to be outwardly directed and inadequate to the task of actually regulating local society. In addition, my argument is that because tribes have assumed the mantle of nations, justice cannot be confined to concepts of the resolution of interpersonal and interfamilial conflict. Instead, tribal justice must incorporate its members' critiques of the "state," in this case the tribe, in the process of revision of tribal public policy. In effect, I am arguing for a more extensive sense of sovereignty, for sovereignty broad enough to allow not only internal critique but also diversity and change in the understanding and practice of culture. If law represents, on one hand, a means whereby rules and values of a society are applied and reinforced, law also "represents where rules and values are challenged and new ways of understanding may emerge" (Asch 1997:ix).

The comparisons between these three cases suggest that it is a dialectical process, an interchange between abstractions of past practice and specifics of current disputes, rather than simply the contemplation of past practices, that enable tribal justice institutions to become effective and acceptable to community members.

To make my argument I advance a somewhat different notion of aboriginal (prior) justice than is present in the ethnographic studies concerning the Coast Salish, none of which have focused on justice per se and which are poorly developed in this regard. I place more weight on local concepts and practices of place and power and on social hierarchy than earlier, more normative and descriptive studies. In addition, I diverge from those justice studies concerning indigenous peoples that treat power unproblematically, place culture outside a historical framework, and advance romanticized notions of Edenic indigenous communities. One widely read observer, for example, holds that somehow there might be a kind of healing-based justice program in which no one gains power over others (Ross 1996:205; see also Krawll 1994; Leresche 1993). The observer dismisses women's fears of abuse under self-government and community-run justice programs by arguing for a hierarchy-free society, thereby confusing the problem with a purported resolution of the problem (Laresche 1993:55). One U.S. tribal justice system is said to be based on tribal common law that is "not the product of hierarchies of power" and arises from a notion of law based by the sharing of normative values among all members of society (Yazzie and Zion 1996:161–62). These dated approaches, in their emphasis on the repetitive reproduction of culture, are remarkably free of people and of agency. In their focus on how systems work rather than how people engage justice, they reflect a conception of society that predates Malinowski's seminal work on law in the Trobriand Islands (1926) (see Moore 1999:102).

A more useful approach has been developed by Nader (1990, 1999) and others who have advanced the idea that indigenous ideologies of law, especially what Nader refers to as "harmony ideologies" or "coercive harmony," have been shaped by the colonial encounter, and that they reflect and mask the internal struggles that arose as a consequence. In this argument, communities are said to manage their relations with the outside world by emphasizing a purportedly cooperative, harmonious past and deemphasizing social conflict and contradiction in the present. Such an ideology dehistoricizes the processes of justice, in particular overlooking influences arising from the difficult experiences of colonization. In addition, harmony ideologies support elite control of present-day communities. Nader wrote that the "harmony ideology in [Zapotec of Mexico] today is both a product of nearly 500 years of colonial encounter and a strategy for resisting the state's political and cultural hegemony" (1990:2). Further, "the harmony model of law and associated ideologies are used to restrict the encroachment of external, superordinate power and are components of a political ideology that is counter-hegemonic" (307). By this, she means that it provides a way to reframe the debate about how justice might be practiced in indigenous communities, moving it away from Western legal concepts and toward concepts that presumably could only be derived and controlled locally. However, if this is the case, the question remains: what are the internal and external effects of such an ideology? Rose, for example, observed that harmony ideologies among the Swazi (emphasizing unity, consensus, cooperation, compliance, passivity, and docility) have been employed differently by various segments of society. The traditional elite legitimate their administrative roles and land tenure systems; the new elite justify their administrative and class positions; both elite justify control; and commoners employ strategic references to harmony in court to resist control (cited in Nader 1990:296).

Nader's recent work reveals a range of difficulties resulting from the naturalization of harmony ideology within indigenous communities. In a penetrating analysis, Nader argues that the Alternative Dispute Resolution Movement (ADR), a movement that arose in legal circles in the United States in the 1970s to find ways to employ venues for cases other than the courts themselves, was promoted by Chief Justice Warren Burger at the same time that indigenous communities, civil rights activities, and activists in the women's movement began to achieve victories in litigation. "Thus, as Indian activists searched for tradition and Pan-Indian themes such as consensus and decision-making through mediation, the U.S. government was launching a movement to get the 'garbage cases' [which were also expensive and time consuming] out of courts and into alternative modes of dispute resolution. Idealized images were fed by both parties—the federal government and Native people" (Nader and Ou 1998:17; see also Haberfeld and Townsend 1993; Barsh and Henderson 1980). Later, in the 1990s, federal negotiators played on idealized images of harmonious indigenous legal systems as a strategy by government and industry to coerce communities into accepting radioactive waste sites on their reservations. Community leaders were compelled to treat tribal legal processes as vehicles for consensus, cooperation, and compliance, even though the best interests of the tribe may have been served by reaching no agreement with the government negotiators or refusing to negotiate in the first place. In this analysis, ADR was but the latest imported legal ideology used by the state to maintain control over indigenous communities (Barsh and Henderson 1980).

Abel (1981) found "informal justice" practices to convey the image of equality and approachability, solicitude and concern, while removing the rights of the powerless to bring suit against the state. Informal justice is said to channel conflict into conservative forms, and by defining the locus of conflict as local, it distracts attention from conflict that could potentially produce change favoring the powerless. In addition, the disadvantaged are rendered more accessible to the state. The inability of alternative dispute resolution programs, including those aimed at restorative justice, to adequately address underlying social contradictions that generate social conflict is of interest here (see Minor and Morrison 1996). In the discussion of British Columbian affairs that follows, one can see a parallel with efforts of the federal justice ministry to import a version of ADR into indigenous communities that might otherwise push for the development of freestanding, community-controlled justice systems.

There are yet other problems associated with the current legal ideologies and discourses. The contemporary justice narratives I consider here reflect the well-documented problems that have resulted from the codification of indigenous concepts worldwide, particularly those recorded by colonial authorities as part of the administration of indigenous peoples. Indigenous justice practices, once unwritten and flexible, are thought to become rigid and unyielding (although codified law is not inflexible, as the Upper Skagit case shows). In addition, because cultural understandings are not shared uniformly, codified law is thought to advantage particular viewpoints and particular sectors of society. Keesing gave a particularly powerful rendering of the problems and possibilities of codification, even when carried out by the communities themselves, concerning the Kwaio of the Solomon Islands. There, he wrote, "Kastomu—as 'culture' externalized, idealized, hypostatized, reified, fetishized—acquires a symbolic power that transcends its contents" (1992:196).

But there is a further problem. Codification of folk law is but one corner of the larger problem of the systematic simplification of images of culture and society of the sort that Nader (1999) references and Povinelli (1993:126) calls "cultural editing." Such simplification is both historically imposed on indigenous peoples and now self-imposed as part of the process of "de-colonization" and the reframing of the relationship with the state. This is not a new circumstance: Harmon (1995) found this process of simplification of Coast Salish society to have begun early on in the period after contact. In the effort to find common ground with newcomers, indigenous people had to "present their complex webs of social relations in simplified form" (Harmon, cited in J. Miller 1999:38) and leave out their traditional beliefs entirely.

In the years before the Second World War, it was sufficient for colonial administrators to create an image of the legal and political practices of the indigenous other to allow convenient, cost-saving vestiges of self-government. In European-controlled sections of Africa and Asia, the practice of indirect rule led to massive efforts to record the folk law of local peoples, producing volumes of "customary law." Customary law has been characterized as an element in the process of internal pacification and as a tool developed by local indigenous elite and colonizers to control resources. This process disguised the expanding coercive and centralizing dominance of the state (Gordon 1989:386; Renteln and Dundes 1994:xv; Havemann 1988; McDonnell 1992; Merry 1991; Glenn 1997). However, in North America, little effort was made to promote indirect rule or self-government until well into the twentieth century. As a consequence, there have been limited reliance on indigenous law in the United States or Canada, few efforts to document local practices, and little study of court records to reveal the presence of any features of indigenous law. There are exceptions to these generalizations, however, and indigenous concepts have entered into American and Canadian mainstream courts, although largely limited to family and estate law (Morse 1988; Renteln 1994:870; Zlotkin 1984; Grant 1982). But now, in British Columbia, the media and the larger public participate in political debates concerning the creation of treaties and associated forms of self-government, and representations need to be ever more concise and comprehensible. These self-representations take the form of narratives that obscure the complexity of social relations in order to advance a "sound byte" image of self-governance plausible enough to develop or consolidate political support for treaties. A current example is the discussion of relations between the chiefs of the clan Houses, the constituent kinship groups that collectively comprise the nation, employed by the Nisga'a Nation in northern British Columbia prior to concluding treaty negotiations and ratification in 2000 (Nisga'a Treaty Negotiations 1996).

My concern is not simply that the current narratives reduce the complexity of aboriginal life. Because these have become public, and sometimes legal, representations, an even greater concern is that communities will be stuck with these in later years when the political issues have shifted and new representations are needed. One can easily see the political terrain in the Coast Salish world. In Puget Sound, where treaties are now nearly a century and a half old, the political focus is not simply on dragging the mainstream society into making equitable arrangements with indigenous peoples but, instead, on living up to ones that already exist. Frequently, this requires documenting the continual presence of indigenous peoples on the landscape so that claims can be made to territory and use rights. In effect, tribes must argue "We were here at the time of the treaty carrying out our activities, so let us continue." In British Columbia, on the other hand, a concerted effort has been made to document the deprivation of indigenous peoples, in the effort to explain to the public that indigenous people are still here and why they are in their current situation. The Stó:lō Nation publication *You Are Asked to Witness* (Carlson 1997b), for example, contains not one but five pictures of smallpox victims in making its visual argument for the impact of disease on Stó:lō society in the eighteenth and nineteenth centuries. One might suspect that, with time, the issues in British Columbia will clearly switch from documenting depopulation and loss to focusing squarely on documenting population continuity, use, and political cohesion.

As I show later, the legal issues facing British Columbian tribes and requiring documentation and the creation of legal "facts" continue to change rapidly. In truth, one can hardly imagine what political issues will emerge, but it is equally difficult to imagine that self-representations of the present will adequately bear the weight of the future.

Motives and Methods and the Anthropology of Indigenous Justice

My own reasons for engaging the issues I have raised here arise from the current direction of anthropology and related disciplines (as well as my own response to the current state of affairs of the discipline) and from the particulars of my own research interests. There is a large literature regarding politics in indigenous communities and another concerning gender and the indigenous world, much of it with a focus on political processes. I have participated in some of these debates based on work primarily with Coast Salish communities beginning in the late 1970s. These publications concern such topics as tribal elections and treaty rights, the analysis of age, gender, and voting patterns, and attributions concerning fitness for public office by gender, and I have explored the connections between income, employment, and success in tribal elections. In addition, my concerns have led to the consideration of prior forms of social organization and the changes that have resulted in communities as a consequence of contact with non-indigenous Americans, Canadians, and Europeans, issues that fall under the rubric of ethnohistory. My work with several communities trying to restore or establish treaty rights and create a new category of rights has led to my participation in creating anthropological material for litigation and to service as an expert witness (see B. Miller 1999).

Primarily, however, my focus has been on current-day struggles within communities wishing to establish themselves as politically autonomous and economically and socially healthy. I have been influenced by the work of such contemporary anthropologists as Dara Culhane (Culhane [Speck] 1987, 1995, 1998), who has forcefully described the struggle of the Nimpkish of Alert Bay, British Columbia, to overcome a medical delivery system that was unresponsive to their needs. She thereby revealed the connections between internal economic and political control and the integration and health of a community. Joseph Jorgensen (1978) began the process of systematically exposing the political economy of indigenous communities and the ways in which power is appropriated and resources are alienated from communities for the benefit of others elsewhere. Patricia Albers and Beatrice Medicine (1983) revealed the ways in which the indigenous political economy is gendered and how the reconstruction of indigenous communities builds on continually changing men's and women's roles. Albers's work both historicized and localized issues of gender and political economy by moving the emerging literature on women and colonization away from globalizing statements to point out variability. Eric Wolf (1982) showed the effects of an advancing European economic and political system, not on isolated communities, but across time, vast reaches, and many indigenous populations.

Many others within anthropology—and, more recently, in related disciplines such as history, political science, and sociology—have carefully worked out and described the interaction between the state and indigenous communities from a political economic viewpoint, particularly within core-periphery and other world systems models. The most important of these studies for Northwest Coast peoples has been the work of Daniel Boxberger (1989), who has connected the rapid changes of the participation of Coast Salish peoples in the critical salmon fisheries to political economic forces originating beyond their communities. Recently, the interpretive, poststructural work of Crisca Bierwert (1999) has focused attention on other ways of comprehending the struggles of Coast Salish and other indigenous peoples, namely from multiple vantage points that embed various perspectives and avoid the creation of dominant interpretive narratives. This stance points to another way of understanding the emerging differentiation within the indigenous world, a process that is likely accelerating with the rapid political and economic mobilization of communities and heightened class distinctions. In addition, the attention to discourse serves as a useful counterpoint to the political economic studies. Bierwert's approach draws attention to the dialogic features of indigenous texts, to engagement, and to the openness to multiple interpretations and responses and new insights (see also Sarris 1993:131).

In advancing my own interest in internal political processes and their connections to cultural understandings, social organization, and the larger political economy, I became aware that U.S. indigenous communities have begun the process of debate on how to approach their own futures as legal entities with significant jurisdiction in criminal and civil matters. The debates, in fact, were culminating in concrete outcomes, albeit continually changing, in the form of tribal code. I found that this development has been largely overlooked in anthropology and has been a passing concern for a small number of scholars in other fields who are not otherwise directly concerned with the life of the community. This is puzzling, particularly in light of the overwhelming scholarly interest in the legal affairs of the mainstream society. The focus of research has been on large-scale jurisdictional issues, which involve concrete features of case law and legislation and which connect to philosophical discussions of nations, rights, and European enlightenment traditions.

Americanist anthropologists, and others, have devoted so much attention to indigenous legal issues that it can be said to have had a profound, albeit poorly understood, impact on access to the field and to the sort of information gathered (see, for example, Mills 1994 for her discussion of her work as an expert witness for the Wetsuwet'in and how this influenced her fieldwork; and Dyck and Waldram 1993). Indeed, the creation of a special court, the Court of Claims, in the United States in the 1940s mobilized anthropologists to help in the legal process of adjudicating treaty and other claims by U.S. tribes. The process spawned a new subfield, ethnohistory, as celebrated in the creation of a then new scholarly journal, *Ethnohistory*, that integrated various sources of information, including oral traditions. More recently, efforts at the international level, particularly the United Nations, to produce agreements on indigenous rights regarding such issues as sovereignty and intellectual property have seized the attention of a sizeable portion of the scholarly community. Perhaps as a consequence, there have been few detailed, ethnographic studies of the operation of tribal courts and other justice programs.

In Canada and other British Commonwealth countries, there has been a great deal of attention given to indigenous rights and issues, but these, too, have been focused differently. In the 1960s and 1970s, Canadian anthropology broke new ground in the effort to provide legal testimony concerning the persistence of aboriginal lifeways. The hope was that communities might receive compensation for environmental destruction due to development projects such as the Alaskan pipeline and the James Bay Hydro Project or might stop such projects altogether. This attention to applied anthropology became a hallmark of Canadian anthropology (Hedican 1995; Darnell 1998). Attention has since focused on diversionary justice, the overrepresentation of indigenous peoples in prison, policing practice, and related criminology issues (Green 1998). In particular, sentencing circles have received a great deal of attention. Recently, to a limited extent, efforts have been made to explicate indigenous common law or traditional law, particularly by circuit judges, law professors, and, less commonly, anthropologists (noted examples are anthropologist Joan Ryan [1995] and crown attorney Rupert Ross [1992, 1996]). As with the U.S. case, little of this has been in the form of critical, ethnographic study of ongoing community processes, and still less attention has been given to what the rank-and-file community members think of justice developments in their communities. The diversity of community viewpoints has been largely overlooked in the effort to demonstrate the significance of consensus, as if consensus can only be understood to mean the existence of fundamental agreement by all parties, rather than the working of power relations behind the scenes (for exceptions see Hoyle 1995; Depew 1996). What is lacking in both the U.S. and Canadian cases, then, is a critical examination of community justice practices informed by both an ethnographic examination and a historical, comparative framework that accounts for community discourses and practices.

In order to carry out such a study, I have relied on previous research relationships with two of the communities considered here. I began working with the Upper Skagit as a graduate student in the mid-1980s, serving as an ethnohistorian for the tribal council in preparation for litigation and, for a year, as the early childhood educator (ECE) on the reservation. This latter work required that I visit family homes of three- and four-year-olds and, to my chagrin, model parenting and bring resources for the parents to use in working with their children. Although I was a certified teacher and underwent a brief training period for the ECE job at the neighboring Nooksack reservation, I felt ill-prepared for this work but found it engaging and a wonderful way to come to know community members and issues. Later, I testified for the tribe in a phase of the successful landmark multitribal case *United States v. Washington*, which concerned treaty rights to shellfish and to the determination of Upper Skagit villages and resource procurement stations in the mid–nineteenth century. Since then, I have participated in a variety of projects with the tribe.

My relationship with the Stó:lō Nation began in 1992 when the nation invited members of the Department of Anthropology and Sociology at the University of British Columbia to establish an ongoing research relationship with them. This led to the formation of an ethnographic field school, held on-site in Stó:lō territory. The first year, Professor Julie Cruikshank and I conducted the field school, bringing six graduate students who conducted various sorts of projects identified by the nation as being of interest. In later years, I directed this project with other UBC faculty members. In 1995 I began a project with the Stó:lō to begin to identify Stó:lō practices and values associated with justice. I was joined in this project at various times by two graduate students, and the project has continued over several years and has incorporated work with the related Coast Salish peoples of Vancouver Island. I recount more of this work in later chapters.

My own field work with the Coast Salish peoples has primarily concerned two of the three geographic branches, those in the south: the branch in the Puget Sound region and the branch along the Fraser River. My connections with the Coast Salish of Vancouver Island and the adjacent mainland are much less developed. However, one of the UBC graduate students working with me, Andy Everson of the Comox Nation, researched the complex issues of identity at the very edge of a region on Vancouver Island where Coast Salish people mingled with and were displaced by Kwakwaka'wakw in the middle of the nineteenth century (see Everson 2000). Many undergraduate students in my courses over the years have kindly informed me of their views of their own communities; among the many are Louie Williams of Cowichan and Doug White of Nanaimo. I am grateful to them and to other Coast Salish students living in Stó:lō and other communities on the lower mainland, including Melanie Repada and Kathy Sparrow, a Haida woman married into a Coast Salish family and a UBC graduate student. Other UBC graduate students with whom I have worked, particularly archaeology students, have carried out research with Vancouver Island communities. As part of the preparation of materials for the Stó:lō justice project, I interviewed senior people in the Coast Salish community on Vancouver Island, and I later interviewed social scientists and justice personnel associated with the South Island Justice Project.

My hope is that this study will be helpful to communities examining their own justice practices or contemplating the development of new programs and will broaden the academic discussion of contemporary indigenous communities. I break from much of the literature by my critique of the healing discourse and the metaphor of healing as justice. I do not wish to dismiss the strength of this approach; indeed, I have seen firsthand the power of redemption in individuals' lives through their participation in Syowen and other spiritual practices (see also Jilek 1974). Nor do I wish to overlook the powerful, pervasive social problems that have resulted from contact and colonialism. Because of the persistence of social problems, state paternalism, and the widely held view among non-indigenous peoples that outsiders should oversee band and tribal programs, I reject the suggestion that we are now in a postcolonial era. My aim is to historicize the current discourses and to move beyond disempowering, essentializing dialogues in order to help provide a basis for redirecting justice discourses and practices more to localized problems of power relations within communities. I wish to direct attention away from what might be called "world justice" to make an analogy with "world beat," a category of music that seems to be constructed on the notion that non-European derived music traditions can be regarded as a single category. Similarly, much of the debate on justice is built on the erroneous unexamined assumption that contact histories and colonial processes are similar processes everywhere.

Despite the critique of anthropology as a manifestation of colonialism and the related critiques of anthropological methods, commentary by outsiders regarding indigenous communities cannot afford to be in the form of softened analysis, pulled punches. If anthropology has a history of engagement within the processes of colonialism, it might equally be anthropology of the colonial encounter and of precolonial or postcolonial contexts (Comaroff and Comaroff 1991:xiii). At this moment in history, many leaders of indigenous communities have well-developed insights into public policy, current discourses, and media issues, and, consequently, they stand to benefit only from the most thoughtful efforts of outsiders, academics or otherwise. They do benefit from thoughtful presentations of the views of others and frequently seek it out. This may be a good time for dialogue as part of a strategy of change. Pommerscheim, a noted participant and observer of tribal courts, wrote of "using the gifts of culture and education and the tools of analysis and action both to describe and to transform the inimical pressure of oppressive historical and contemporary circumstance to advance a flourishing way of life" (1995:5). Although continually challenged by the mainstream society and, in most cases, regularly in court defending gains and fighting off challenges, many communities are now in a different political circumstance than even just a few years ago. Across North America, a process of institutional growth that began in earnest in the 1970s is paying dividends today, and for these and many other reasons, the communities are no longer voiceless and vulnerable in the same way they previously were. Dyck (1993) wisely observed that seeing indigenous communities through rose-colored glasses is both poor ethnography and potentially damaging to communities in that it provides a set of false baseline observations against which the communities can later be measured and found lacking. In the effort to continue to build the infrastructure of self-governance, contemporary communities can sometimes benefit from a critical appraisal from the outside, and to the degree to which they cannot or will not benefit, external commentary can be disregarded. Indeed, Elbridge Coochise, the chief justice of the Northwest Intertribal Court System and former head of the U.S. Intertribal Court Judges, commented that the system is too busy handling its responsibilities to monitor its own tendencies (personal communication, 5 April 1995).

In addition, the tribal councils of today are governments, and their activities must be subject to the same oversight as other governments in order that the rank-and-file membership maintain some control over their own personal destinies, independent of the interests of the emergent government. Finally, tribal codes and justice systems are public in the sense that community members—and, in some cases, outsiders—are, or potentially are, subject to their authority. Although the discourses surrounding them often concern the sacred, this is not sufficient to shield from view the public practice of justice. One might argue that indigenous courts and justice systems, although aimed primarily at servicing indigenous people, are public concerns, part of public debate and public policy. In this additional sense, then, careful scrutiny is merited and even required. In particular, I emphatically disagree with the notion (perhaps most vigorously held by those who eschew contact with contemporary indigenous communities) that the gulf in understanding between members of the mainstream community and members of indigenous communities, expressed in academic terms as the intrusiveness of colonialism and modernity, should cast a shroud of anonymity over the public conduct of the law and of justice (see Denis's argument otherwise in *We Are Not You*, 1997).

Writing Strategies and Organization of the Book

I have chosen not to obscure my own limited participation in the projects I describe, although I had no role in the now defunct South Island Justice Project and have had a very minor one in the development of the Stó:lō justice system that I describe in a subsequent chapter. My role is primarily that of an observer. But as observers, the University of British Columbia graduate students (Cindy McMullen and Jane McMillan) and I have been best able to get the sense of community viewpoints and political activities when we have participated and made contributions to the best of our abilities. In this sense, the analysis is informed ethnographically. I employ the strategy of describing portions of events and transcribing portions of conversations to which the students and I have been party in order to convey immediacy, to reveal something of how we carried out the interviewing process and how community members chose to respond, and to indicate something of the sense of the communities. Furthermore, revealing my own views and participation enables me to more adequately convey how I came to my present view of justice issues. In addition, although I recognize that the outcome of debates about justice properly belongs to community members and leaders themselves, I wish to present my own views of the fundamental issues facing communities attempting to develop justice initiatives. I do not wish to suggest that these descriptive passages concern pivotal moments in the history of the development of community justice, however. In addition, I appreciate that employing this writing strategy runs the risk of appearing to exaggerate our participation. This reflexive writing strategy is most apparent in a chapter in which I transcribe portions of an unusual conversation between leaders of Coast Salish communities on both sides of the U.S.-Canadian border. I do this in order to give a feeling for the divergence between the two in historical experience, to present the similarities of issues the two are facing, and to make clear the relevance of the conversations between indigenous communities around the world, but especially within a single, divided culture group. In this case, community officials have told me the meeting has had some influence on the development of community policy. In the interests of provoking debate and rethinking in what seems to be a stagnant area, I would rather run the risk of unsupported conclusions than of timidity.

In chapter 1, I briefly describe several of the most significant recent developments in the relationship between the state and indigenous communities to enable readers to form a picture of the milieu in which the present justice debates are taking place, prior to articulating a more developed, historicized picture in other chapters. In addition to describing political and legal developments of direct significance, I also describe current intellectual trends in the interpretation of problems of the sort I treat here. In particular, I point to the concepts of tradition, culture, and the sacred and to treatments of the issues of colonialism and differentiation, domination, resistance and accommodation, and ethnonationalism. I provide a brief consideration of the issues of public sentiment and media representations of indigenous justice. Finally, I consider issues internal to the indigenous nations—namely the challenges to their own political authority, intergenerational disputes, and long-term issues of internal affiliation and disaffiliation. At this point, I begin to make my analysis specific to a particular place, the Coast Salish world, and to specific communities within that larger grouping.

Chapter 2 focuses on historicizing Coast Salish aboriginal justice. I begin by addressing several of the intellectual problems inherent in undertaking such an exercise in communities faced with language loss, the results of generations of forced assimilation, and associated difficulties. It is current community understandings of justice that are most relevant to the project of (re)establishing community-controlled justice, rather than reconstructions of the past created by outsiders or community understandings of earlier periods. But because community members form their own understandings of aboriginal justice through dialogue about the past and about tradition, I provide my own view of significant features of aboriginal justice that might be considered in the present. To do this, I provide a discussion of the self, of the landscape, and of Coast Salish concepts of power that, I argue, underlie the framing of justice and that appear to be inadequately considered in academic and community discourses. This is an explicitly ethnographic section, reflecting my own training and viewpoint. The next two sections of this chapter are historical; the first is a description of political economic forces at work in the nineteenth century, and in the second I examine changes in the legal consciousness of Coast Salish peoples. In doing this, I consider the gaps in the existing ethnographic and historic literatures and the lacunae in the analyses of changing justice practices in the nineteenth and early twentieth centuries. In particular, I critique explanations that focused on the failure of indigenous communities to internally regulate themselves, to provide justice and order, and instead I point to problems of colonial administration, disease, and dislocation.

In chapter 3 I move from a regional view to the particulars of the history of the Upper Skagit community as it concerns justice. I consider the development of the tribal court, tribal participation in a larger, regional court system, and the current nature of justice service delivery. But beyond these descriptions, I consider how the community has addressed pressing issues facing a self-determined justice system. To do this, I broaden the scope of the discussion briefly to incorporate materials from seven of the other tribes of Puget Sound in examining how the individual is contextualized in current tribal codes, including the legal status of individuals and other constituent units of society. Finally, I provide a view of an internal study of aboriginal justice created by the Northwest Intertribal Court System (see Northwest Intertribal Court System 1991a, 1991b, n.d.; Zotto 1998), an intertribal legal consortium that included the Upper Skagit until recently, and point to the inherent conservatism of the study despite the ethnographic richness.

The Stó:lō Nation is the subject of chapter 4. I provide a sketch of the political history and a description of the current political organization prior to examining Stó:lō justice narratives, beginning with the middle of the century. Much of the chapter takes up contemporary Stó:lō views of justice, largely based on interviews. The chapter concludes with a consideration of the official discourse of the Stó:lō tribal government and community reactions to the tribal government practices and to the issues as members define them.

In chapter 5, I record parts of a 1998 dialogue between officials of two tribal governments, Upper Skagit and Stó:lō, and include my own analysis of the most pressing issues brought out in the meeting. These issues include obligations to nonlocal indigenous peoples residing in the Coast Salish communities (including whether the nonlocals' concepts of justice can be incorporated), resource law, relations between families, and the incorporation of diverse modes of justice within a single system.

Chapter 6 concerns the South Island Justice Project (SIJP). I briefly describe the postcontact history of the communities involved and move to "the preamble," a diversionary justice case concerning custody of a Coast Salish child, which received a great deal of attention in the 1980s and which helped produce the climate for the creation of the SIJP. I describe why this was not the model case that it is presented as in the academic literature due to its failure to account for real community issues of power. Next, I examine the "texts," the writings of the SIJP elders that constitute a statement of aboriginal law from their viewpoint. By doing so, I run the risk of critiquing community elders. But I do so not to undermine the pivotal role of elders in justice, but, rather, to underscore that they, too, as in the past, are politically positioned as members of particular families and with their own personal histories (see also LaPrairie 1992 concerning elders). Finally, I look at outcomes of the cases adjudicated by the SIJP.

In the conclusion, I consider all of these diverse materials together.

I

Foreground

The Legal Landscape

CANADA

Canadian policy regarding the implementation of indigenous justice in British Columbia is framed by the absence of treaties that might provide direction concerning leadership, governance, and law (with the exception of fourteen mid-nineteenth-century agreements with small bands on Vancouver Island that have been interpreted to have the force of treaty). Nor is there a judicial precedent equivalent to the nineteenth-century Marshall court decisions in the United States, which established the limiting idea of "domestic sovereign nations" but which allowed for rights to the self-administration of folk law, or indigenous common law, as it is sometimes called. In addition, Canadian policy has not followed the U.S. lead in establishing sovereignty as a policy priority. As a consequence, there is little development of the infrastructure of tribal justice, and almost none outside of the imposition of the state. Following the repudiation of the efforts of the Pierre Trudeau administration at enforced assimilation and the termination of tribes, as articulated in the infamous White Paper of 1969, there have been some feeble efforts at the indigenization of justice. The 1975 National Conference on Native People, put on by the solicitor general of Canada and the Department of Justice Canada, prompted a call for more attention to justice issues as they pertained to indigenous people, and more than twenty government reports voiced the same recommendations between 1975 and 1990 (Clairmont 1998:5). Although there has been widespread recognition of the failure of federal and provincial justice practices for indigenous peoples, the federal initiatives in the 1970s and early 1980s were limited to programs to indigenize criminal justice personnel (that is, to hire indigenous people), to provide cross-cultural awareness programs for criminal justice personnel, and to provide more culturally sensitive services to inmates (Warry 1998:183).

Since the late 1980s, efforts have been directed at research and demonstration projects in a variety of locations, particularly the Northwest Territories (Ross 1996, Warry 1998, Royal Commission 1996). These programs, in Warry's words, present the "*appearance of radical change when in fact the state has abandoned absolutely none of its control over dispute processing*" (1998:187; emphasis in original). The three central government strategies for aboriginal justice remain indigenization, the delegation of minor powers, and a surface acknowledgment of aboriginal culture (183). Government initiatives have included the use of panels of elders during sentencing and indigenous justices of the peace who hear minor offenses following training in the mainstream system.

There are several federal government explanations for the otherwise conservative, impoverished program of reform in the light of overwhelming evidence of the failure of the justice system, a system highlighted by the jailing of disproportionate numbers of indigenous peoples (who mockingly refer to the system as "Just Us," a play on the word *justice*). Among these explanations are the vast size of the Canadian landscape and the small size of most bands and tribal councils, circumstances that are said to make the implementation of indigenous-directed systems impractical. In addition, core concepts of tribal justice are said to be widely shared, thereby allowing for the use of generic models of justice that can be transported in a cost-efficient way from the state to various communities in a top-down system and administered by local indigenous people trained in government programs (Suo, interview).

In 1992 the federal government established the Aboriginal Justice Learning Network in order to mobilize key players in the justice system, including judges, crown attorneys, and indigenous leaders to work toward common objectives, particularly culturally appropriate justice processes. The Department of Justice Canada formed the Aboriginal Justice Directorate (renewed in 1996 as the Aboriginal Justice Strategy) to study community-based strategies through the funding of pilot projects (Clairmont 1998:6).

In the early twenty-first century, then, British Columbia has yet to create a political climate in which the indigenous peoples and communities can act on their own perceptions of law and justice within forums of their own devising. The province remains distinct in North America for its historical failure to negotiate treaties. However, treaty negotiations are underway with many bands and tribal councils, and the Nisga'a Nation has concluded a treaty now ratified by the federal and provincial governments. In the meantime, British Columbian indigenous communities are engaged in a great variety of initiatives as part of their larger struggle with the mainstream society over power and meaning. Some initiatives are formalized interventions with the mainstream, as I subsequently describe here, and others are one-time efforts at indigenizing justice. An example is the cleansing ceremony for a rapist and his victims in Nuu-chah-nulth territory on the west coast of Vancouver Island in 1993 (Griffiths and Hamilton 1996; Hamilton 1994). Other initiatives are quasi-legal, including urban sentencing circles of military veterans.

There are, in fact, so many localized, informal initiatives that the Department of Justice is not able to keep track of them all (Warry 1998; Suo, interview). Indeed, the disinclination of indigenous people to report to the government all of their justice activities is best regarded as strategic. Warry (1998:180) astutely noted that "Aboriginal people have the right to identify what constitutes an offence in their community. Failure to notify the external system must be interpreted as instances of individual or collective resistance to state justice."

This form of resistance to the system of justice imposed by the state is part of a wider effort. Indigenous leaders continue to employ many tactics in British Columbia, including the use of barricades blocking roads and railroad tracks, short-term political alliances with ecology groups over the preservation of forests, lobbying, and regular efforts to mold public opinion through the media. The law, however, is the primary venue for this struggle. Important conflicts have arisen over land claims, compensation for residential school victims, rights to resources, and other issues and have been fought out in court. Among the notable cases was the Vanderpeet case, which concerned the right of Stó:lō people to sell fish to non-indigenous people without provincial license. This case raised the issue of whether aboriginal rights are "frozen" in the manner in which they may be practiced. These jurisdictional struggles are the subject of a considerable academic and popular literature. Tribal leaders and criminologists are well along in the process of documenting the numbers of and issues for indigenous prisoners in the federal prison system, and proposals are underway for turning over custody of some prisoners to local band and tribal councils. In British Columbia, as elsewhere, an effort is underway to indigenize policing, by training First

Nations police for service in indigenous communities, by indigenizing methods and concepts underlying policing, and by freeing them from oaths of loyalty to the Crown (Jim Maloney, interview).

The Nisga'a Nation of British Columbia, in common with some other indigenous nations, intends to open legal space for its own justice ideas through the creation of tribal courts. In significant ways, the creation of new, indigenized legal venues lies at the heart of all the energetic efforts by First Nations to resist the imposition of the outside, reorganize their communities, and create sovereignty. It is through tribal legal processes that indigenous concepts can be applied to a range of critical internal disputes, over fisheries and other resources, and to the role of indigenous officers. "Peacekeepers" can be relieved of the burden of administering law created outside their own communities and of facilitating the imposition of restrictions on indigenous rights. Further, indigenous legal venues remove outside control over routine community life and allow communities to define community issues for themselves through the creation of the mechanisms whereby problems are translated into legal discourses and conflict is dampened or resolved (see Merry 1990). Tribal legal systems also permit the employment of local sentencing and related concepts of punishment, deterrence, restitution, or restoration.

A significant recent development in Canadian law arose from a reinterpretation of the folk law in the appeal of the Delgamuukw case. This case concerned a land claim in northern British Columbia by two tribes, the Git'ksan and Wet'suwet'en, and was filed by House chiefs (clan leaders) who entered as evidence *aadox*, traditional chiefly narratives of House history and the relationships to territory (B. Miller 1992b). The Reasons for Judgement (McEachern 1991) in this case provides a new test for determining aboriginal title to land in emphasizing what the members of the indigenous society regarded as their rights and title, rather than the prior tests of custom, tradition, or practice. Aboriginal law, then, has new relevance as a determinant of title and is "welcomed into the common law." In addition, the decision gave a new role to indigenous oral history in Canadian courts. Oral history entered as evidence could bear the weight of proof if it is more convincing than the other side and if it has an "air of reality" (Lambert 1998). It remains to be seen how the courts will treat oral history and, significantly, who within communities will be entered as experts in oral history and on what grounds. Nevertheless, the emphasis on tribal law, or folk law, as a factor in determining title underscores the increased significance of the articulation of indigenous concepts of justice in Canada.

In late 1999, the federal government's minister of Indian Affairs announced plans to once again modernize the Indian Act, which regulates indigenous people and communities by dealing with grievances with the past and, possibly, new forms of justice. Minister Robert Nault was quoted as saying, "I am interested in attempting to deal with pilots of different judicial processes [although any First Nations justice system], even though its structured differently, will have to run parallel with our own system" (*Vancouver Sun*, 27 September 1999, A9).

UNITED STATES

In the United States, the legal field is dramatically different. American tribes have long-established tribal courts with significant, though limited, civil and criminal jurisdiction. The U.S. tribal court system has been constructed on a series of Supreme Court decisions written by Chief Justice John Marshall, which held that Indian nations in the United States retained some form of inherent right of self-government, even though they could not be viewed as fully sovereign foreign nations. In the landmark 1832 case *Worcester v. Georgia*, the Supreme Court struck down laws passed by the state of Georgia that were aimed at supplanting the Cherokee Nation's constitution and codified system of law, thereby imposing Georgia law and assisting in the confiscation of Cherokee territory (Royal Commission 1996:180–81).

Tribal courts have largely unlimited jurisdiction over civil law matters that arise between tribal members on the reservations and have resolved cases involving millions of dollars. In a significant decision treating the issue of jurisdiction over cases involving non-Indian litigants, a test (a legal statement of the criteria to decide an issue) in *Williams v. Lee* (1959) was imposed that addressed the question of whether the matter concerned tribal rights of self-government. In criminal cases, tribal jurisdiction is limited by the terms of the Major Crimes Act of 1885, which reserves the prosecution of major offenses, including murder, rape, and drug offenses, for federal court. The Indian Civil Rights Act of 1968 limits penalties to $5,000 or one year in jail or both and imposes some of the protection of the U.S. Bill of Rights. However, in some cases tribal officials attempt to get around these limitations by seeking to prosecute when federal prosecutors fail to act and by reserving the rights to exclude members from communities. Further, tribal communities have chosen to interpret the provisions of the Bill of Rights in their own ways.

American tribal communities, such as Upper Skagit, face a somewhat different set of issues than their Canadian counterparts in contesting the reach of the mainstream society into their communities (see Deloria and Lytle 1984; Harring 1994). In part this takes the form of extending tribal jurisdiction by creating tribal code that specifies the manner in which tribal youth can be treated in nontribal incarceration (forbidding hair cuts, for instance). The creation of such code builds on the inclination of local towns to cooperate with increasingly powerful and influential tribal councils and industries. The contest also takes the form of a legal struggle over defining who is within the reach of tribal justice, including nonmembers, non-natives living on reservation lands, and Indian people who are nonmembers but resident on tribal lands.

A 1990 U.S. Supreme Court decision, *Druro v. Reina*, restricted tribal court jurisdiction to members of the tribe where the court was sitting. The decision "resulted in a jurisdictional void on Indian reservations . . . and raised the problem of how tribes could maintain law and order when significant numbers of the reservation population were beyond the reach of tribal justice" (Royal Commission, 1996:218). Later, congressional legislation in large measure overturned *Duro*, thereby restoring "the jurisdictional morass in the tribal courts to the pre-Duro days of simple confusion" (218).

Another form of struggle is the effort to define access to tribal resources, including natural resources and treaty-linked health and human resources. In one case, for example, a long debate has ensued over whether nonmember spouses ought to have rights to tribal treaty fishing in order to feed their family members who are tribal members (B. Miller 1994c). These struggles are exacerbated by reductions in levels of federal funding for health, education, and social services.

The Landscape of Ideas

TRADITION, CULTURE, AND THE SACRED

There are several distinctive issues, and idioms of expression, influencing the current discourses regarding justice in indigenous communities. Although these justice discourses take place within, and are part of, a political field of resistance and accommodation to the dominant society, some are derived locally and concern long-term community issues, and others have more recently spread across indigenous North America. But the discourses and politics are also connected to larger, international developments in indigenous-mainstream society affairs as well and can be captured analytically by the concept of ethnonationalist movements that are directed toward gaining some measure of internal control, or even political autonomy, in opposition to the values and practices of the encompassing nation-state.

Perhaps most significantly, present-day discourses about justice in Coast Salish communities employ concepts of tradition, culture, and the sacred. These are ambiguous, symbolic terms that do not mean the same thing to all people, but that carry great weight and meaning and have the capacity of moving people to action. I do not wish to engage in now-dated debates concerning whether tradition is best regarded as imagined, constructed, invented, or transmitted intact from the past. Rather, my use of the term *tradition* points to its place in the discourses produced and the play of power in present-day communities. Fiske observed that "concepts of 'customary,' 'traditional' or 'Indian' laws are drawn upon as a political resource" and "constitute 'materials of identity' " that arise from a "consciousness of colonization" and that are "defined by strategies of decolonization" (1995:185).

Mauze noted that "tradition is a metaphor for identity. This means it encompasses and illustrates a past, a present and a future. It is not only the memory of the past frozen in time that reemerges; it is also a reference necessary for elaborating a version of the contemporary world, which is the 'space' where traditional and modern social life occur side by side. *Tradition is primarily a political instrument for regulating both internal and external relations*" (1997:12; emphasis mine). This emphasis on the present-day instrumental qualities of tradition avoids the issues of whether tradition is simply false or true, alive or dead, destructive of the claims of living indigenous peoples or supportive of their claims against the state, a manipulation of the indigenous elite or the stuff of the broad mass of the population, and other related debates. Indeed, tradition may be all of these.

It is worth noting that the idea of tradition among the indigenous peoples of North America is widely associated with values and practices worth aspiring to; that tradition, as an amorphous quality, has a certain face validity. Harkin wrote that among the peoples of the Northwest Coast and elsewhere, "traditions may be authentic, in the sense that they move people affectively (and move them to action), despite the fact that they may be 'artificially' constructed and framed." Further, the invocation of tradition, by its nature, involves the selection and reframing of recognizable cultural symbols, whose content becomes available for the process of creating solidarity and social identity. Those who employ these symbols bask in their reflected significance and obtain a measure of authority (Harkin 1997:98). However, this authority rarely remains unchallenged. The Comaroffs observed that the "encounter" between indigenous peoples and colonizers in South Africa "led to the objectification of 'the' culture of the colonized in opposition to that of the whites. The 'natives,' that is, began to conceive of their own conventions as an integrated, closed 'system.' . . . Not only did colonialism produce reified cultural orders; it gave rise to a new hegemony amidst—and despite—cultural contestation" (1991:18). History, they point out, is everywhere actively made in a dialectic of order and disorder, consensus and contest.

In part because of the significance placed on the past, and on ancestors whose names are borne in the present and whose lives are thought to have been well lived and worthy of replication, there is stiff competition for the past, for control over the resource that it represents. This competition has both destructive consequences (I consider this issue in more detail below) and constructive outcomes. In indigenous communities there is a constant dialogue concerning tradition, the "right" ways to do things, and the underlying values. The dialogue is sometimes quiet, concerned with minor issues or obscure details. These debates are ordinarily covered over, but sometimes they are on public display. It is the public nature of the debate that points back to the significance of the practices and beliefs held to be traditional and that demonstrates the seriousness of the efforts to conform to tradition. This public debate and affirmation of tradition simultaneously allow for differentiation to appear among families and communities and for those from outside the community to be alerted to the direction in which the communities wish to go.

Debates about aboriginal law (folk law or, more recently, *indigenous common law*), including those I consider here, lie at the heart of the current struggles for communities and individuals to define themselves, both as psychological and concrete political issues. As I argue below, *law*, for indigenous people, is sometimes equated with the whole of tradition itself (as in "our law determines how land is to be used," or "we are to marry according to how the old ones did this"). In other instances law is synonymous with the *culture* of the people (as in "the ways we are to act is our culture and our law"). Sometimes law is held to be sacred, immutable, and primordial (as in "our law was given us by X̱á:ls, the Transformer," sometimes referred to as Xals, Hals, or, in the plural, X̱exá:ls). In other settings, and for other people, law is equated with the imposed legal practices of non-indigenous peoples, the activities of tribal governments, or the current ways traditional concepts are practiced. Just as the manipulation of tradition relies on a selective process of symbolic display, so, too, do justice and law.

In his work on ethnogenesis, Sharp (1996) connects the idea of sacredness to the current debate about the positioning of ethnic groups and aboriginal identity. Sharp observes that the "sacred" belongs to a primordial discourse that locks local groups into a particular identity construction that itself builds on the idea of critical differences between indigenous and dominant societies. Indeed, for American Indians and Canadian First Nations, the issue of presenting themselves as protectors of the sacred is emblematic of their "opposition ideology" (Hornborg 1994:253). The issue may be even more fundamental than this, in that some members of aboriginal and mainstream communities hold differing views of culture itself. Whitten (1996:204), in commenting on the significance of confrontational, ethnic-bloc nationalist discourse, observed that for many indigenous people, culture "is that which is worthy of reverential homage." Further, "indigenous culture, as such concepts are manifest in practical and spiritual conflict, [is] characterized by reverential webs of signification." (205). To members of the majority community, on the other hand, culture may remain less problematic, even invisible. The Comaroffs, responding to critical postmodernism, described culture not as an overdetermining, closed system of signs but as a "set of polyvalent practices, texts, and images that may, at any time, be contested," and power as always implicated in culture, consciousness, and representation (1991:17). Sarris, an indigenous scholar, referenced Kashaya understandings of tradition as not fixed, as an ongoing process, and as subjective and dependent on the viewer (1993:179).

In order to consider specifically how discourses about tradition and indigenous justice are linked to current practice and contemporary legal circumstances, I examine the following set of issues and draw out the implications of these differences in approach in subsequent chapters:

1. The ways in which the three systems are articulated in relationship to their own band or tribal governments. At Upper Skagit, the court is created and sanctioned by the tribal government but maintains judicial independence; in the South Island case, the justice system emerged as an enterprise of the elders' council and rejected the control of the tribal government; at Stó:lō, the incipient system is directly integrated into the government with an as-of-yet unarticulated separation of powers.

2. The relationships to the constituent family groups that compose the tribes. Because Coast Salish communities are composed of competing but interconnected family networks, and because these families vary in size and influence, the way in which the justice systems propose to manage the relationships between families is a central issue. The question of nepotism and how it is defined and managed is a critical component. The Upper Skagit code restricts, in limited ways, the ability of families to dominate tribal life. At Stó:lō, these concerns are unclarified, although an imported model of family group conferencing has been employed. In the South Island Justice Project, families were recognized as constituent units with rights to "family law." This was not operationalized, although tribal law was thought to be a composite of family law.

3. The justice model that is presented as underlying the practice and that suggests the aims of the system. At Upper Skagit, the tribe holds jurisdiction, and crimes are officially against society, but resolution can be carried out within a model of family-to-family restitution. This system, then, has features of punitive justice, rehabilitation, restitution, and restoration; at Stó:lō, the system is primarily healing and restorative and is based on the diversion of authority from the state; the South Island model was diversionary and restorative.

4. The law-justice concept. At Upper Skagit, the law is derived from the authority of the tribal council and ultimately the general membership; at Stó:lō, the law is an outcome of discussion between the elders and the chiefs; at South Island, the law was articulated by elders and was said to derive from primordial teachings given the elders by the Creator.

5. The ways in which the justice systems are tied to indigenous

spiritual practices. At Upper Skagit an indirect connection exists between spiritual practice and justice practices, but with the possibility of intervention and representation by spiritual practitioners. Religious groups participate in the drafting of code of direct concern. At Stó:lo and South Island, participation in Spirit Dancing is viewed as one significant route to justice.

6. The ways in which those said to be "culture bearers," especially elders, are incorporated. Elders are allowed to participate as advisers at the point of intake of a case, in the body of the trial, or in sentencing at Upper Skagit. In the Stó:lō Nation, there is a formal House of Elders that advises the chiefs and House of Justice. The South Island program was elder driven with elder-articulated laws.

7. The paths to the creation of law (or code). At Upper Skagit, boilerplate laws (those from other jurisdictions) have been gradually transformed by code writers and tribal committees to meet local needs and viewpoints. For the Stó:lō, a code writer has been hired to record the folk law, through conversation with elders, chiefs, and justice workers. In the South Island program, an elders committee articulated the Creator's laws.

8. The manner in which the systems articulate with the outside world. The Upper Skagit system holds jurisdiction and employs its own police and court officials. Agreements concerning extradition and other issues have been reached with other jurisdictions. Code has been written to attempt to regulate members in outside jurisdictions. In addition, there are provisions for the use of legal language from other jurisdictions (federal, state, municipal, tribal) if desired. The Stó:lō system is diversionary only, although agreements with the state will change this; police are cross-trained with the Royal Canadian Mounted Police. The South Island project was an official diversion project, with no associated police and with outsider consultative judges and court officials.

9. The "reach" of the system. The Upper Skagit system asserts jurisdiction over members and others on reservation lands, without habeas corpus to other jurisdictions. Violators can be banned from reservation lands. The Stó:lō system, to date, incorporates those willing to participate in criminal issues and has incipient jurisdiction over child welfare. Member bands can leave the tribal council. The South Island program was limited to cases in which all parties were willing to participate.

10. The nature of internal critiques and the ways in which problems within the system are addressed. The Upper Skagit justice officials have asked constituent groups to draft code concerning their own issues; tribal code is continually revised and is tied to licensure (houses, fishing, etc.). The Stó:lō have faced critiques of their own "central government" and of the importation of outside justice models that have been addressed by consultation. The South Island program failed to address critiques concerning the protection of women and the efforts by families to protect their own interests. The primordialist elder-based tribal law lay beyond critique.

COLONIALISM, INTERNAL CONFLICT, AND DIFFERENTIATION

Seen from another vantage point, my concern is with the ways in which culture, tradition, and justice are understood within a single, although divided, indigenous cultural group and the ways in which historical forces, including public policy and its implementation, intrude in the production of various understandings and in various configurations of contemporary justice practices. A starting point is the view that indigenous justice policies and practices emerge, dialectically, in response to the actions of representatives of the nation-state who shape policy and practice, while simultaneously addressing critical voices from within, voices that shape and distort tribal politics. Justice practices, then, are neither inventions nor strictly imaginings; nor are they necessarily clearly articulated. Rather, they are emergent, the product of rational dialogue, of distrust, of chance, and, sometimes, the path of least resistance. The justice initiatives are strategic and nonstrategic, examined and unexamined.

In establishing the context in which these late-twentieth-century justice initiatives occurred, I wish to point to the historical process of internal differentiation as a result of colonialism and the consequent problem of how to make sense of the past in the current world. Coast Salish people confront not only the "other" within their own larger grouping, but their own past. Sider, in his study of race, ethnicity, and identity among the Lumbee tribe, noted that "Native American peoples have been forced to claim and to continually negotiate not only their public identity but also their public 'presence.' *They have done so from colonial times to the present in ways that create substantial internal struggles*" (1993:8, emphasis mine). The fluidity of their situation and the "difficulty of developing a strategy for coping even in part with these pressures, and especially the importance of maintaining at least some significant aspect so their own ways, their own social relations, their own values, in the midst of this turmoil—all of this often confronts Native American peoples with an unavoidable and irresolvable antagonism between their past and their present" (9).

The three justice systems considered here reveal fundamental differences that derive from differences in the ways domination, resistance, and accommodation have worked within the communities (see Sider 1993:xxi). Sider argues for "bringing the flow of history" directly into otherwise lifeless analytic categories in order to see diversity, both between and within subcultures. He suggests that in the midst of diversity and the context of domination people construct their own humanity and dignity not merely by applying cultural rules or an ensemble of values (25). Analysis, in short, must go beyond the notion of culture in understanding the tension between the past and the present.

The justice discourses address themselves to a range of issues, including healing, the play of power, separation and moral distance from the mainstream, rejection of the institutions of the mainstream, diversity within, and the recognition of current problems within the communities themselves. Although these are overarching themes attached to the current justice discourses of indigenous peoples of North America and elsewhere, there are less visible streams of thought and practical dilemmas that are commonly overlooked analytically and that are of concern here. Furthermore, these materials demonstrate the ways in which oral traditions, including those that address justice, do not merely speak for themselves but, rather, explicate the current predicament. These oral traditions have arisen from earlier interpretations of the past that themselves incorporate Western concepts and that are now received wisdom within communities (Cruikshank 1998). The current content of *tradition* is understood here to reflect a winnowing out, a selection process, that has highlighted particular understandings while excluding other understandings and, by implication, other voices. The orality of the past and the literacy of the present, then, far from being "mutually contradictory poles, can interact and support each other" (Finnegan 1988:10). What is highlighted and what is excluded itself varies within the single culture group, or *nation*, as it is sometimes referred to locally, a process that reveals the historically situated property of justice narratives, oral traditions, and culture itself. In some cases, justice narratives and practices appear highly ideologically driven. In others, the justice practices are rooted in a grounded sense of what the current community problems are, independent of a global political economy that generates dilemmas that are beyond the reach of the justice system. The ways in which *culture* and *tradition* enter the justice undertakings emerge as critical variables in the viability of the program.

The three systems considered here, then, offer a view of the alternative ways in which Coast Salish peoples have attempted to resist or accommodate the fragmentation of their own communities and the imposition of outside notions of legal order. These systems present substantially different views of such critical issues as the nature of relations between families and the definition of personhood. Taken together, they form a picture of the internal dialogue and dispute within the larger Coast Salish society over meaning, over control, and over relations with the state. More than this, the justice projects encapsulate and orient this dialogue through the processes of being recorded. Community responses to the justice initiatives further illuminate this process.

Merry (1988:891) situated the study of such developments within the then "new" legal pluralism. She noted that "to examine the ever-changing conceptions of the normal and the cultural and the constant struggle of interpretation of the symbols and forms of legality in small places and large legal systems at the same time is, at the least, challenging." She directed attention to "the specificity of each situation, to the variation in minute social processes and to the complex texture of ideological meanings formed within particular historical situations" (892; see also Just 1992). The legal systems reveal the tension between the reliance on deeply embedded cultural meaning as a means of facing the state and on more explicitly political strategies. One might describe a sort of legal pluralism within the Coast Salish communities, a perspective that "examines the ways social groups conceive of ordering, of social relationships, and of ways of determining truth and justice" (Merry, 1988:889). Fiske and Ginn observed that "It is time to turn our gaze to the construction of plural legalisms within a single legal order and to ask how, and with what implications, are some citizens enabled to reconstruct their identity and subject position before the law while others are not" (20).

Foreground

INDIGENOUS RHETORIC, ETHNONATIONALIST MOVEMENTS, AND THE STATE

The current political and justice practices of Coast Salish peoples in both the United States and Canada (in common with other First Nations, American Indian, and Alaska Native groups) can be viewed from the broad analytic frame of indigenous actions of resistance and accommodation and, it might be argued, examined through their connection to the widespread late-twentieth-century ethnonationalist movements. Comaroff (1996) observed that ethnic identity usually arises in relations of inequality and emerges dialectically through attribution and self-assertation. In this view, identities should be thought of as relations, not as things, and as revealed in the minutiae of everyday practice. The current period of transformation, which Comaroff likens to the Age of Revolution, is characterized by, among other things, the accelerated processes of globilization, the weakening of the nation-state, and the rise of identity politics. The globalization of communications is said to subvert the power exercised by the state, just as the globalization of the economy undermines the nation-state by deconstructing the currency, customs, boundaries, and national economy. However, these developments are thought not to destroy local culture; in fact, the opposite is the case, and the experience of globalism reinforces the awareness of localism. Consequently, the explosion of ethnonationalism is broadly linked to the claims of sovereign self-determination in a period of convergence between ethnic consciousness and assertions of nationalist (as opposed to nested) identities.

The emergent ethnonationalism, then, is dependent on the moral, the particular, and the nonrational in contrast to mainstream, European-derived, modernist nation-state claims of secularism, universalism, and rationalism (see also Connor 1994; Levin 1993; Fleras and Elliott 1992). In addition, the institutional entailments of the nation-state, particularly the centralization of political and juridical authority and bureaucratization, stand in contrast to the rhetorical positions of leaders within the ethnonationalist movements. Ethnonationalist rhetoric envisions a nation-state that is immoral in its positioning outside the embrace of a sanctioning cosmology, in its reliance on a universalism that denies what appear to be salient differences between peoples (those who subscribe to, for example, the "Great Law" and those who do not, or those who are spiritual leaders and those who are not), in its emphasis on defining membership within geographical borders, rather than landscapes of meaning, in the emphasis on the individual rather than the group, and in the control exercised in the center, by an elite. Taiaiake Alfred, a Rotinohshonni (Mohawk) political scientist and political leader, articulates this viewpoint:

> The state's power, including European concepts such as "taxation," "citizenship," "executive authority," and "sovereignty" must be eradicated from politics in Native communities.
>
> In fact, traditional philosophy is crucially relevant to the contemporary indigenous situation. In the Rotinohshonni tradition, the natural order accepts and celebrates the coexistence of opposites: human purpose consists in the perpetual quest for balance and harmony; and peace is achieved by extending the respect, rights, and responsibilities of family relations to other peoples. Even stripped down to a skeleton, these teachings speak with power to the fundamental questions that a philosophy of governance must address. Among the original peoples of North America, the cultural ideal of respectful coexistence as a tolerant and harmony-seeking first principle of government is widespread. Diametrically opposed to the possessive individualism that is central to the systems imposed on our communities, this single principle expresses the hope that tradition offers for a future beyond division and conflict. (1999, xiv)

To the rationalists of the mainstream community, the speakers of ethnonationalist discourses appear incompetent in their appeals to particularism, to the spiritual, and to the decentralization of authority. They appear unsuited for the tasks of present-day administration and management. They appear anti-democratic and insufficiently progressive; indeed, they seem to overvalue ancestors and old ways and to be living a fictionalized past. To those within a Euro-nationalist frame of reference, the ethnonationalist stance appears to justify and confirm federal and provincial government fears and restraint in allowing or facilitating the development of band and tribal procedures, institutions, and agencies, including justice. Basic, nonnegotiable features of Canadian society, it is said, will not be protected, or adequately protected, by band councils that permit nepotism and that fail to protect individual rights.

Fears have been publicly and regularly expressed about the rights of workers to collective bargaining (for example, the *National Post*, 19

November 1998, 1), about the rights of community members outside of the powerful families and, most vociferously, the rights of non-indigenous residents on reserve lands. A headline in the *Vancouver Province* read "Longtime Lessees Cry Foul" (10 February 1999, A10), one of an endless stream of reports. The Nisga'a treaty negotiations brought this latter issue to public attention in British Columbia when it was discovered by the media that the Nisga'a council, following ratification of the treaty, would have taxation rights over Canadian citizens who would lack both the vote and representation on the council. Front-page headlines of the *Vancouver Sun* (15 February 1996) proclaimed that "Tribe Gets Own Legal System," and the story reported that "the tentative deal gives the Nisga'a control over many government services, a Sun reporter discovers." While the Nisga'a treaty contains provisions for the establishment of a tribal court, neither public nor official discourses took note of the fact that this court would offer remedies for all those within the jurisdiction, including non-indigenous peoples. This gap apparently reflects a widely held fear that Nisga'a governance would be simply incompetent and biased. Similarly, following public protest, federal officials moved to rewrite legislation, Bill C-49, aimed at enhancing band control over reserve lands by providing the right to condemn property for tribal purposes. A *Province* (25 April 1999, A28) headline read "Natives Fear for Their Land," noting "Bill C-49 gives band councils too much power, women say." Meanwhile, huge increases in lease rates for tenants on Musqueam land in Vancouver led to public demands for accountability outside of indigenous authority, amid claims of incompetence, disinterest, or favoritism to the enrolled membership. A three-quarter-page "Forum" section of the *Vancouver Sun* (14 August 1998, A3) was entitled "Living as Leaseholders, Living without Rights." The *Vancouver Sun* reported "Band Chief Accused of Vote Fraud" (10 April 1999, B5); the paper's front page of 16 March 1999 read "Kamloops Indian Band Defies Ottawa, Sets Own Labour Code," and written commentary noted that the band is "abusing the principle of self-government by trying to deny their employees many basic labour rights." The paper employed military language on its 3 May 1999 front-page headline and accompanying article, noting "Battle Looms over Indian Band Union Issue."

But the ethnonationalist sword cuts both ways, and there is another side to the critique, aimed from the inside at band and tribal councils that appear to the members to adapt the reviled characteristics of mainstream governance. By the early 2000s, these very well publicized critiques appear to threaten the viability of band governance for several related reasons. First, they undermined the "politics of embarrassment" employed by band and tribal leadership as a political tool in the ongoing contest with the mainstream governments by exposing the leaders themselves to public censure. The media was all too willing to report the controversy within indigenous communities. In 1999, for example, a national newspaper, the *Globe and Mail*, featured a front-page series on corruption in tribal government, and the *Vancouver Sun* regularly runs pieces on the mishandling of budgets by tribal leadership. The *Vancouver Province* (19 September 1999, A40) reported the conclusion drawn by Alberta judge John Reilly that Stoney Indian reserve leaders intentionally divert money from programs in order "to keep the people under-educated, unwell and unemployed so that they can be dominated and controlled."

Second, these critiques strengthen the programs of the political right in British Columbia, as expressed through the radio show of commentator Raif Mair, commentaries by pundit Mel Smith, and others who oppose treaties, land claims, and, especially, the development of indigenous justice initiatives. This has created a convergence between indigenous ethnonationalist political rhetoric, as characterized by Alfred above, and right-wing Alliance Party political slogans. One First Nations chief astutely described this development as "the new frontier thesis." Chief Stanley Arcand argued that nineteenth-century Canadian society absolved itself of any role in the displacement and destruction of indigenous societies by the idea that savage society must give way to advanced civilization. Further, society would wither away due to profound and innate problems within their culture and political structures. He wrote:

> Today, this antiquated thesis has found new life within the media . . . , [arguing] our problems today are explained away as arising—again—from within our culture and political structures. In recent editorials and commentaries the current system of First Nations governance is deemed so "vicious" . . . that it would test the "virtue of angels"—that a "perverted power relationship" now exists between First Nations leaders and their members at the grassroots. . . . This assumption is that First Nations people are incapable of managing their own

affairs—that when given the chance they invariably botch things horribly. (*Globe and Mail*, 10 May 1999, A13)

In addition to the public focus on the issues of particularism (privileging one's own family), corruption, and alleged disinterest in the rights of minorities on their reserves, recent discourses have also attacked tribal leaders for their purported internalization of mainstream patriarchal viewpoints and mistreatment of women (see, as examples, LaRocque 1997; Fiske 1993, 1996, 1997–98; Nahanee 1993; Monture-Angus 1995; see also Bell 1988). A headline in the *Vancouver Sun* (30 March 1992:A7) reported that "Aboriginal Men Have Learned Sexism, Women Fearing Self-Rule on Reserve Say." In this piece former Musqueam chief Wendy Grant is reported to have argued that the insistence of the Canadian Charter of Rights "on individual rights would jeopardize key elements of traditional native government, law, and society." These issues were particularly evident during the constitutional debates surrounding the Charlottetown (Constitutional) Accord in 1992, when a variety of fissure points within indigenous communities were publicly exposed during television ads run by indigenous groups and aimed at supporting or rejecting the Accord. These discourses have featured an emphasis on re-indigenization and on the diminishment of women's role under the capitalist, colonialist, centrist state, as shown by the following headlines: "Native-Managed Lands: A Threat to Women" (*National Post*, Toronto, 2 February 1999, A18); "Fearful Native Women Plead for Protection against Ancient Rituals" (*Vancouver Sun*, 3 March 1992, 1); and "Indian Women Say Fraud, Nepotism Rife on Reserves" (*Vancouver Sun*, 13 April 1992, 1). These problems, and the public outcry about such issues, played a prominent role in the collapse of the South Island Justice Program, as I show later.

However, in this period of internal crisis and of critique of both the mainstream society and indigenous leadership, ethnonationalist demands by community members for retributive justice—to correct wrongs and reward good based on moral law—appear to be dependent on national, impartial, universalistic apparatuses of government, law, and courts. For many, the incomparability between tribal government rhetoric and practice creates a sense of corruption associated with tribal government and the efforts to create justice practices. The dilemma for tribal government is that although governments must employ the rhetoric of retributive justice in their struggle with the state, many of their own members reject the claims to authority and the right to govern. This distinguishes North American indigenous governments from the several contemporary national governments that employ retributive justice efforts to gain legitimacy and buoy their regimes, including central and eastern European states and South Africa through its Peace and Reconciliation tribunal (see Borneman 1997). But tribal leaders have positioned their emergent governments as nations with institutions characteristic of the state. The contradiction emerges, then, from the need to gain legitimacy within the ethnonationalist, indigenous idiom and the requirement of rules, procedures, and practices similar to the surrounding state. Although the whole political movement rests on the repudiation of European Enlightenment values, nonetheless, these are relied on in the creation of retributive justice. For these reasons, the sort of justice discourse generated within indigenous communities at the moment depends in good measure on its source, such as from the seat of administrative power, from the vantage point of community elders, from urban women, from indigenous intellectuals, or from young, reserve-based people.

CONTEMPORARY GENERATIONAL AND RESIDENTIAL DISCORD

The situation is complicated further still within indigenous communities because of the fracturing of relations along generational lines, and in some locations a highly visible contest for authority is being played out between elders (variously defined), middle-aged political leaders, and newly organized youth. Fienup-Riordan (1990a) captured the sense of this dislocation among Yup'ik Eskimos of Alaska in their efforts to reform leadership in order to achieve tribal sovereignty. Elders indicated that, in earlier times, it was "the duty of elders to talk about the rules and the duty of young people to listen" (206). The problems of the present were associated with the failure of the elders to speak and the young to listen (209) and with the diminished primacy of orality. This selective presentation of values and practices emphasized the role of elders in justice practices. Indigenous youth have publicly and pointedly contested the rights of elected leaders to establish the terms of treaty making and leadership generally, and they have also contested the rhetoric of elderhood. LaPrairie has pointed out that youths who get into trouble are the ones most likely not to hold elders in esteem or to regard them as appropriate to resolving conflict (cited in Ross 1996:224; see also 1992), an issue that emerged in the South Island Justice Project.

There are still other sources of discord, including the different voices of those who have grown up off reserve and who now seek out connections to ancestral communities. Many women and their children have sought residences on reserves following a political struggle in the 1980s resulting in federal legislation (Bill C-31) that reversed the discriminatory practice of stripping women of tribal membership for marrying non-indigenous men. These returnees are sometimes repudiated by those who grew up on reserves, and their experiences and viewpoints disregarded, because they are thought not to be traditional.

INTERNAL DIFFERENTIATION

Although it is clear that Coast Salish communities are now differentiated on many dimensions, this is not to argue that differentiation in new. Coast Salish communities have never been organizationally simple or homogeneous. As a consequence, justice issues cannot be fully explained from either colonialist or ethnonationalist analytic frames. I argue from yet another vantage point that the present-day internal differentiation and conflict are not solely the result of colonization and contact (see Brown 1991; Gledhill 1994:70). Rather, the Coast Salish communities themselves have never been seamless cultural units, nor have community members ever been "cultural automatons," an idea ridiculed by Malinowski (1926) in his effort to establish the anthropology of law within a framework that accounts for conflict. In his seminal work on the Tlingits, a northern Northwest Coast people, Kan (1989) noted the opposing ideologies of hierarchy and clan solidarity and the endemic internal struggles around these irreconcilable themes. The Coast Salish, too, although not organized into clans, suffer the problems of unity within an ideology of solidarity and the practice of hierarchy.

Current public discourses within the Coast Salish communities do not ordinarily emphasize the issues of conflict or problems of contradictory cultural values. More generally, contemporary social problems are publicly attributed to contact processes, social dislocation, and the loss of language, ritual practice, territory, identity, mental and physical health, and economic security. In addition, efforts at forced assimilation, especially the introduction of alcohol, residential schooling, and the repression of indigenous spiritual practices are linked to contemporary problems (NICS report 1991a; see Fournier and Crey 1997). These factors are understood in one Coast Salish community to constitute a particularly explosive threat to youth, who are not yet strong in their identities and who have internalized a "pervasive sense of personal doom." This response is regarded as a postcontact analog to post-traumatic stress syndrome (Swinomish Tribal Mental Health 1991:54).

However, Snyder (1964) described what she called the major "fissure points" within Coast Salish societies in the pre-reservation period as being the social contradictions arising between in-laws, between members of the same family of different social class, and between men and women, especially postmenopausal women establishing political careers. In each of these cases, cultural values stood in contrast to one another, thereby creating alternative grounds on which claims to resources and authority could be made, albeit with difficulty and with the potential for conflict. Snyder's work implies the need for mechanisms for addressing conflict, dissent, and interpersonal violence. Her unpublished fieldnotes (Snyder n.d.) further this claim, revealing both cases of unresolved conflict and mechanisms for resolution.

Concerning women and gender roles, Snyder wrote about "the ethnographic evidence of the weakness of the social system to provide an unchallenged and stable position for women and to effect simple clarity for their identity. . . . Analysis shows not only that a bewilderingly ambiguous situation existed, but more significantly, that feelings about women's roles were nearly explosive" (1964:255–56).

Regarding in-laws and "aliens," by which she meant indigenous people with whom one had no tie of kinship, Snyder reported: "In the past, although kinsmen might quarrel and even physically harm one another, disputes among them were hushed. But feuds between in-laws were open. . . . Old Skagits never rallied to the aid of in-laws in debt or in need of property for a wealth exchange because these were the very persons who were rivals in the class struggle" (1964:389).

Difficulties in relations between families continue to be a significant obstacle to the development of self-governance, a circumstance of long standing. Kew and Miller (1999) see conflict, rather than simply cooperation and consensus, as a regular feature of historic and contemporary Stó:lō political processes. They describe the processes of dispute at several levels of social organization and emphasize "affiliation, disaffiliation, and reaffiliation":

> In addition to the properties of coherence and permanence of affiliation, Coast Salish social networks allow for short-term bouts of disaffiliation by individual members, communities, bands, or other constituent groups without substantively affecting the long-term social universe, disrupting cultural continuity, or dissolving the boundaries of the Coast Salish moral universe. Example of this in recent years include actions by bands to disaffiliate themselves from tribal councils or the refusal to participate in meetings of common interest to First Nations, such as fisheries meetings. Individual people, including leaders, sometimes practice what one Stó:lō chief called a "pulling-out strategy" to express reservations about decisions taken by the collective, or to influence internal political processes. Perhaps the most important aspect of this strategy is that, eventually, such people or groups are reaffiliated into the larger Coast Salish political community without penalty. Such actions are best understood as routine political actions rather than as schisms and ought not to be taken as evidence of political collapse or ineptitude. Instead, this property of the social network is a resource that allows for changing configurations of public opinion and for the establishment of alternative directions. One might argue that Stó:lō people can choose between alternative political approaches before a consensus gradually emerges among the leaders of the constituent bands. This property of the social network rests on the idea of permanence and continuity; the First Nations understand that their ancestors affiliated, disaffiliated, and reaffiliated over very long periods and that their descendants and heirs will do the same. (1999:58–59)

What Kew and Miller saw as potentially a strength, albeit one that posed occasional difficulties, Suttles saw as a deficit: "It seems to me rather probable that Coast Salish society suffered chronically from a need for more bases of leadership because of its poverty of political institutions. This need may have led to occasional internal crises that permitted the rise of prophets who used religious concepts and ceremonies to exercise more than usual authority" (1987c:198).

In brief, then, the approach here focuses on long-term (pre-contact) issues of power and authority and those that derive specifically from colonialism and oppression because both sorts of issues continue to concern communities, members, and leaders.

On a practical level, the three examples of indigenous justice systems described here reveal the difficulties facing justice systems that are established with minimal jurisdictional resources and highly ideological aims in comparison to a system that has emerged from the practical problem of managing a tangible asset—in this case, fisheries. Indigenous peoples struggling with the state and with local governments for autonomy, self-expression, and a sense of control, then, have assembled a range of responses, some sustainable and others not. The nature of these responses cannot be captured by an analysis that focuses exclusively or largely on the current overarching narratives of healing and justice (see Tanner 1998; Depew 1996). The issues at hand are not simply about healing individuals or divisions between community members and families; they also reflect irresolvable differences that have emerged historically and that are reflected in the dramatically different views about justice. Indeed, the possibility of irreconciability concerning particular issues or between particular people seems to have been well recognized by Coast Salish people in earlier eras and was accounted for by a pattern of avoidance, if necessary, or of allowing issues simply to remain unsolved. Current narratives of healing and justice reflect an inadequate sense of the enormously increased internal variability and complexity of indigenous communities and appear to point to a notion of culture as, at heart, homogeneous and capturable as an entity. In this sense, narratives of healing are both too grand and too simple. In addition, the notion of healing unproblematically assumes the priority of collective rights over those of individuals, a conception that romanticizes and misrepresents indigenous concepts of the individual. La Rocque (1997:83), citing Plains, Métis, and Northwest Coast examples, argued that the safety and dignity of individuals in indigenous communities was, as a rule, not sacrificed for the collectivity. The notion of healing as justice, however, is built on the idea that individuals must submit to the collective good. This view creates particular problems for female victims of violence who must give up their own rights to security in favor of collective rights that favor the offender (81). The problem of individual rights and collective healing became a major problem in the South Island Justice Project, as described in a later chapter.

In this chapter I have pointed to a need for an ethnographically informed, historical, and comparative analysis of tribal justice that accounts for local discourses and local understandings and engagements of power. This analysis considers tradition in its manifestations as a political instrument as well as an asset in directing and regulating community life. Several forms of internal differentiation have resulted from colonialism, particularly the emergence of new social classes, new means of wealth, privilege, and power, and generational discord. But I argue that community diversity is also the result of deeper, older processes, and these, too, need attention in the study of indigenous justice in the present day. Finally, I suggest that communities have assumed an outward-looking stance in response to an ever-intruding mainstream society that has historically fluctuated wildly in its responses and policies toward indigenous peoples and communities. A current, widespread expression of this is captured, to a degree, by the notion of an ethnonationalist discourse set in opposition to a bureaucratic nationalism derived from European sources.

2

Background

Historicizing Coast Salish Aboriginal Justice

In the early 2000s it is difficult to adequately characterize the practices of aboriginal justice as they existed early on in the era following intrusion by Euro-American outsiders. Indeed, attempting to do so replicates the difficulties encountered within the three programs whose efforts I describe here. Efforts to reconstruct mid-nineteenth-century justice practices are tripped up by several conceptual hurdles, among these the problems of relying on memory culture, especially current pressures to present idealized versions of honored predecessors' lives. Even if elders are knowledgeable, one cannot unproblematically assume that elder testimony about justice primarily addresses the past. Fienup-Riordan states, "Elders' testimony addressed as much what they hoped for the future as what they remembered of the past. . . . Here it is important to look at both what Yupiit Nation elders chose to say and what they omitted. . . . Their testimony also was rhetorical: They presented the problems of today as proof that ignoring the traditional framework inevitably led to disaster. Their testimony was an ideal view of the past recalled in the present in an effort to influence the future. *The value of the testimony is not its documentation of the past*" (1990a:197; emphasis mine).

In addition, many of the current generation of Coast Salish elders grew up in circumstances that limited their access to justice practices. Barnett (n.d.; folder 1–5) was told by one elder Coast Salish informant in the 1930s that children were never allowed to watch the work conducted to resolve difficulties. Although this practice does not seem to have been universal in the Coast Salish world, it is suggestive. Further, many attended residential schools that removed them from observing and hearing about how their elders handled conflict and contradiction (see, for example, Carlson 1997b). Officials at residential schools worked to break the transmission of indigenous languages and, thereby, the transmission of key ideas. Most of the current elders grew up in the period after the effective repression of Coast Salish languages, but, in addition, communities were restricted by Indian agents in their ability to apply culturally appropriate sanctions and to control their own communities (Kew 1990b). In sum, justice practices have been subject to government intervention and are, consequently, historically volatile.

In considering aboriginal practices in collaboration with the Stó:lō Nation, my graduate students and I faced the same problems Llewellyn and Hoebel (1941; see also Hoebel 1967) faced earlier in the century in reconstructing the law of the Cheyennes and other American Indian tribes. These scholars responded, in part, by searching for general principles of the law through a process of boiling down case law as described by elder informants. This approach runs the risk of assuming that indigenous practices were bound to general principles and that one can generalize across family and community boundaries. We described this method as follows:

> One method of thinking about aboriginal justice is to work with descriptions of actual cases and to infer general principles. Some of these have been presented to us by elders as a means of showing general principals, but we do not think that Stó:lo justice likely depended on abstract principles, case law or the use of precedent in the same sense as Canadian law. Rather, these cases provide ways to think through issues rather than suggest resolutions, as we discuss below. There are, therefore, limits to the case analysis approach. Instead of looking for legal principles, the cases presented to us, and also the ones we have read about, seem to be useful in reflecting underlying spiritual values which give guidance. (Miller and McMullen 1997)

As I point out later concerning the South Island Justice Project, justice was reduced to finding the lowest common denominator, merely those things held in common, a critique Vincent addressed concerning Hoebel's attempts to eliminate contradictions between elder informants (Vincent 1994). Elders reminded us of the variability in cultural practice among the families that comprise the Coast Salish bands and tribes.

We addressed our reservations in a report to the Stó:lō Nation Justice Committee, noting that we analyzed a variety of materials thematically in order to potentially meet the test of practicality. Current efforts to understand aboriginal practice are only of use if they can be comprehended and applied across the community, regardless of what might once have been the practice or the cultural ideal. This idea is well understood among some in indigenous communities themselves, where many hold a "fluid understanding of traditional law." Ryan noted, for example, concerning collaborative efforts to restore Dene justice, that "our goal is to explore what traditional values people can take forward upon which to build a current rational way of dealing with problems of social and personal control" (1995:66). Warry invoked the distinction between custom, a particular cultural practice, and tradition, "the appeal to values and actions that sustain customs or provide continuity to a social group over time," in arguing for a centrist view (1998:174–75).

At best, one can report on how members of the current community understand the practices of their own predecessors (see Fienup-Riordan 1990a) and supplement this with how elders and others of earlier generations understood and explained these issues in their own times. Some inferences can be drawn from historical materials (see Harmon 1998 for a detailed effort to do so). This creates a sort of suggestive pastiche, specific to no particular place or time. Because many of the present-day elders have themselves read the available ethnographic materials about their own relatives, ancestors, and communities, there is a curious reverberation effect in interviewing elders and searching through the ethnographic materials of predecessor anthropologists. For example, Chief Frank Malloway, a host for the ethnographic field school organized collaboratively by the University of British Columbia and the Stó:lō Nation, is an avid reader of the work of Wilson Duff (1952), Franz Boas (1894), and other ethnographers (B. Miller 1994d). We described these issues as follows:

> All of these materials, but especially our work with the Stó:lō elders, have helped us create a frame for the material presented here. We do not represent that our organization of the materials falls within Stó:lō ways of knowing, but rather, allow us to reflect this knowledge and to create relevant contrasts with the concepts of law and justice within the Canadian system. Our frame allows us, we believe, to illuminate ideas both in their integration into Stó:lō thought and in relation to the mainstream society. We first introduce our project and our methods, then comment on the relationship between Stó:lō justice and community values and spiritual practices. By so doing, we attempt to discern pragmatic "premises" of Stó:lō justice. Next, we describe

major causes of conflict. Then, we consider the aims of Stó:lō justice practices. Although we describe the Stó:lō aboriginal justice as not procedural in nature, there are legal procedures, and we describe some of these in the next section.

This draft is perhaps weakest in integrating ideas of aboriginal justice with ideas of spirituality and spiritual practice. In part, this is because our report reflects the ways in which the community elders to date have wished to describe aboriginal justice to us. All have provided an implicit reference to spirituality, and this is reflected here, but not many specifics of Longhouse practice. We wish to respect the elders' manner of treating the topic. We hope, however, with time, to build up this section. In addition, we have not attempted to present specifics of law in particular domains such as property law, resource law, family law and so on. This reflects the issues the elders have chosen to present to us. Much of what we have been told concerns the regulation of affairs between, rather than within, families.

We have, at points, felt the pull between ideal representations of aboriginal law, that is, how it ought to have been and ought to be, and the real world enactment of aboriginal justice by community members. As with all communities, there is sometimes a gulf between the ideal and the real. For the most part, we have chosen to present the ideal. However, justice deals with disagreement, conflict, dispute, wrongdoing, and the real as opposed to the ideal, by its very nature. It is often in conflict that the tension between the ideal and the real is most felt. We approach the Stó:lō material as reflective of a society with deep cultural values, including a value placed on finding new ways to address the constantly changing issues. We think that justice has likely always had this feature and that we may capture, to some degree, snapshots of aboriginal justice at one or more moments, but that the practice of justice itself continues to change.

All of the material we have examined is situated in some particular moment and significant changes arose after regular, sustained contact with non-natives in the 19th century. We characterize this as being reflected in historical shifts, and, likely, with increased regimentation of justice practices. However, we have not made the study of these historical shifts our concern here. We do wish to point out that accounts of aboriginal justice vary somewhat depending on the time period under consideration. It is also worth noting that it is precisely

> the ability to practice aboriginal justice that was most restricted by colonial authorities, and elders have told us frankly that much of what they remember is from a period in which outside agencies (especially Indian agents, missionaries, school administrators, and so on) held control over much of the administration of justice.
>
> There is also the issue of differences in teachings by family and by individual. As with other cultural practices, members of various families do not think in precisely the same terms concerning aboriginal justice. We have found that the toleration for some differences in practices and viewpoint is, in fact, a hallmark of Stó:lō society, and that the practice of aboriginal justice reflects this.
>
> Finally, consistent with [our understanding of] Stó:lō philosophy, we believe, we employ the concepts of "wrong doer" rather than criminal, and of "dispute management" or "dispute resolution" rather than the Canadian conceptions of punishment, the payment of an individual's debt to society and so on. In this paper we address both what might be regarded as civil law, that is non-criminal disputes between individuals, and criminal law. Unlike the Canadian system, the Stó:lō system of justice does not draw clear boundaries between civil and criminal law. (Miller and McMullen 1997)

There have been two significant prior efforts to comprehend Coast Salish aboriginal justice practices. One is the study by the Northwest Intertribal Court System (NICS:1991a). A panel of elders was convened to describe these practices for the consideration of the conduct of their own tribal courts in Washington State. The other major work was the report of Vancouver Island elders for the South Island Justice Project (First Nations 1987). I consider both of these works in detail in later chapters.

The Self, Place, Theories of Power, and Coast Salish Justice

Despite having noted these reservations about making claims about aboriginal law in the Coast Salish region, I venture some characterizations. An adequate theory of aboriginal justice depends on an articulation of the ideas of the self, of the social individual, of place, and of local theories of power. In the early-reservation period, and to some extent today, Coast Salish cultural ideas of the self have emphasized human subordination to and dependence on more powerful, nonhuman forces.

These forces, some of which are anthropomorphized beings and others not, are potentially beneficial and dangerous and sometimes form relationships with humans who may be "favored by power" (Jenness 1955; Kew 1990b). But the nature of human relations with nonhumans is never fully revealed to others, and the source and extent of their power is thereby unknown (Amoss 1977, 1978). The human being is made up of several components, these being the body; the soul, which only some can see, which continues after death, and which can be lost; the breath, vitality, or life, which is not a condition, which can be disassociated from the body, thereby creating a state of illness, and which can be returned; and the shadow or reflection, which also can be lost or stolen. Although everyone has all four of these components, they are not well integrated in the young, the feeble, the ill, and others who are consequently vulnerable to spiritual dangers.

There is another part of the self that not all acquire: Sil'ye, the guardian spirit power. This power is gained in various ways, coming unbidden to some, and to others through the rigorous process of fasting, training, and purification necessary to become acceptable prior to undergoing a quest for the spirit power. Once a relationship is established, a human becomes a different kind of human being. This relationship is invoked in the complex known as Spirit Dancing, or Syowen, a term that refers to the visible aspects of the nonhuman world given to humans. The initiate into Spirit Dancing draws closer to the nonhuman sphere and, eventually, gains new powers and abilities once the relationship becomes properly managed. The private relationship with the spirit power becomes dangerous if spoken of and if the spirit is offended, and an upset in the relationship can cause the death of the human partner. Healthy persons, then, know who they are (their selves) and maintain a proper spirit relationship.

Coast Salish concepts of power follow from these conceptions of the self as a spiritual, psychological state and conceptions of the individual located within society. Power is not seen as a property of an abstract entity, such as society, which might act on individuals or groups, or of social institutions, such as the family, but rather as a manifestation of largely unspoken human-nonhuman relations. Some individuals, however, were and are known publicly to occupy particular social roles as a consequence of their recognizable spirit powers. These include, among others, warriors, shamans, carvers, and public speakers. Although these ideas describe concepts widely shared in earlier generations, they still influence present-day conceptions and are still directly taught in the Winter Dance houses that are the centers of Spirit Dancing throughout Coast Salish territory.

There are particular features of Coast Salish theories of power that complicate their comprehension by non-indigenous peoples both today and in the early contact period (I do not consider the present time to be outside the contact period, although the history of relations is now of some time depth). First, the locus of power in individuals or nonhuman beings rather than institutions or national groups complicates the idea of domination by an outside group. In addition, the authority of an individual was not thought to be easily generalized; efficacy depended on circumstance, so someone skilled in one area of life was not necessarily an overall leader (Harmon 1998:22). Third, virtually all appropriate adults had access to spiritual power of some sort, such as the ability to acquire wealth, gamble successfully, cure, hold one's breath underwater to repair fishing weirs, eat prodigious amounts without manifesting a swollen stomach, and seduce women, among others. Those without spiritual helpers were thought to be insignificant and weak. But because spirits might associate with anyone, even those without "advice" (including proper spiritual training), prudent people avoided giving offense to anyone. Amoss wrote that "Coast Salish Indians are . . . genuinely afraid of offending those whom they believe have strong spirit powers, because the spirits may take umbrage at the insult offered their human partners and retaliate without the conscious participation of the injured person" (1977:134). One interpreter concluded that power "was not so much a means to dominate others as insurance against domination" (Harmon 1998:23).

Bierwert commented on Coast Salish concepts of power and the lack of intersubjective agreement that continues to characterize life and that imposes limits on the exercise of power:

> The fact that a local culture works without having a master narrative has resulted in a lot of very bumpy roads in Indian country. Coast Salish social structures have been comparatively decentered, a phenomenon attributable to the history of colonial oppression, but also reflecting laterally distributed power. . . . Here, local knowledge fits together loosely and contains contradictory statements about human dynamics

> and human natures. The "text of culture" is episodic, open to accretion of meaning. To use postmodern terms, the culture is destabilized and decentered; to use more classic terms, power is diffuse, laws and characterizations are applied ad hominem, and judgements are ad hoc. (1999:5–6)

But one must not assume that there was no operation of domination among the Coast Salish. Indeed, efforts to avoid domination suggest the presence of efforts to dominate. Over a long period, longer than the historical frame of reference here, one could read Coast Salish society as oscillating between periods characterized by efforts to centralize and dominate and reactions against this. Thom (1995), for example, connected the rise and fall of the practice of building elaborate burial mounds to a period of consolidation of regional authority by political elites and subsequent successful resistance to this consolidation. Stó:lō cultural adviser and historian Sonny McHalsie has argued that both a class system and social conflict are deeply rooted within Stó:lō history and that oral histories provide a glimpse of powerful leaders capable of controlling and regulating others (McHalsie 1999).

The social field was not level in the historic period, and the local play of power by dominant members of society must also be taken into account in considering prior justice. In the Coast Salish world, domination did not ordinarily take the form of physical intimidation or direct attack. Rather, it was manifested through indirection, subtle intimidation, and efforts to control public discourses about appropriate behavior. Duff (1952:80) observes, concerning what he called the "Upper Stalo," that birth into high-ranked family "constituted a tremendous advantage." Such birth brought control of wealth, the possibility to be bestowed important ancestral names, and the opportunity to train for positions of respect. In addition, Duff writes, Stó:lō beliefs were that children inherited the characteristics of parents and that the families of great people were thought to be superior and worthy of deference. He notes that despite the expected humility and mock denial of status by elites, "there was never any doubt in anyone's mind that high-rank people were superior individuals. All children were thoroughly taught who were their social equals, and who were their inferiors" (80). Barnett (field notes, 1935–36; folder 1–7) gives the sense of this by indicating that the practice of the payment of blankets in the event of a murder was not extended to "low people," who were said to be just good for clam digging and drying fish.

It is worth noting that this domination, as elsewhere, was regularly quietly contested by subordinated people in such forms as storytelling and in the constant monitoring of elite people to see if they would maintain their propriety. For example, elite nonhuman beings (stand-ins for the local human elites) are revealed as pretentious and without the knowledge and bearing they claim in the oral traditions such as the story of Crow's marriage. Crow's claims to upper-class standing are belied by her reliance on slaves to make her marriage arrangements and on her crude voice (see Bierwert 1996; for a fuller development of this theme see Holden 1976).

For the Coast Salish, then, power was not ordinarily consolidated in social institutions that served to protect and reproduce the advantage of the elites, nor were there social boundaries insulating the elites from continual interaction with the non-elites. Power was regularly contested, and the capacity of others could be underestimated only at one's peril. Although power was thought to be an attribute of individuals with strong spirit helpers, access to power was not simply or easily passed intergenerationally. Power had both spiritual and material dimensions, and power differentials reflected raw demographic variables, primarily the size of one's family network, in addition to control over important resources such as salmon procurement stations, and the personal abilities of leaders (Kew 1976). But important differences existed between individuals and families at any given moment, as indicated by the elites' abilities to influence community affairs and to impose their viewpoint in defining and redefining community goals and values. Differences in power were displayed publicly as well in the layout of longhouses (with the location of family quarters indicating status), in the conduct of potlatches, in control over important resources, and in deference shown at public gatherings.

Ancestors of the members of the current communities created justice practices that accounted for these views of the self, the social individual, and the nature of human power. They employed a range of sanctions to control behavior and restore communities in the event of a breach. These sanctions included restitution, ostracism, social pressures, and even violent recrimination and are well documented in ethnographic literature. Public ceremonies were, and continue to be, carried out in the process of the public debate and resolution of conflicts. In addition, the region has been characterized by a cultural emphasis on the avoidance of conflict through proper training in the absence of coercive authority in order to avoid disruption of economic activities. Ethnographic materials suggest that local kin groups bore responsibility for the behavior of members, and that damage to the personnel or property of another family constituted grounds for compensation (as in the wergild). Meetings were held between senior members of the families to work out the terms of compensation, but if these were unsuccessful, rivalries or blood feuds could develop. The offender also had to undergo seclusion in the woods in order to fast and bathe to obtain purity and become acceptable to society. Although the ethnographic materials emphasize compensation in the event of a killing (accidental or otherwise), this may in some measure reflect the transformed, dangerous, more violent environment in the middle and late nineteenth century, and these processes also applied to other difficulties between families.

Although there are significant risks in making comparison to Western legal concepts, there is some advantage in considering the issues of guilt and intention from the vantage point of social hierarchy. Perhaps the closest ethnographic examination of the intersections of justice and social hierarchy is found in the work of Snyder (1964), who combined her ethnographic work in the 1940s and early 1950s with an analysis of folkloric reflections on community values and practices. Snyder's Puget Sound materials derived from her work with elders from Swinomish, Samish, Lower Skagit, Upper Skagit, and other communities. In 1953 a Swinomish elder told Snyder a story about his father concerning an episode that brought relations between members of two groups (Swinomish and Stillaguamish) to a dangerous point.

> When HbE's father was a small boy he was once walking home along the beach at dusk. He was half lost, and came to a Stillaguamish camp in front of which he had to pass. Nightguards had already been posted there, and the child skulked along the shoreline in hopes that they would not see him. But they did, and his suspicious activity led them to think that he was trying to steal a canoe. They held him at their camp overnight. The next morning a man there recognized the boy and warned the others that they had made a grave mistake, that

> he was the son of important people and that they [the boy's people] would soon find out why he was detained—as a captive for slave-trade. The Stillaguamish hurriedly released the boy and were ready to face a charge against them. Soon the boy's family arrived at their camp bringing a canoeload of valuables to the Stillaguamish and obsequious apologies for having a youngster foolish enough to lose his way at night. That was, of course, an insinuation of the Stillaguamish's guilt—one which could have been played up as an abduction and not a natural error. But all of this was supererogatory for the already anxious Stillaguamish who accepted the Skagits' offerings and then gave their visitors in return far more than they had received. (Snyder 1964:433–34)

This story reveals both the critical role of class and status in Coast Salish society and the pragmatic side of justice. Upper-class people in this telling overawe lower-ranked people and dominate their thoughts and actions without resorting to force. Here, the critical issue was not the boy's guilt or his intentions (apparently no one, neither his family nor his captors, made any attempt to determine if he had or had not tried to steal a canoe) but, rather, power relations. But there is a second issue, namely the costs to elite people anxious to maintain their position in society. Snyder's field notes provide more detail, and the importance of this story is the interpretation given it by the elder while speaking to Snyder. He said that his grandfather's motives were that he "wanted to keep their record clean; to wipe out the accusation, rather than the crime or the supposed crime." Elmendorf (1993:192) provides a similar example of a Skokomish man who paid the father of a wronged slave in order to avoid trouble with the Klallam.

Snyder's field notes, recorded in 1953 with a knowledgeable Swimonish elder, provide insight into the related issue of intentionality: "If a [murder] is accidental a slayer will sacrifice some of his things as a sort of apology to that family of the deceased and then there will be no ill-feelings towards them. If you have intentionally committed a murder and still 'apologize' to seem innocent of intention, someone would know you had ill-feeling towards that person, he would still revenge."

Another Swinomish elder told Snyder in 1953: "Accidents had to be covered by payment, whether accidental or intentional. Intentional murders turn into long grudges between families, and a feeling to get even." Yet another Swinomish elder told Snyder that "with theft, if you didn't know who stole, you let it go, because you couldn't prove anything." The elder noted that if the murderer was not known, the wronged party would hire a person to find out. This was done spiritually, according to the way the *skedelich* (animated spirit board held by someone with a specific, strong spiritual power and by an assistant) was interpreted. "This is just between the family and the hired party." This implies that the evidence of guilt produced spiritually did not create the grounds for demanding compensation or asserting guilt.

Snyder's work gives a picture of the occasional employment of secrecy, both in the commission of wrongdoing and in response. One elder gave an example of a murder within a family that was revenged by someone outside of the family "without the other parties knowing it." The same elder noted that intermarried families having a quarrel (blood feud) would "usually hire an Indian doctor to get rid of the guilty party, or hire a woman to poison, get him without shooting." The implication is that shooting would be more public and cause further difficulties. This elder also told Snyder that "One can shoot another who has gotten off his own territory and no one will know." A present-day Stó:lō elder pointed out that "I've heard stories too, where one or two people have had something happen to them while they're in the wrong people's territory but they won't be able to prove so they won't be able to do anything about it really because they can't prove why that person was harmed or injured or killed. But that thing is there, that maybe you could say, 'well that person was hunting in the wrong territory, see what happened?' But no one could say or find out how that person died."

Barnett, working with Squamish elders in the 1930s, notes that the practice of a face-saving potlatch ("wash blood") was held only if a fight was witnessed or if the damage was apparent. If the fight was not witnessed, the father of the combatant would "pay maybe $10," and the injured party would "give maybe $5," at which point, the combatants would "shake hands, just like married." Similarly, if a man sickened and died, there would be no "wash blood" unless the death was accidental or violent and was witnessed (n.d., folder 1–5).

There are several distinct views concerning execution held by the elders with whom Snyder worked. One Upper Skagit man observed that murderers had to be killed for "make even," and that the punishers would be "the next generation down." A Swinomish elder said that murderers performed acts of sacrifice and apology. If they did not, there were revenge murders in retaliation. A second Swinomish elder spoke of execution by the chief for the crime of theft. A second Upper Skagit man reported that "murderers paid funeral expenses, and otherwise, they weren't punished. Murderers usually leave." A Swinomish elder told Snyder in 1953 that "Murderers usually leave, lives with another tribe. If they [members of another village] let him in, they watch him closely." In other situations people involved in an interfamily dispute could become disgruntled and leave the community when other attempts at solving the dispute had failed. These differences in practice likely reflect historical shifts, such as the consolidation of the Upper Skagit in the 1850s under a powerful prophet (who practiced corporal punishments of his followers), or differences between communities.

Ethnographic materials provide some insights into what might be known as rules of evidence and the use of precedent, to again make analogy to Western legal categories. Although the terms are foreign, the ideas are not. Coast Salish people, in common with others, faced the issue of what might be said about a given dispute or case of wrongdoing, by whom, and what weight might be assigned to a particular person's views of the matter. Present-day Puget Sound elders point out that people were free to make their views known. Yet, if some people did not want to talk publicly they could hire a public speaker to talk for them. Stories of family and village history, genealogy, and legends could be presented to provide guidelines for resolving current disputes (NICS 1991a). However, these histories were not referred to for rules of precedent. A problem was not resolved in the same manner as a previous problem because of the implicit understanding that no two circumstances are precisely alike.

There is overlap between the features of indigenous views of knowledge, which would be categorized as science in Western thought, and justice concepts. Kidwell (1991) argues that Western science has been constructed around the search for law-like regularities and for predictive generalization, but indigenous systems of knowledge have, instead, been framed around the idea of understanding the spiritual uniqueness or will of entities in nature, which might also yield a predictive capacity. So, too, the circumstances of the people involved in wrongdoing or disputes could not be just the same as those involved in earlier cases, and, consequently, a resolution can only be reached if the particulars of the case are understood. Just as in indigenous "science" knowledge, there seems therefore not to have been an emphasis on generalization and anything resembling the creation of binding precedent that allows the facts of a case to fit into an existing legal category. Zion (1988) makes a similar point, characterizing North American indigenous law generally as structural and procedural, rather than substantive and rule-bound in that relationships, obligations, and group survival are more significant than substantive law (which he notes exists in hero and animal stories).

These details concerning the lack of emphasis on guilt, intention, and precedent can be connected to Coast Salish ideas of power, illness, and the control of will, particularly the notion that individuals can harm others through their failure to control their thoughts. Individuals must therefore guard against their injurious projections onto others (Swinomish 1991). This harm can be unintentional or intentional and yet can produce similar results. In some cases, a spirit helper of an individual has been said to act on the emotions of its human partner to harm enemies. These ideas explain the cultural de-emphasis (but not absence) of guilt and intention as guiding principles of justice since one is thought not to be at fault for such harm, although it is an indicator of a poor upbringing and a failure to consolidate one's relationship with a spirit helper (see Blomfield 1999c for a consideration of the role of guilt and intentionality). Because spiritual power might be exercised inadvertently in some instances, justice practices typically focus on repairing relations between families rather than punishing the individual. Stories reveal, however, that individuals might be restrained from causing further harm or even murdered by family members if it is apparent they cannot or will not stop.

None of the discussions of justice appear to suggest any formal sense of precedent, then, because of the spiritual distinctiveness of each situation and because of the ambiguity of oral materials and the ability of tellers to apply them in a variety of ways. But there is another related issue, the nature of landscape, which has been poorly understood in its connection to aboriginal justice practices. This issue is hinted at in one sentence in the NICS study, above, for example, but remains unclarified. The landscape is perceived within a set of cultural, historical, and spiritual understandings and serves as a mnemonic trigger for ideas that have important application to conflict and wrongdoing.

Landscape, Place, and Place-Names

Studies of landscape, place, and place-names are undergoing a rebirth in anthropological studies and within indigenous communities in the effort to gain a greater understanding of indigenous concepts of knowledge and history (Thornton 1997). Scholars have noted the importance of place-names as a domain of knowledge and their great density. Thornton, for example, cites early-twentieth-century ethnographer T. T. Waterman's claim of 10,000 indigenous place-names in Puget Sound (216). Basso, a leading exponent of the study of place, observes that distinguished anthropologist Edward Spicer erroneously believed that Western Apache people "showed very little interest in becoming tribal historians" (1996:30), apparently failing to perceive that Apache practices of interpreting the past are different than those of Western historiography. This is worth considering because, although the details of Apache landscape and historiography are not the same as among the Coast Salish, there are important parallels.

"Anglo-American practices, such as crafting extended chronicles and presenting autobiographies[, are] tangential to their interests and unsuited to their tastes," Basso writes (1996:31). He observes that Apache history is "Weakly empirical, thinly chronological, and rarely written down, advances no theories, tests no hypotheses, and offers no general models. What it does instead, and likely has done for centuries, is fashion possible worlds, give them expressive shape, and present them for contemplation as images of the past that can deepen and enlarge awareness of the present. *In the country of the past, as Apaches like to explore it, the place-maker is an indispensable guide*" (32, emphasis mine).

In Basso's rendering, Apaches "speak the past into being," to give it dramatic form, by speaking as a witness of what happened at a particular location and could be happening now. Within the narrative frame, ancestors moved through their lives, and "most of the time things are done correctly. But now and again mistakes are made, serious trouble comes, and life is shattered. Pathos reigns and the air is charged with suspense. What will happen next? What will the ancestors do? How will they survive?" (1996:32–33). The principle themes are survival, community and kin, and moral norms. Therefore, one aim of the landscape-linked histories is to create empathy and admiration for the ancestors and to hold them up to emulation "except, of course, when they fail to do what is right and threatened by their actions the welfare of the group; then, they are punished or killed" (33).

While Western historiography is obsessed with time, indigenous practice is more concerned with place—with the actions of ancestors and the nonhuman beings their ancestors encountered in a particular place (Sider 1993). Comparatively, Western history "lies silent and inert on the printed English page . . . it also seems unconnected to daily affairs and concerns; it is history without discernible applications" (Basso 1996:33). Indigenous communities, then, embrace a "spatial sense of history" (Vine Deloria Jr., cited in Basso, 34). Basso concludes that "knowledge of place is therefore closely linked to knowledge of the self, to grasping one's position in the larger scheme of things, including one's community" (34).

In British Columbia, place-name studies (often subsumed within "traditional use studies") have an important connection to the processes of making claims to land and to establishing the terms of treaty negotiations. These connections have been investigated for several years by Sonny McHalsie, a Stó:lō employed by the nation as a cultural adviser, in order to record the several existing stories associated with place (see "*Halq'emeylem* Names Hold Timeless Histories of These Places," *Sqwelqwel* 3, no. 1 [January–February 1994]: 12). These stories are not so much contending as alternative stories inasmuch as families have their own particular points of reference to place. There has been no single dominant narrative in which all members of the community participate, and in this sense, Stó:lō place-name histories are not "histories within history" (Sider and Smith 1997), that is, local histories that contest overarching narratives. Stó:lō histories come into contest, however, with white society over the meaning of place and Stó:lō people's role in it. Carlson, for example, took note of the relationship between Stó:lō place-names and adverse interactions with non-indigenous people in the gold rush period of the late 1850s: "*Halq'emeylem* place names from the area of the most intense mining activities between Hope and Yale also reflect aspects of the relationships between the Stó:lō and the *Xwelitem* ['hungry peoples'—a term that has come to mean whites] miners. Elders Susan Peters and Amelia Douglas explained that the *Halq'emeylem* name for one of the gold rush Bar's translates into English as 'cleared away.' This term describes the rocks that had been stripped of moss through the mining process" (Carlson 1997b:62).

Background

An academic interpreter of Coast Salish concepts of the landscape, of place and space, Bierwert (1986, 1999), points to the creative potential and the possibility of discovery inherent in human interaction with the landscape. "Salish people," writes Bierwert, "see power as being within a place, not only inscribed upon it" (1999:39). Further, the texts of place, rather than being merely authoritative and literal, "question" the tellers and the listeners to produce their own understandings (66). Place is experienced subjectively, synesthetically, in a manner that opens up human understanding, beyond thought, to extraordinary perception.

Landmarks are personified and serve as guides for the Stó:lō. Bierwert describes Mt. Cheam, in Stó:lō territory, for example, in these terms:

> The Mountain is a lady spoken of with affection; a woman grieving; a sleeping giant; an Indian; an elder and ancestor; a grandparent, strong, loved, and respected. I can generalize the Stó:lō interpretations of the mountain in the statement that the mountains are part of the continuum of Stó:lō life, regarded by the people as ancestral both in time and . . . in their beneficence and strength. . . . But for all the warmth in that generalization, it lacks the vividness of the individual images given to me. Each image focuses on a set of experiences: a lady's attributes, a trauma of family life. . . . Each image is cryptic and does not exclude other interpretations. (1986:39)

Further, "Each image draws on teachings of the past and a complexity of explication fuller than its moment of discourse provides. The little text is also an abstract in relation to the full text of reference in the speaker's memory. But in use it is more than an abstract: it not only abbreviates but it stands for the full text of references: it is metonmymic for that full text" (40–41).

In the Stó:lō world, then, and, one might argue, the larger Coast Salish world, the images of landscape can be brought together into significance, but this process is "creative and intrinsic to the individual" (Bierwert, 1986:55) and contains an element of surprise or gestalt.

A central thematic element of the oral materials of indigenous peoples of the Americas is travel and change (Momaday 1991). This holds true, too, for the Stó:lō, for whom space is defined through traveling—as in the travel of the sun, of the cyclicity of seasons, of the flow of the rivers, and of humans on the landscape. People "follow a trail," and trails "inscribe lives on the face of the earth." The Stó:lō people conceive that they follow their ancestors on these trails, "tracing the same patterns in their environment" (Bierwert 1986:150). Stó:lō people move through these patterns, reenacting tradition. Necessarily, their actions also involve recollections, both from their own lives and from oral tradition. "Thus, the geographic mapping . . . is inscribed in memory, together with experience" (151).

Stó:lō experiences of the landscape include stories of travel to encounter immortal beings in their spiritual homes, such as caves, pools of water, or underwater locations. From these risky encounters, humans gain spiritual helpers or, in some cases, fail to return. It is the travel to worlds other than the normal world of everyday life that brought shock, transformation, and new power. Travel on the physical landscape, then, connects Stó:lō people to other experiences: "Today, getting a powerful sense from the river or the cedars or a particular rock . . . is recognized as part of supernatural communication. The old stories of supernatural contact fit into this more immediate spiritual experience. . . . Thus, there is a linking of episodes: immediate and personal spiritual awareness is related to the histories of supernatural contact and both are also related to the myth time marking of the land" (Bierwert 1986:206).

Transformer stories concern a being who transformed the landscape in the myth time and provide examples of how place can have agency, intelligence, and will. X̱á:ls, for example, is said to have punished three chiefs who refused to protect Stó:lō knowledge by turning them into a transformer stone, located in the town of Mission BC (Carlson 1997b:97). This and other transformer stones are not inert, nor are they simply identified with a story of spiritual failure; they also provoke an understanding of power and capacity in the landscape. The chiefs are not simply dead but, rather, are transformed, and the stones themselves have spiritual efficacy to this day.

There is yet another feature of human interaction with the landscape that impinges on justice. Coast Salish people maintain a system of "Indian names," or ancestral names, which connect the holder of the name (the incumbent) to a line of predecessors and, in due course, successors, and ultimately to a location where an ancestor had a spiritual encounter with a nonhuman being. The name implies rights to a location and obligations to the site and the relationship with the spiritual being. In the process of giving the name to a family member, speakers often describe the place and the resources there that enable the family to remain prosperous and healthy. Names, then, capture the ancestral relationships between humans and place and, sometimes, the transformations between them in those cases where humans were changed into salmon, cedar, and other beings (Thom and Cameron 1997:167). There have been recent efforts to rethink and reestablish the connection between names and justice. Anthropologist Michael Kew (personal communication) attempted to draw on his detailed record of names to help establish claims to title and thereby help mediate overlapping band claims made to land within Vancouver prior to legal proceedings; McHalsie (n.d.) has referred to names in his effort to understand contemporary rights to Stó:lō fishing locations.

Jay Miller, drawing on his experience with Coast Salish of Puget Sound and other indigenous peoples, observed the connection between place and social authority: "dominant features of the landscape, believed to be inhabited by powerful spirits, were associated with predominant families, which often formed a regional elite. Known as 'real' people, members of such elite families, relying on the security of their strong ties to a particular landscape, were connected by obligation, ritual, trade, or marriage. *Every terrain was saturated with memories, which compressed generations of experience—ranging from daily routine to great crises—into useful knowledge*" (1991:306, emphasis mine).

Spiritually efficacious "real" people" (as opposed to those who are not real to spiritual beings) regulated subsistence and other practices by managing relations with the nonhuman real people. It was not until senior people conducted first salmon ceremonies, for example, that fishing could begin.

To summarize, landscape connects Coast Salish people to their spiritual relations, to their histories, to one's sense of self, and to teachings that point (rather than direct) the way to a life well lived. All of these are comprehended by each person in his or her own manner and yet provide the means to think through a dilemma facing a family or community. As with the Apache case described by Basso, the sense of place provides guidance and meaning and a way to find commonality with others with whom one is in conflict. The sense of place may even lead to new understandings that can be drawn on in resolving problems.

Nineteenth-Century Public Policy and Political Economy

As I have shown, Coast Salish peoples' contact with whites and other non-indigenous peoples in the late eighteenth century started a process with gradual but serious consequences for indigenous justice practices and the justice practices that I have just described. In this section, I consider what happened in indigenous communities and how these changes have been understood and described. To a considerable degree, extant theories of change in Coast Salish have been inadequate to understand shifts in justice practice and associated legal consciousness. One line of argument suggests that early contact was benign and that, later, especially following the relocation to reserves and reservations, breakdown of the family unit reduced the capacity for social control. However, this viewpoint makes it difficult to perceive just how indigenous justice shifted in the late eighteenth and the nineteenth centuries. Among the notable changes of this period were the rise of new sorts of leaders, including warriors and prophets who came to dominate society, and new wealth and class divisions. In addition, communities expropriated white legal practices and institutions for their own benefit, and interactions with whites in the "middle ground" between cultures wrought changes in both directions.

The first recorded contact between Europeans and Coast Salish people occurred in 1790 when a Spanish expedition under the command of Quimper explored the Strait of Juan de Fuca. Another Spaniard, Eliza, sailed through Padilla Bay and Bellingham Bay and the southern end of Georgia Strait and then sailed south through Haro Strait. George Vancouver explored Puget Sound and Georgia Strait. These explorers provide the first written reports of Coast Salish Culture (Suttles 1954:37–38). Following these forays by British and Spanish explorers, who did not stay, came a period of interest in the commercial possibilities of a coastal fur trade. Simon Fraser, of the Northwest Company, traveled overland to the mouth of the Fraser River in 1808 and contacted the Musqueam and other indigenous peoples. Regular contact with non-indigenous people, however, began for those on the Skagit and Fraser Rivers following the establishment of Fort Langley in 1827 (Collins 1950:355).

Analysts have written of an early period of relatively little disruption of indigenous life or, possibly, of a florescence of aboriginal culture (Fisher 1992). Suttles reports that fur traders had no wish to seriously alter native culture other than to get the indigenous people to spend more time hunting fur-bearing animals and "less time quarrelling among themselves. . . . The additions that they made to native culture were mainly in material culture rather than in social organization and religion" (Suttles 1954:39). Collins notes that among the Skagit new techniques of obtaining food stabilized the economy, and the availability of nonsubsistence goods such as blankets and cloth made it possible for more families to stockpile gifts and food for guests and thereby have more and more elaborate potlatches than previously (Collins 1950:336).

But this benign interpretation overlooks several significant developments. The first is the massive depopulation that occurred as a result of a smallpox epidemic derived from white contact with indigenous peoples in the Americas but before the first whites arrived in the area, and the impact of which has not been fully understood and described. Harris, however, has recently written of the emotional, organizational, and political consequences of depopulation in Stó:lō territory along the Fraser River (Harris 1997; see also Duff 1964; Boyd 1990; Guilmet et al. 1991). Swinomish and Skagit chief Martin Sampson gave some sense of the emotional impact and the rapidity of the indigenous adaptation of new ideas of the treatment of disease:

> Epidemics of some disease, probably smallpox, almost wiped out the whole tribe [of Noo-wha-ah, a predecessor band to the present-day Upper Skagit]. There were still many Indians left after the first epidemic in the 1700s, since the people living on the upland lakes and prairies were not affected, but the last scourge in the 1830s reached every village, leaving only about 200 out of over 1000 people.
>
> Only one out of a village on Jarman Prairie was saved, a baby girl. A visiting uncle found her in her dead mother's arms, moved her to the north side of the Prairie, and left her in a shelter. He then went back to the houses on the banks of the Samish River, and after making sure that no others were alive, set the torch to all of the buildings. . . . Stripped naked and with the bare little orphan in his arms, he then set out . . . to the village. . . . Arriving, he did not enter his house, but called from a distance for clothing and food which he took to the girl. . . . As a final precaution, he made three different shelters, and fumigated each. . . . They spent a few more days away from the houses until he was sure they were free of the dread smallpox. (Sampson 1972:25)

Guilmet and colleagues (1991) have connected the epidemics with a systematic erosion of senior leadership and, consequently, of cultural and practical knowledge, the reduction of the work force necessary for subsistence activities, and the disruption of kin networks. All this, they believe, destroyed faith in community health practitioners who were overloaded by patients and unprepared for previous unseen diseases and, ultimately, eroded the underlying cosmology. These events then softened up the community for new ideas introduced by the settler state. Guilmet et al., and others, have argued that indigenous peoples came to believe American and European people, practices, and ideas to be superior because the newcomers seemed less vulnerable to epidemics and were able to fend off "northern raiders," indigenous peoples from the north, especially the Haida and Kwakwaka'wakw, who so thoroughly disturbed the Coast Salish communities. Harmon (1998) convincingly disputes the "loss of cultural confidence argument" on several grounds. She notes that "This argument is seductive because Puget Sound natives had recently suffered catastrophes capable of daunting anyone. First, thousands of people had discovered that their powers were insufficient to defeat new agents of illness and death loose in the land. So many natives had sickened and died from imported pathogens that some could not make sense of their afflictions and loss in the usual ways" (39).

But Harmon points out that the Coast Salish were accustomed to consulting healers from outside their communities and, in any case, believed that they had found ways to come to grips with the new diseases, as indicated by Sampson's (1972) reflections on the importance of shamans during the early reservation period. In addition, Snyder's notes (n.d.) indicate that some Upper Skagits had come to believe they could cure smallpox. Rather, Harmon suggests, the Puget Salish persisted in self-confidence and, in some cases, attempted to usurp the spiritual power of missionaries for their own purposes, as I show below. In addition, Harmon notes that the deficiencies of Bostons (Americans) and King George men (English) were all too apparent to those looking from a Coast Salish viewpoint, no doubt dissuading them from regarding their own societies in an unfavorable light. The whites were ignorant of fishing techniques, they often were without wives and children (indicators of class), they appeared lazy (as indicated by their reliance on underlings to work for them), and they failed to control their tempers, among other failings (Harmon 1998:40).

In any case, although the epidemics neither paved the way for Christianity nor eroded healing and spiritual beliefs connected to justice, they did reduce the Coast Salish population sufficiently that the survivors could be managed by the relatively small non-indigenous population in the middle nineteenth century and, ultimately, could come under a new and quite different legal regime. In addition, the way was open for a drastic alteration in residence patterns, social hierarchy, and political authority.

Another issue concerns the shifting patterns of authority and power within indigenous communities as Coast Salish people sought out ways to benefit themselves and their families (Littlefield 1995; Norton 1985). Up and down the Northwest Coast, political innovators maneuvered to control the exchange of goods between the fur traders and indigenous peoples. Suttles observes that "The fur trade, while not accompanied by much external pressure, may have led to some internal causes of social disruption. It permitted [indigenous] hunters and trappers to accumulate wealth more rapidly than before and probably enabled them to rise socially at the expense of the hereditary owners of fishing locations and other productive sites. This increase in social mobility may have stimulated others to seek out sources of prestige and authority" (1987c:197).

As I show below, precisely this sort of development occurred among the Upper Skagit, Stó:lō, and Coast Salish of southern Vancouver Island. The implications of the rise of newly rich people with political and, frequently, marriage ties to powerful outsiders (Suttles 1954:47) for the practice of justice are considerable. In general, the stratification of society became more pronounced. There was a relative increase of both those people with the wealth to compete for high status and the people who dropped into the lower class as a result of deaths from epidemics and raids and the consequent loss of family history and other information necessary for attaining high status. In addition, there was an increase in the number of slaves in the region and in the number of lower-class villages that lost their small cohort of adult upper-class residents to disease (Suttles 1954:45; Collins 1950). Segments of the communities thereby became carefully regulated and controlled by powerful members of their own groups who demanded conformity. In the Upper Skagit case in the mid–nineteenth century, for example, as elsewhere in Puget Sound, the leader of a prophetic cult subjected villagers under his domain to regular policing. This religious leader created his own summary court and placed miscreants in stocks at his headquarters near Concrete, Washington. Collins wrote that the prophet merged indigenous and Catholic beliefs and practices to create an idiosyncratic new belief system that required strict obedience: "Sk'ubebt'kud instructed Indians to make the sign of the cross before meals, to kneel in prayer on both knees with head bowed, eyes closed, and hands folded on the breast and to observe Sunday." Further, "Persons who disturbed the peace by quarreling or fighting might also be punished by whipping. Those who violated moral rules such as the one forbidding extra-marital sexual relations were bound and left exposed for several days" (Collins 1974b:686).

Third, relations between men and women became altered in ways that gradually favored the authority of men over female relatives (Donaldson 1985), a development that eventuated in all-male judicial bodies at Sauk-Suiattle, for example (NICS 1991a), and all-male tribal councils (B. Miller 1992a). The new hereditary male chiefs were recognized as legal authorities and now handled all communications between government and the Indian communities, thereby removing women from direct participation in key aspects of political life. In addition, men played an increasingly significant role because of their capacity to direct warfare and defense and in the leadership in the new prophetic sects (Collins 1950:341).

A fourth development was the growth of violence between families and communities in the mid–nineteenth century, as economic and political dislocation increased. Collins argues that warfare between Puget Salish and Gulf of Georgia Salish probably occurred in pre-white times (1950:335), a view affirmed by Sampson (1972:25), although Suttles (1989) suggests warfare must have increased after 1792. In any case, warriors, who had a specific warrior-spirit power and were widely regarded as ferocious and potentially dangerous, began to exercise more influence than in the immediate prior period (see Carlson 1997a). Melville and Elizabeth Jacobs recorded a story of a warrior told by Thomas Paul, Saanich, in 1930, which gives a sense of the fear of warriors and of violence, particularly in the period immediately prior to Paul's story. The story, which I paraphrase here, concerns a warrior with a strong power, wolf power,

> who could "shoot an arrow through ten men" and fought all the time, "all around." The warrior shot an arrow in the air and split himself

> in two in order to have someone to practice fighting with. He felt bad because he could not defeat this "brother" and so he departed. He encountered a woman whose family was threatened by neighbors and whose brother and sister had been seized for slavery. The woman offered money to pay for a champion. Following a journey to the woman's home, the warrior entered a sweathouse with the woman's father. He rolled a big rock in front of the entrance and awaited the arrival of the woman's families' enemies. These enemies entered the sweat lodge one at a time and were pulled apart by the warrior and thrown aside, until the lodge was full of dead. At first light, the warrior put on his war coat, which made him impervious to arrows and placed a mask in front of his face. He got up and ran, and the remaining enemies shot arrows at him. The warrior turned around, and with his knife, cut off the enemies' heads. He fought this way all day until 2, 3, or four o'clock, when he went to the "old man's house" and stayed there, taking the woman as a wife. He called on his wolf power to clean up, and 1000 wolves circled the house, cleaning up the blood and dead bodies. Nobody bothered them. (Jacobs and Jacobs, n.d., box 80, notebook 71)

Seen from a viewpoint of an unchanging Coast Salish society built around social consensus, these developments are thought to be associated with a general breakdown of the "social control that previously had been effective in reducing conflict" (NICS 1991a:52). Collins added another piece to this line of thought, associating the turmoil of the period and the loss of social control with the weakening of the control of the elders over the young so that they could no longer "check aggressive acts" (1950:337). However, if Coast Salish society is more fully historicized, it becomes apparent that much of the difficulty was not simply about the loss of internal social control. Rather, the problems were in good measure external. With regular epidemic outbreaks (smallpox, a scourge in the 1780s, hit the Coast Salish again in the 1830s, and measles and other epidemics hit in between), a pattern of movement arose in which groups scrambled to take over vacated lands (see Elmendorf 1993 for descriptions of such activities in Twana-Skokomish areas of Washington State). In addition, the dislocation of peoples to the north, including the Haida and Kwakwaka'wakw (Kwakiutl), led to predatory raids into Coast Salish areas in order to take slaves for work parties and for the emerging, profitable slave trade. These raids are widely reported among Coast Salish people and occupy an important place in oral traditions. Elmendorf (1993), for example, describes an intergroup Coast Salish effort to defeat "northern raiders," and the Hudson's Bay Company officials at Fort Langley in British Columbia made efforts to defeat the Kwakwaka'wakw raiders who threatened to disrupt their fur-trading activities in the 1830s. Collins writes: "Capture, murder or lesser injury in pre-white times could be vindicated only by equivalent treatment of the offender or one of his relatives, or by payment of property. The breakdown of the old controls operating to preserve the peace meant that retaliation by fighting rather than settlement by parlay and payment became more frequent. Some salt-water [ocean] villages came to have bands of warriors under the leadership of a single man. While these bands defended their own villages, they also raided and took slaves, who could be sold or returned so that their services could be utilized, and who, in either case, were a source of wealth" (1950:338).

Eventually, changes came to be imposed by outsiders, rather than simply arising indirectly as the outcomes of trading activities and other economic practices of the whites. Fur trading was replaced by a brief surge of gold-mining activity on the Skagit and Fraser Rivers in 1858, and a simultaneous push for settlement and seizure of lands, in part due to British fears of American designs on the territory along the Fraser River. This fear, in turn, led to a drastic push to quickly resolve the question of land title.

In Washington State the negotiation of treaties in the mid-1850s and the eventual placement of most, but not all, indigenous peoples of northern Puget Sound on reservations in the 1870s brought other changes to the indigenous political and justice practices. First, a system of hereditary chiefs emerged as the demand grew for indigenous communities to develop specialist leaders to deal with the American state and, in addition, as an outgrowth of demands by American treaty negotiators for chiefs to sign treaties (Miller and Boxberger 1994). The growth of this form of centralized authority largely supplanted the earlier development of aggressive warriors, prophets, and intermediary traders, although the descendants of these leaders maintained their position in society in many cases. These new chiefs were predominantly, although not exclusively, male, and this helped consolidate a new system of authority and social control in which one person spoke for all. These emergent chiefs and their successors did not necessarily have the support of all segments of society. However, when families were settled on reservations, these chiefs were expected by Indian agents to maintain law and order and administer justice, even though the prior system allowed the exercise of control only within their own household. Suttles states: "The majority of offences were punishable by the household, not the larger community. The house-head may have been judge within his own house and represented his house in friendly dealings with others, but in the case of an offence from a member of another house he seems to have temporarily given over his leadership to a warrior. *Now the chief was expected to represent all households in dealing with offences against any and to suppress the exercising of private justice*" (1954:68, emphasis mine). One such category of "private justice," perhaps the most significant one—the practice of interfamily feasting and the negotiation of payments to resolve problems between families—was not permitted (NICS 1991a:63).

A new system of hereditary chiefs emerged in communities along the Fraser River in British Columbia as well. As in the Puget Sound case, often the chiefs appointed by state authority were men of high standing, but in other cases they were simply men who were useful to white authorities. Contemporary Stó:lō chief Frank Malloway (S'íyemches) described the process of selection of chiefs this way: "So these are the chiefs that were not really from chief's [high standing] families but they were appointed by the Department of Indian Affairs because of their knowledge; their education. Billy Hall was well educated, Joe Hall's great-grandfather, he could read and write, and that's what the Indian agents were looking for—people to write letters to them and report to them" (quoted in Carlson 1997b:26).

The American settler societies imposed other changes on the Coast Salish. Slavery was outlawed in the Treaty of Point Elliott; later, in 1871, the Bureau of Indian Affairs banned Spirit Dancing and the performance of indigenous medicine (Roberts 1975:252). In addition, potlatches were prohibited. All of this was done with the express intention of undermining existing systems of leadership and spiritual values and practices and because "the religions made the tribes strong and the individuals of the tribes immune to intimidation and corruption" (253). In turn, these changes eroded indigenous justice practices that depended both on the existing system of leadership and on the socialization of the young into the underlying system.

Similar developments arose in Canada. The Gradual Enfranchisement Act of 1869, and its application to British Columbia after the province entered the Dominion in 1871, enabled government officials to remove leaders within the indigenous system and replace them with elected councils or, simply, to appoint chiefs. The Indian agents characteristically appointed people selected by missionaries working in the communities. In 1880 and 1895 amendments to the Indian Act strengthened government control over indigenous leadership by prohibiting leaders from exercising power unless elected. As a result, communities that retained their leaders (*sí:yá:m*) selected within the indigenous system had less legal authority than those communities that had elected or appointed chiefs. Potlatches were outlawed under the Indian Act in 1884, making it illegal for indigenous people to congregate to celebrate marriages, funerals, namings, or other events where distributions of gifts occurred. The first person to be convicted under this act was Bill Uslick, a Stó:lō man from Chilliwack, who was arrested in 1896 following a report by the Indian agent to the police (Carlson 1996:98–99).

In common with the experience of indigenous peoples elsewhere in the Americas, the Coast Salish suffered from a series of public policy decisions that were expected to erode the prior culture. There is now vigorous debate about the extent to which Coast Salish culture was actually eroded, although the considerable suffering is well documented. The aim of the U.S. government was to move all indigenous peoples west of the mountains to a single reservation; however, delays in signing the treaties allowed time for settlers to move into the intended area, and the government was unwilling to dislodge them (Suttles 1990). When reservations were established, they were intended to provide for indigenous peoples from a wide area. As a consequence, peoples without a history of joint residence were forced to move into a vastly diminished area already occupied by an indigenous group. Some, such as one group of Upper Skagits, refused to move and instead sought to stay beyond the reach of American authorities. Others moved into new and difficult circumstances. Suttles writes, concerning the Lummi reservation, "Despite the fact that no Samish, Semiahmoo, or Nooksack names appear on the treaty, these tribes were to occupy the reservation with the Lummi. This arrangement did not work out well. Members of other tribes came for the annuity goods which the Government passed out yearly at Lummi, but it is doubtful if many tried to settle on the reservation. Those who did became discouraged at the Government's negligence in surveying the reservation and giving out individual allotments, and most of them eventually drifted away. Also, they were probably unwilling to settle on the land of another tribe" (1954:55–56).

However, many did settle on reserves, and the tensions and disagreements that resulted produced the period of "evil doctors," in which shamans attempted to spiritually defend their own family groups against the others with whom they were now co-resident. Roberts provides this graphic description of shamanic activity, which parallels the anxiety concerning warriors: "The spiritual power they [Indian doctors] acquired was used to protect their families from neighboring enemies—other Indian families. Eventually there were more Indian doctors than ever before. Almost every family had its own protector, if not several. A syndrome of competitive threats and bluffs began to build up between the Indian doctors, and they began to create fearsome reputations. Some of them were so 'mean' that they would make others sick, just because they were annoyed, even kill them. People were especially afraid for helpless little children. Mothers would run and grab up their children and hide them" (1975:254).

The previous practice of avoidance and movement, even of whole villages, to avoid conflict was now more difficult to carry out as settlers gradually occupied much of the landscape. The use of the longhouses as places where justice practices of debate and mediation were carried out was no doubt eroded, although there is little evidence on this point. In addition, competitive games and contests, notably gambling, which are thought to allow the dissipation of antagonism between families, and which might have taken on new significance in this period of crowding onto reservations, were discouraged (NICS 1991a:63).

Other policies directly affected the lives of Coast Salish peoples, including the establishment of schools, both residential and day, the system of surveillance under Indian agents within a system of agencies, the establishment of religious missions, and the establishment of tribal police and courts. Residential school policies banned the use of indigenous languages, subject to severe punishment. The residential schools also took children out of homes for long periods, thereby depriving them of much of their opportunity to observe and learn how problems were defined and resolved by senior members of their communities. The schools took as their explicit task the eradication of indigenous values, beliefs, and practices and the instruction in non-indigenous practices. The language loss also kept children from learning the linguistic nuance that tied directly to justice ideas and practices. For example, Upper Skagit elder and scholar Vi Hilbert told the NICS researchers of the Lushootseed word *yoloxalgwic*, which has no direct English gloss, but which approximates "justice by council" and means that "there are two sides to each situation that needs to be addressed" (NICS 1991a:60).

Indian agencies were established in the 1860s in Washington State in order to more efficiently impose order on the indigenous peoples. Indian agents, assisted by resident farmers, carpenters, and physicians, embarked on their "civilizing" mission, employing schooling and agriculture as their primary tools. The Coast Salish people, whose subsistence relied heavily on salmon fisheries, had experience in horticulture, especially women's cultivation of roots, but the government hoped to produce farmers within the Jeffersonian, Enlightenment framework. In the 1870s, President Ulysses S. Grant initiated the Peace Policy of assigning the Indian agencies to missionaries and humanitarians. In Puget Sound, this meant the arrival of Roman Catholics (at the Tulalip agency that oversaw Tulalip, Port Madison, Swinomish, and Lummi reservations and the Neah Bay Agency on the Makah reservation) and Protestants, particularly Methodists and Congregationalists (who controlled the Quinault and Skokomish agencies) (Marino 1990:172–73). In some cases, missionary Indian agents, such as Myron Eels at Skokomish, had a particular interest in disrupting Spirit Dancing, shamanic curing, and other spiritual practices and in creating converts to Christianity. Marino notes: "Overall, Indian children experienced the same cultural ambivalence that was felt among older generations. Despite nominal conversion of many Indians, Christian denominations had not succeed in eradicating aboriginal beliefs and rituals" (174).

Indian agents attempted to erode indigenous concepts of ownership and land title in addition to health and religious views. Efforts to cultivate the nuclear family as the key social organizational element were combined with the attempt to move families to separate, privately owned allotments of land. Under this system, every nuclear family was to receive land so that land might not be held in common. However, the Coast Salish already had concepts of private ownership, although it was largely limited to heads of important kin groups (Marino 1990:175).

In British Columbia, the colonial government failed to develop an explicit policy regarding indigenous peoples. Following entry into the Dominion, the superintendent of Indian affairs for the new province, Israel W. Powell, followed precedent in eastern Canada and developed administrative units, initially called "superintendencies" and later renamed as "agencies." Each agency contained a number of reserves and bands. The Fraser River Agency contained the mainland Coast Salish, and the Cowichan Agency contained all the Vancouver Island Coast Salish (Kew 1990a:160–61). As was the case in the United States, policy toward indigenous peoples remained primarily the responsibility of the federal government.

The ethnography and history literatures point to a number of possible consequences of all these changes for the existing patterns of justice, although some arguments seem unsupportable or slightly miscast. Prior patterns of residence in multinuclear-family longhouses came to an end as single-family residences became the common practice. Suttles notes, for example, that the last Lummi bighouse was no longer occupied by the middle or late 1880s (1954:61). The NICS report noted the connection between residence style and justice: "Fifty to sixty people in one longhouse would be well aware of each other's behavior and could restrain undisciplined actions and violence" (1991a:57). Contemporary Stó:lō cultural and political leaders make the same argument in examining how existing housing stock can be altered (such as the removal of walls) to produce multifamily residences (Ginn 1998). However, if the point is that co-residence made peoples' behavior apparent, thereby inhibiting misbehavior, this implies a sort of "shame" society in which internal restraints and a sense of guilt was of little significance. This view seems out of line with the Coast Salish practice of the internalization of significant, unspoken spirit relations and of the belief in a highly personal moral system. Second, this line of argument connecting residence and justice overlooks the ongoing reality of inadequate, frequently overcrowded housing, the regular movement of people between relatives' houses, and the high number of residents per house. Further, the bighouses afforded some privacy through the use of mat partitions between family sections. One could argue that people remain under the regular scrutiny of relatives, both at home and in the community, and that this form of purported social restraint continues. In addition, Amoss's (1977) concept of the element of spiritual secrecy in Coast Salish society, in spite of the regular elbow-to-elbow nature of life, argues against this purported connection between the loss of longhouse life and decline of social control.

However, Bennett, taking the issue further, argues that the movement to the reservation implies a "breakdown of the family structure" and speculates that this breakdown "necessitated finding another means to inhibit anti-social behavior. The policemen of the reservation assumed this function. The court system decided on matters concerning the reservation of the whole, replacing the pre-contact influence of the council of elders" (1972:22). More recent literature, however, demonstrates that the structure of family organization was not irretrievably damaged and, in fact, has persisted despite tremendous pressure. Mooney (1976), for example, shows the persistence of interfamily cooperation, exchange, and pooling of resources as survival tactics, and Miller (1989a) describes the immediate redeployment of family networks as fisheries cooperatives by Upper Skagits following the restoration of salmon fishing rights in 1974. Rather, the new practices of residences in single-family dwellings and of tribal police and courts reflect more a domination of indigenous peoples by the state rather than erosion of indigenous conceptions. NICS interviews with contemporary Puget Salish elders provide some confirmation of this, noting that the Indian police may not have enforced the rules against spiritual beliefs (NICS 1991a:67). The report further concludes that, despite persecution of the Salish for their religious practices, the "belief that allowed individual freedom of expression, but not at the expense of the family or community, continued to be held" (64). Similarly, Marino (1990:174) concludes that "After years of Christian control of Indian affairs, it became clear that throughout western Washington the traditional patterns of subsistence, kinship networks and intervillage ties persisted, fostering Indian values and the maintenance of Indian identity." In sum, external forces imposed by colonization, rather than the internal collapse of family organization and the system of social control, produced changes in the practice of justice.

Changes in Legal Consciousness in the Nineteenth Century

Although the changes in the political economy of the Coat Salish did not wholly derail indigenous society, such changes did, however, produce some changes in viewpoint concerning justice. The most detailed study of early- and mid-nineteenth-century indigenous Puget Salish processes of adjustment to contact is the work of Harmon (1998), who carefully examined British, American, and indigenous theories of power in order to understand the "cultural space where people from dissimilar societies could serve their separate interests by observing common, specialized rules. Richard White has coined the term 'middle ground' to describe a comparable culture of relations" (1998:31; see also White 1980, 1991). Harmon further states:

> However native people made sense of sermons and Sabbath rituals—and they probably did so in assorted ways—their responses became part of the decorum that eased relations between natives and newcomers. Thus, they and King George men [British] gradually constructed a cultural edifice that bridged the gulf between them. It was a bridge fashioned of mutually agreeable etiquette, including gifts and favors, shard pipes and libations, interpreters and the Chinook jargon, bluffs and bargains, Sunday sermons and dances. All architects of the bridge made concessions to the perceived sensibilities of the people across the gulf, yet the result of their concessions was neither a merger of the two societies nor the subordination of one to the other. What they built was a specialized, ever-widening structure located between the two societies. To use the bridge did not require a fundamental change of course: people could approach each other without renouncing their own distinctive habits and values. Strategic congruities in their values enabled them to benefit from each other's sensibilities and desires while pursuing separate agendas. Beyond either end of the bridge, there remained realms that people on the opposite side saw but dimly, if at all. (1998:34–35)

These bridge builders, Harmon notes, made choices that had "transformative repercussions in their respective societies" (1998:34–35). In the early and mid-nineteenth century, indigenous peoples had their earliest opportunities to observe American and British legal systems in practice. White officials were anxious to use the courts to help impose their own system of power and to create and reinforce racial categories previously unknown among indigenous peoples. There were several such trials, and colonizers hoped that the message of a powerful state with fair and clear rules and procedures would be clear to the indigenous population. However, in this period "[whites were] projecting onto Indians thoughts the latter almost certainly did not have. To indigenous people of the Puget Sound region, state power, universal laws, and crimes against society were alien, untranslatable concepts. . . . Rather than a righteous American sovereign with power to assign them all a new status, native people probably saw only a small, if formidable, tribe of Bostons [Americans] who had responded in an exotic way to the harm done by particular local people" (57).

The settler population of Puget Sound remained at a numerical disadvantage through the middle of the century, and much of the early adaptation to the circumstances was undertaken by needy whites. A settler diary, for example, observes that "We were guided entirely in dealing with the Indians by their own laws and not ours" (cited in Harmon 1998:60). Harmon proposes, however, that this pioneer has oversimplified and that "The code that native people expected Bostons to follow was a hybrid one that had evolved to facilitate the relations of King George men and natives; and while Americans learned that code, they also proposed amendments" (60).

There were several innovations by Coast Salish people and transformations in approach in the mid- and late-nineteenth century, a period that might be characterized by the coexistence of several justice systems and, in some instances, an uneasy legal pluralism. This remains incompletely documented (but see Asher 1999), yet it is clear that adept community members sought out ways to use courts for their own purposes, both to resist the imposition of white law and to use the courts of the mainstream society to their own advantage or in their own defense. This is not unexpected: current research concerning other colonized areas emphasizes the abilities of dominated peoples, including slaves, to use available legal remedies (Lazarus-Black 1994:252–81). Jay Miller noted that the Hudson Bay Company's efforts at indirect rule early in the nineteenth century included reliance on indigenous trading leaders and, at Fort Nisqually in what became Washington State, the use of "native judges from Yelm noted for their arbitration skills" (1999:39). Asher (1993, 1994–95; see also 1999) described the use of white law, rather than existing indigenous practices, by Indians in Washington Territory wishing to impose sanctions on other Indians in the period before statehood. In an ingenious 1870 case, a Snohomish man, Charley Julles, asked that a claim made against him for back wages be thrown out because he was an Indian and therefore could not make a legally binding contract with anyone in his employ under then current law applicable to indigenous peoples of Washington Territory (Asher 1999:60). In cases involving murder and property, Indian people themselves brought complaints to white courts. For example, children of mixed ancestry attempted to sue for their inheritance from a white father. They were denied because of a legal ban on mixed marriages from 1855 to 1866 (Harmon, cited in Jay Miller 1999:42). Similarly, when settler livestock at Ebey's Landing on Whidbey Island destroyed Klallam potato fields, Klallam protests in 1853 led to cash compensation of three hundred dollars (Jay Miller 1999:44). In addition, indigenous people of Washington Territory played rival federal Indian agents and territorial courts against each other in order to maximize their own autonomy (Asher 1999:58–59). In other cases, Coast Salish Indians of Washington Territory warned agents of the federal government not to intervene in instances where existing practices were carried out (Asher 1993).

In a related development, Coast Salish people of the period also argued for their own legal concepts within the mainstream courts as a means of obtaining acquittals. Asher (1994–95), for example, documents a case of murder by a community member, Harry Fisk, who represented that he was attempting to stop a Squaxin shaman, Dr. Jackson, from killing his wife, Susie, with bad medicine (*tamanawas*). He was acquitted by an all-white jury instructed by the judge to base their decision on "Fisk's standards" (20) as an Indian man (albeit one with a white father) with Indian beliefs. But the issue did not end there. Some Indian leaders in the area were upset with the decision and "challenged the superintendent to live up to the policy of punishing Indian killers" (23). Others apparently attempted to kill Fisk upon his release by white authorities. After Fisk had used other shamans and medicines to attempt to remedy Dr. Jackson's use of evil power against his wife to no avail, Susie demanded that he kill Dr. Jackson to save her. Half a day after Fisk killed Dr. Jackson, and as Susie lay dying, she gloated, speaking in the voice of Dr. Jackson and claiming responsibility for the murder. Jay Miller pointed out that, in the view of indigenous witnesses to the affair, Fisk had "taken the right course at the wrong time, waiting a week too long to save his wife" (1999:47). Dr. Jackson's guilt was obvious to these witnesses because of his boastful confession from the grave, but the release of Fisk from incarceration by Americans provided an unfulfilled counterclaim of revenge on the part of Dr. Jackson's relatives (48).

In the nearby Coast Salish areas of British Columbia, leaders prodded officials to intervene legally in the case of the lynching of Louie Sam, a fifteen-year-old Stó:lō boy who was thought by vigilantes to have killed a shopkeeper, James Bell, in the border community of Nooksack in 1884. A "delegation of approximately 200 Stó:lō from over twenty communities . . . gathered in a Chilliwack village to 'consider the best means of obtaining justice' " (Carlson 1996:68). The conference lasted over a week and included a visit by a Canadian Indian agent who was summoned by the sons of Stó:lō leaders. The Indian leaders believed that they would have to identify the murderer to achieve justice, and they contemplated crossing the international line to avenge the hanging of Louie Sam. In this case, as with those in Puget Sound, Indian people weighed the merits of using their own systems of justice and those of the mainstream, or a combination of the two. This reflects a changing legal consciousness and a growing familiarity with Canadian and American systems.

Hill-Tout gave insight into another indigenous practice that suggests, as was also true with healing practices, a willingness to try a variety of approaches in legal affairs involving the state. Hill-Tout writes that at the time of his fieldwork with the Pilalt (a Stó:lō group) around 1900, spiritual means were employed to disrupt activities in white-imposed courts or to punish court officials: "The *seuwel* [described as a witch or sorcerer] is by no means an institution of the past among the Pilalt, notwithstanding the influence of the priests. The *seuwel* still flourishes. . . . My informants told me that the services of the *seuwel* are invariably employed to protect any of them when brought before a police court for some misdemeanor or other; and to harm the policeman who arrested the person and the magistrate who sentenced him" (1978:61).

Later, beginning in the 1920s, indigenous people of Puget Sound began to use state and federal courts to construct a common identity based on a common history of oppression and loss. The many meetings held in communities to develop legal claims for compensation under treaties, such as those held by the Upper Skagit described in a later chapter, brought people together on the basis of a legal standing and with particular rights as indigenous people. However, the Puget Salish people continued to rely on another legal sensibility, namely their ideas of kinship and connections to place and ideas of ownership of territory (Harmon 1998; Jay Miller 1999:44–45).

Coast Salish peoples' concepts of justice have continued to shift, but there are difficult problems inherent in pointing out what these concepts might have once been in the mid-nineteenth century and, consequently, precisely how they have changed. Despite these problems, there are concepts and practices embedded in community oral traditions and ethnographic and other writings as hallmarks of Coast Salish indigenous justice. These include the reliance on family teachings and pressure to avoid difficulties with others, a disinclination to allow problems to be aired outside of the family if possible, the use of senior, respected people in problem solving, a spiritual understanding of the resolution of many issues, which implies an ethic of non-interference, and a pragmatic sense of the necessity of getting along with others in close proximity and with whom one shared the resource base. There are other, significant features of Coast Salish culture, in addition to these well-known features of justice, with important implications for justice. These features emerge from a consideration of concepts of power, of the individual in a social context, and of landscape and place. Especially significant is the relationship between the human and nonhuman domains, including humans' relations with immortal spirit helpers and with a vital, animated landscape, which together decenter human efforts at control and which open individuals to the possibilities of new understandings. Implicit within the system of rank and class is a form of differentiation and domination that is itself a feature of justice, and that is embedded in the spiritual and physical landscapes through the device of heritable ancestral names.

In the emergent "middle ground" of contact with non-indigenous peoples in the nineteenth century, Coast Salish peoples shifted ground to defend their practices and to extend their reach through the use of white legal institutions and procedures. But external forces—such as depopulation, loss of lands, the loss of language through assimilative government education programs, and predatory slaving—eroded Coast Salish people's capacity for self-regulation. The academic literature points to a breakdown in family organization, a decline in the ability to practice internal social control, and a loss of self-confidence in Coast Salish culture as critical features in understanding indigenous justice by the mid–twentieth century. However, neither the family system nor the underlying cultural concepts disappeared, and the argument for a crisis in confidence appears unfounded. Instead, some features of local justice, such as interfamily feasting, continued to be practiced, and others remained in the minds of some community members.

3

Upper Skagit Justice

A Historical Narrative

In this chapter I consider in detail how justice practices changed in a single community, Upper Skagit, over a century and a half. During the period from the middle of the nineteenth century to the start of the twenty-first, Upper Skagit people lost control of much of their territory and the regulation of community life. Community members developed ways to respond under new sorts of leaders, especially those skilled in interacting with the mainstream society, and to act on legal traditions in new ways. This has not been achieved without difficulty, and Upper Skagit people have been forced to address fundamental questions about the nature of the community and where they wish to head as a group, particularly in light of the vastly increased diversity. Among the key issues have been defining what the relationship between individuals, families, and the tribe should be, and the Upper Skagit tribe has chosen a somewhat different route than some of the Puget Salish tribes. Part of the effort to reconfigure their justice practices after the establishment of their current legal system in the 1970s has been a study of prior justice conducted by the Northwest Intertribal Court System (NICS).

Ancestors of the present-day Upper Skagit people were no doubt aware of the arrival of Captain George Vancouver of the British Navy when he dispatched longboats to examine indigenous villages on Whidbey Island in Puget Sound in 1792. This visit had little direct effect on the upriver members of the community, however, and the first permanent white settlement on the Skagit River drainage was not established until 1850, although nearby Fort Langley (1827) and Fort Victoria (1843) were created earlier. The controversy between the United States and Great Britain over possession of the Northwest slowed down white settlement in the Skagit Valley until the United States gained clear title in 1846, and the Oregon Territory was established in 1849. In 1853 Washington became a separate territory, and Congress allocated funds to negotiate treaties with the indigenous communities of the new territory, in the hopes of quickly opening the area to settlement (Roberts 1975:184). The most influential of the Upper Skagit leaders, Slabebtkud, would not sign the Point Elliot Treaty in 1855, but he allowed his subordinates to do so, and two of them are signatories. Congress ratified the treaty in 1859, and reservations were created in the 1870s. Yet, there was less direct disruption of Upper Skagit life than for most other local tribes until after 1875, when settlers moved into the area (Snyder 1964:vi). Few Upper Skagit people were drawn into the fur trade, nor were they involved in the so-called Washington state Indian Wars of 1855–59. There were significant results of indirect contact, however, in the period before 1875. Although the effects of epidemics were likely greater in saltwater areas than upriver, there is evidence of epidemics in larger Upper Skagit upriver villages as well as saltwater locations. Further, increased raiding and slaving by other indigenous groups, especially from the British Columbia coast, led to increased contacts between indigenous groups for defensive purposes and favored consolidation under a powerful leader. A third effect of indirect contact was the "growth of class distinctions" (Collins 1950:331). New sources of wealth eventually filtered into the system and facilitated status acquisition by potlatches (336).

The upper Skagit Valley experienced a short-lived gold rush after 1858, and miners traveled a trail along the Skagit River to gold fields, some heading into British Columbia (Collins 1974b:38). A naturally occurring, two-mile-long logjam at the site of the present-day town of Mount Vernon discouraged settlement along the Skagit River, although one settler arrived in 1867 at what is now the town of Hamilton. The logjam was removed by dynamite in 1878, but shortly before this, in 1876, several young men attempted to move into the upper reaches of the Skagit Valley and were rebuffed by armed Upper Skagit people (*Illustrated History* 1906:472), as were early surveyors to the region. Sometime after 1886 the Upper Skagit people protested these incursions on their lands. Collins observes that the protest was touched off by the apprehension by white authorities of a suspect in the murder of an Upper Skagit person (1974b:40–41). The Upper Skagit people believed they should deal with the murder, and this episode suggests that even at this late date, the relatively isolated indigenous people living on the upper stretches of the Skagit River believed that authority over justice remained in their hands.

Soon after the subsequent murder trial, a white surveyor attempting to establish boundaries was ordered to leave by Upper Skagit people, who proceeded to smash the surveyor's compass when he did not comply (Collins 1974b:40–41). The Upper Skagit people then warned all settlers to leave the area or be harmed. White settlers moved down the river and held a parlay at a ranch, calling for five unarmed Upper Skagits to meet with them. More than one hundred canoes of people eventually showed up at the ranch, and the indigenous people protested the seizure of their lands, saying that they had not signed a treaty nor received money for the lands. No agreement was reached between the groups, and the Upper Skagit people left the ranch and camped nearby. One settler, however, wired the military, and a company of soldiers was sent to the ranch from Tacoma, to the south. Conflicting accounts obscure what happened next, but eventually the soldiers, under Colonel Simmons, and the Upper Skagits held council. Colonel Simmons suggested the Upper Skagit people contact the Department of Justice for assistance, and the Upper Skagits agreed not to harm the settlers. Some Upper Skagit people moved even farther up the river valley, away from white settlers and influences. Later, five Upper Skagit leaders asked territorial judge Roger S. Green for assistance in the problem of encroachments on their land. He responded by asking them to apply to Congress concerning their problems (42).

By the 1890s some Upper Skagit individuals obtained allotments under the federal Homestead and Allotment Act of 1862 and the Indian Homestead Act of 1884. However, some failed to fulfill the terms under the acts for acquiring the land and were removed in favor of settlers. In 1907 and 1909 Upper Skagits were granted allotments on the Suiattle River, a tributary of the Skagit River (Boxberger 1987:9). The Upper Skagit people believed that they would be given a reservation there, and traditional longhouses were constructed and land cleared. The effect of this activity was to further increase isolation from the settler population, and as of 1921 it was reported that no Upper Skagit children were in school (B. Miller 1989b). But by 1917 many allotments in the Suiattle area were cancelled, and thereafter the Upper Skagit people were forced to disperse and move into regular contact with the mainstream society. Further, they effectively lost the ability to continue traditional land use patterns.

As Upper Skagit families moved out of the upper reaches of the

Suiattle River and into nearby towns such as Concrete, men found employment in the booming logging industry, and families participated in seasonal hop and berry picking. Others were forced to move out of the valley altogether in search of work. However, new developments helped in the effort to maintain cohesion during this difficult period. One development was the establishment the Indian Shaker Church among the Upper Skagit people; this indigenous religion was founded near Olympia, Washington, at the end of the nineteenth century. Shakerism is Christian in orientation and consequently was tolerated by Indian agents of the period who had banned Syowen, or Spirit Dancing, on reservations (the Upper Skagit people, though, had no reservation at the time and were not compelled to stop the practice). A Shaker Church was constructed in Concrete in 1926 and became the central meeting place for tribal events until the construction of the tribal center in Sedro-Woolley in 1981. The long-term effort to force the government to pay compensation for the cession of land under the terms of the Point Elliot Treaty was a second issue prompting tribal cohesion. In 1915, tribal members gathered at Concrete under Chief Campbell to organize their attempt to obtain a settlement. A tribal council structure, with a chief and subchiefs who were headmen from the traditional villages, was created to help carry out this task (Sampson 1972:24). The land compensation issue came to take on great symbolic significance and became a preoccupation of tribal leaders until the issue was resolved in the 1960s. Regular social events, such as salmon bakes open to the public, were conducted over many years to raise money to employ counsel to wage a legal fight for compensation.

The Upper Skagit tribe sought relief in a suit brought by several tribes in 1926 (*Duwamish et al. v the United States* 79 C Cls. 530). Another suit in 1951 (Docket 92), under the Indian Claims Commission, sought compensation for 1,769,804 acres. The petition was amended in 1958 (Ruby and Brown 1986:253). In 1968 the federal government settled the longstanding suit, awarding the tribe $385,471.42, or $271 per capita. The pitiful settlement, based on land values of the 1850s and with deductions for government expenses incurred on behalf of the Upper Skagit tribe, was the cause of great dismay. Some were frustrated by the dispersal of funds to people who claimed tribal membership under descent from the 1942 baseline roll but who had no other involvement in tribal affairs. One Upper Skagit recalled the pain of having money "sent to Germany!" In fact, the settlement of the land compensation issue precipitated a crisis because of the compounding effect of handling other serious issues at the same moment. Some felt that the settlement could be derailed if the tribe pushed for federal recognition or fishing rights. These members argued that individual cash settlements should be allocated and the formal tribal organization, originally created for the purpose of bringing suit, be disbanded. In effect, the tribe would cease to exist as a recognizable entity. This position was outvoted in a tribal referendum, and the leadership geared up for the even greater battles for fishing rights and federal recognition. Ultimately, both issues were tied together by a landmark court ruling in 1974.

The struggle for fishing rights among Puget Salish peoples has a long, complex history. In 1890 the state of Washington began to regulate the salmon fisheries in order to aid the new industrial fishery. Then, in 1897, the state began to restrict off-reservation fishing (Boxberger 1989), and the Upper Skagit people, who had no reservation, began to loose their ability to make a living by fishing. Officials of the Departments of Game and Fisheries sometimes ignored the limited subsistence fishing efforts by Upper Skagit people, but contemporary elders recall difficulties attempting to fish in the 1920s through 1960s. In the 1950s and 1960s Washington State began to actively prosecute indigenous fishing because of the demands made by the industrial fishing fleet on a declining resource. Several Upper Skagit fishermen who openly fished in order to publically challenge the restrictions were arrested and incarcerated for terms of up to ninety days (*Concrete Herald*, 5 January 1963; *Skagit Valley Herald*, 28 July 1962). Life became hard with the loss of lands, fishing areas, and gathering sites and with the diminishment of the remaining resources. But in 1974, U.S. district judge George Boldt, presiding in the case of *U.S. v. State of Washington* (384 F. Supp. 312 W.D. Washington 1974), made the surprise ruling that treaty Indians of western Washington were entitled to roughly 50 percent of the harvestable salmon and steelhead. This ruling was subsequently upheld in the Ninth Circuit Court of Appeals, and the U.S. Supreme Court refused to hear an appeal. The 50 percent share was to be divided between the federally acknowledged tribes. In the process of clarifying which were the acknowledged treaty tribes, the Upper Skagits successfully pressed a claim for acknowledgment as a federally recognized tribe. This claim succeeded because of a congressional appropriation in 1913 to the Upper Skagit tribe for the purchase of a cemetery, an act held to constitute proof of congressional recognition of the tribe.

In the banner year of 1974, then, the tribe received both federal recognition and fishing rights. With these changes came urgent needs: a new tribal constitution and political system, fisheries regulation and management, and a way to accommodate all of the tribal members who returned to the valley to take up fishing. The present governing body, the Upper Skagik Tribal Council, the constitution, and the bylaws were created under the terms of the Indian Reorganization Act of 1934 and were approved by the secretary of the interior on 4 December 1974. The council has seven members with staggered three-year terms so that annually two to five new members are elected. The whole electorate elects a chair and vice-chair from among council members.

Subsequently, the tribe has achieved other landmarks, including the creation of a reservation. Between 1977 and 1982 the tribe received several federal grants to purchase a twenty-four-acre parcel and a seventy-four-acre reservation. Both were taken into trust status by the federal government despite ferocious opposition by Skagit County officials who attempted to bring suit against the federal government. In 1982, the tribe received a federal grant from the Department of Housing and Urban Development, HUD, which was used to build their tribal center and, later, fifty housing units. Meanwhile, leaders developed the infrastructure necessary for governance. This included the establishment of the tribal court system and, in 1976, a system of fisheries management (the Skagit Systems Cooperative), which they created jointly with the Swinomish and Sauk-Suiattle tribes. The Upper Skagit tribe also joined the Northwest Washington Service Unit of the Indian Health Service and began providing medical care to tribal members on their own reservation. The tribe established Cascade Inter-tribal Housing Authority (CITHA), a housing administration to plan and administer the new reservation housing, together with the Sauk-Suiattle and Stillaguamish tribes.

The most spectacular development of recent years has been the creation of a $26 million "destination gaming" facility, originally operated for the tribe by a high-visibility national gaming corporation. Disputes about details of the operation led the tribe to cancel the contract and assume the operation of the facility themselves. The tribe, whose members had come to be dependent on the mainstream community for employment by virtue of the erosion of control over their abundant resources, suddenly reversed this relationship and became one of the largest employers in the county. A hotel, constructed next to the gaming complex, opened in 2001 and will likely enhance the tribal economic situation. Other tribal efforts at economic self-sufficiency included the creation of the Tribal Enterprises project with two divisions. Timberline Services was established in 1985 to provide fire-fighting crews, tree planting, slash burning, and other income-generating operations, and the second division, also established in 1985, was a woodshop to produce replica Northwest Coast Indian bentwood boxes for the retail market.

Political Leadership and Law

After several decades of contact with Europeans and Americans in the nineteenth century, the Upper Skagit tribe developed new concepts of political organization, leadership, and law. A mid-nineteenth-century Skagit innovator, Slabebtkud, described earlier in the chapter (and spelled variously), organized loosely affiliated villages and imposed a new form of rule based on coercion. He established a system of subchiefs who enforced new, Christian-influenced concepts through the threat of incarceration in stocks (Collins 1974a). He also established a new system of hereditary chiefs that persists in the same line into the twenty-first century.

Snyder reports, concerning this prophet's justice practices:

> Capital punishment for murder provides a less-satisfactory revenge than does blood revenge partly because of its depersonalization. And with this it is tacit that the offense is one against society as well as against particular persons and is a matter of public rather than private responsibility. But such a principle was probably utterly foreign to precontact Skagits. It would have made little sense in a reciprocal system wherein acts never concerned society at large (because society did not exist in the abstract) but only those who were personally affected by them, and wherein those persons who were intimately associated with the doer were held jointly responsible for his deeds. (1964:399–400)

These changes in procedures and concepts have been attributed to the influence of Catholic missionaries in the early nineteenth century (Collins 1974a). Snyder notes that "One informant maybe rightfully claimed that peaceful settlements came in with Catholicism and with the Western legal tactics brought to the salt-water bands in the early nineteenth century" (1964:395). However, it may also be true that the rapid innovation of political styles and processes emerged from within a stock of culturally sanctioned practices within the political ideology. Although the ethnographic record emphasizes the role of "quiet" statesman-like leaders who employed the tools of indirection and example rather than coercion, the likelihood is that capable people could appeal to a broader range of options. Certainly, the model of warrior leaders already existed, and several people with warrior spirit power quickly emerged as powerful intermediaries in Puget Sound as the demands of leadership continued to change in the nineteenth and twentieth centuries.

Later, the U.S. Bureau of Indian Affairs (BIA) authorized the creation of Courts of Indian Offenses (CFR courts) in 1883 for reservation people in order to fill a perceived leadership void following an apparent decline in traditional authority. The BIA hoped to diminish the residual authority of traditional chiefs (Johnson and Paschal 1991). It exercised great authority over this court system, selecting the police and judges and promulgating the rules and procedures. These courts were charged with enforcing the Code of Federal Regulations, designed to assimilate Indians, and hence were known as CFR courts (O'Brien 1989:203). BIA authority over this court system was diminished with the Indian Reorganization Act of 1934. Tribes were encouraged to establish governments and court systems modeled on those of the dominant society, although the BIA is said to have simply imposed its own bylaws on "tribes . . . ill-prepared for self-government" (Burnett 1972:565). Later, there was little money available for tribal legal systems during the termination period of the 1950s when federal policy was aimed at ending the trust relationship between tribes and the federal government (Johnson and Pascal 1991:3).

In the 1970s federal policy again produced contradictory effects on Indian courts. The new federal policy of encouraging tribal self-determination was accompanied by efforts of tribes with independent courts and those within the BIA system to rewrite their codes for their own ends. However, the Indian Civil Rights Act of 1968 imposed most of the federal Bill of Rights on tribes, thereby reducing self-governance and imposing new requirements on tribal courts. For example, it became unlawful for a tribal government to enact a law that imposes punishment without a jury trial (Johnson and Paschal 1991:3). The passage of the Self-Determination Act of 1976 required that further regulations be adopted. In some cases, specific provisions must be contained in tribal law so that jurisdiction may be obtained (such as provisions for the detention of criminals and specific provisions for recourse under the law) or so that funding requirements be fulfilled. Today tribal courts, CFR courts, and traditional dispute settlement institutions all still exist in Indian country.

The Northwest Intertribal Court System

The Northwest Intertribal Court System (NICS), a judicial services consortium of some fifteen tribes (the number fluctuates), was established in 1979 following the 1974 fishing litigation U.S. *v. Washington*, which held that the treaties of the mid–nineteenth century gave Indians of Washington State half the salmon catch in state waters. The ruling created a need for fish and game codes and a venue to adjudicate violations. The NICS court system has been of some interest to Canadians, and a commission of inquiry into aboriginal justice in Manitoba notes that the NICS provides "court services to . . . tribes in the Pacific northwest, whose populations range from 200 to 500 [sic] people and whose reservations are relatively small" (cited in Royal Commission 1996:191). The NICS-affiliated tribes were thought to be similar in size and population to many indigenous communities in Canada. Although the commission apparently failed to recognize that the NICS judges apply the code of each separate tribe when serving their community, it recommended: "In establishing Aboriginal justice systems, the Aboriginal people of Manitoba consider using a regional model patterned on the Northwest Intertribal Court System in the State of Washington" (196).

The NICS courts exercise general jurisdiction over tribal members, as limited by the tribal code and constitution and by federal law. In the case of Upper Skagit, for example, jurisdiction is exercised over civil, traffic, fisheries, and some elements of criminal domains over Indians and non-Indians. Upper Skagit has now left the consortium to act independently, but the origins of the tribal court lie within this system.

Each tribe has its own processes to compose laws. At Upper Skagit there are a number of means whereby law can be created. One route is through the work of the Law Committee, which consults with a code writer in making recommendations to the tribal council. The council can then refine the language and vote to accept or reject the proposed legislation. It is particularly at the committee level that notions of folk law and practice are entertained most significantly. However, ordinarily the code writers are not indigenous, and frequently they are not community members, so the code writers face the difficult task of finding a way to fit the ideas emerging from the community and the Law Committee into the legal structure already in place. This process opens the possibility of miscommunication between committee and code writer.

Composed of elected representatives of the enrolled members, the tribal council can pass legislation on its own initiative or vote on suggestions coming directly from the membership or others. In some cases, tribal councils have created formal advisory boards to advise the code writers. Finally, the general membership of the tribe can instruct the council to prepare legislation by vote at the annual general membership meeting. Procedures of other tribes resemble those of Upper Skagit. There is, as of yet, limited development of case law (but see B. Miller 1997).

Court is convened on the Upper Skagit reservation once a month, or more often if needed, at the community center on the reservation near Sedro-Woolley, Washington. The court staff includes one part-time clerk and one part-time deputy prosecutor. Previously NICS provided the other personnel, most notably the judge, but now Upper Skagit contracts court officials. The source of the law is the tribal constitution, approved in 1974 and amended in 1977, and customary law. The tribal code may "codify or refer to customary practices. The sitting judge may also have discretion to consider and apply custom in individual cases" (Johnson and Paschal 1991:37). In fiscal year 1990, the Upper Skagit court, which serves 740 tribal members, heard 43 criminal cases and 15 civil cases. NICS data (which do not include Lummi, the largest of the tribes) give some measure of court activity. The data show that in 1990, the court heard 147 criminal cases (ranging from 8 to 43 per tribe, with a mean of 21) and 21 civil cases (with a range from 0 to 15; six of the seven tribes had no civil litigation) (data compiled from Johnson and Paschal 1991).

The formal court system is thought to be used as a last resort after a variety of informal mechanisms have been exhausted, especially in the case of intrafamily disputes, and the "sorting-out" process applied. In one case, for example, the judge ordered a young married couple to "work out their problems" after a restraining order was brought against the husband at the suggestion of tribal Social Service staff. Interfamily disputes, public disorder, fishing violations, and vandalism are more likely to end up in court than intrafamily problems. For these reasons, the court hears more criminal cases than civil. There is so far a limited infrastructure of lawyers versed in tribal law to help bring civil action in the court. In addition, the prosecutors are frequently non-Indian and nonresident and must work with police reports, thereby making the application of nonjudicial remedies more difficult. Also, the presence of non-indigenous tribal police, who are not fully informed of community processes, produces a formal initial treatment of cases. Individual non-indigenous tribal police are sometimes described by community members as lacking in compassion and understanding of indigenous philosophy, and thereby unfair or even brutal in their treatment of indigenous people.

Underlying the tribal system of laws is the system of law enforcement. According to Upper Skagit records, in 1991 officers were on active duty patrol 16.9 percent of their hours, a total of 1,478 hours, compared to 2,551 hours in 1990. However, 155 cases involving violations of tribal laws and ordinances were logged in 1991, compared to 87 cases in 1990. Of the 155 offenses, 86 involved adults; 52 of these were alcohol related. Forty-six incidents involved juveniles; 22 of these were alcohol related. Subsequently 13 adult males, 5 adult females, 4 juvenile boys, and 4 juvenile girls were referred to the prosecutor. The offenses can be categorized as in table 1.

The Upper Skagit data, and NICS data generally, conform to the generalization that in the tribal court there is a high volume of cases of crimes against the person associated with alcohol abuse (Brakel 1979:36). Crimes against the person are often offenses against family and children, and these data point to the importance of tribal code for women. Upper Skagit code, unlike that of some other Puget Salish communities, seeks to protect women and family in several distinctive ways. The significant role women play in tribal employment, for example, is recognized by provisions against the harassment of tribal employees and by the emancipation of female minors who are heads of household or who have children, in order that they may seek full-time employment

Table 1. Offenses of the Upper Skagit, 1990–1991

Category	Year 1990 (n = 87)	 1991 (n = 155)
Mixed offenses	5.7%	5.8%
Offenses against property	12.6	8.4
Offenses against public order	35.6	37.4
Offenses against persons	9.5	13.5
Other offenses	26.4	34.8

Source: Data from the Upper Skagit Tribal Police FY91 Activities Report 25 January 1992; B. Miller 1995.

(see B. Miller 1994b for more details concerning tribal code and the gendered implications for men and women).

The Individual, Family, and Tribe Contexualized in Code

The Upper Skagit code is one of several Washington State Coast Salish codes, and I briefly consider it collectively with codes from seven other tribes (the Skokomish, Tulalip, Nooksack, Muckleshoot, Lummi, Sauk-Suiattle, and Nisqually) in order to broaden the discussion of the cultural context of the individual. In addition, the diversity of codes reveals something of the current discourse among Coast Salish peoples. In the codes, the individual is contextualized culturally and also within current Coast Salish codes, not merely as a holder of inalienable rights and worth, but within one or more social roles and within a legal system that allows for aboriginal conceptions of the collective to be considered. Provisions for the application of current understandings of the spirit of tribal law, which pertain in one form or another in the eight codes, allow for contextualizing of the individual litigant at either the point of sentencing or during the trial itself. One tribal youth code provides that "tribal law or custom shall be controlling, and where appropriate, may be based on the written or oral testimony of a qualified elder, historian, or other tribal representative" (cited in B. Miller 1995:155). Another allows that "if the course of the preceding be not specifically pointed out by this code, any suitable process or mode of proceeding may be adapted which may appear most comfortable to the spirit of Tribal Law" (155).

The following examples illustrate the direct application of the "spirit of tribal law." In one case, the tribal appeals court ruled that tribal custom creates a fundamental right of individuals to speak on any matter of concern, including issues being litigated. The ruling recognizes the individual within the cultural setting and localized notion of rules of evidence (B. Miller 1997:127 n.33). In a second case, rights of individuals are restricted. The tribal court held that although the United States imposed a Bill of Rights because of a history of abuse of minorities, the tribe had no such history nor cultural practice, and therefore the Tribal Bill of Rights need have no provision analogous to the Sixth Amendment (127 n.34). In a third case, the tribal court rejected an appeal lodged on the grounds of the failure to employ the exclusionary rule regarding pretrial testimony (which was formulated to proscribe police conduct) because it does not take into account Indian cultural background and community common knowledge (127 n.35). Here, in effect, rights of the individual are limited in favor of the community through the expectation that individuals share cultural understandings.

Tribal code both places community members within a legal context (situating people as members of the community, as adults, as members of extended families, and so forth in relation to others) and serves as a text by which social discord is mediated. Most significantly, the everyday social context, even in the present, incorporates social beings other than human beings; therefore, consideration of the set of human-human relations must be supplemented with human-nonhuman relations as well.

There is another sense in which the individual, kin group, and tribe conceptually merge. Tom and Sarah Pocklington, in considering the issue of nepotism in Indian politics, note that universalistic precepts of the polity stem from a political ideal that stresses personal autonomy (1993). The familial or parochial precepts, which are said to generate nepotism, on the other hand, emerge from a conception of polity that stresses community and the collective. Paradoxically, then, individual rights are connected to the universal, and communal rights to the particular. This is one sense in which drawing a distinction between collective rights and individual rights fails; both individual and collective are connected to some conception of the greater good but are defined in differing ways.

In the case of contemporary Coast Salish societies, corporate extended families make up the tribal community but do not of themselves constitute the collective. In fact, the extended families are widely regarded by Coast Salish people as particularistic in nature and as acting to defend their own interests at the expense of the large collectivity. Some Coast Salish people argue the other side, holding that the creation of legal rights of individuals and of the tribe violates the rights of the corporate extended family, which itself ought to be regarded as the primary social body, the collective. The differing emphases heighten the difficulties facing those creating codes in balancing interests within the tribe.

Legal Statuses in Puget Salish Law

The eight sets of tribal codes and constitutions create complex, overlapping systems of legal statuses, about which some generalizations can be made. Men and women are treated by the codes as undifferentiated individuals with entitlements (interests in community-held resources of various sorts). These legally distinct individuals are restrained in their interests by two other sets of interests, those of the tribe and also, in limited ways, the rights of family networks. Second, men and women are legally members (citizens) of the tribe (and also of the community); as such, they are entitled to residence in Indian country and are shareholders in community assets (such as fisheries resources, education programs, Indian Health Service care, and reservation housing). Community membership alone does not confer these entitlements. Third, in most codes men and women have legal standing as extended family (or family network) members. As such, in some tribes people are entitled to make claims to fishing locations (under customary provisions of use-rights), and rights to oversight over the children of the family network. In addition, the law places restrictions on citizens on the basis of kinship affiliations that overlap in various ways with membership in corporate, temporal family networks. For example, several of the codes restrict individuals from running for office in the event that a relative is a sitting member of council. Finally, people are legally parents, with an array of parental rights and obligations.

The various legal statuses an individual may occupy are not fully compatible (in part because of the long history of federal policy and

Court officials of the Upper Skagit Court, September 2000. (*Left to right*): Martin Bohl, tribal court chief judge; Michele Robbins, court administrator/clerk; Edward Wurtz, tribal prosecutor. The Upper Skagit justice system employs non-indigenous personnel and American Indians from other nations, such as Michele Robbins, in addition to community members. The Upper Skagit constitution and legal code are local, however.

court rulings that have imposed and reconstructed concepts of membership), a circumstance that leads to significant disagreement in the communities. Some people residing on the reservations are legally members of the community but not members of the tribe (some are legally members of other tribes, others are non-Indians). A further complication is that some nontribal members who are resident on the reservation are family network members and hold legal rights as such. They may, for example, have priority in adoption or in provisions for the care of family network children, or they may have legal rights to attend family-sponsored ceremonial events while incarcerated. These incompatible statuses give rise to role conflict. A recent debate on one reservation, for example, arose over whether community members who were not tribal members were entitled to treaty fishing rights, a vital resource. Tribal council members split over this issue by sex, with three council women arguing to allow these community men to keep fishing (and thereby provisioning Indian family members) and three council men arguing against granting permission. In this case women's statuses as tribal members were in conflict with their role in provisioning family members. Table 2 summarizes the primary generalizable legal statuses that individuals occupy and the associated legal entitlements.

The legal codes differentiate on the basis of age and other criteria. Legal minors are distinguished from adults in a variety of ways: voting for public office is a privilege available to tribal members over eighteen, children are restricted from fishing and hunting (with some exceptions when supervised), and in some cases children's movements are restricted by curfews. But some of the codes (Skokomish, Tulalip, Upper Skagit, Nooksack, Muckleshoot) allow for the formal age requirements of adulthood to be set aside under certain circumstances. In two of the codes (Skokomish, Tulalip), children can be emancipated when acting as a household head, a circumstance of special importance to females, who frequently begin families while in their early teens and who assume responsibility for the provisioning of their offspring. Emancipation releases minors from restrictions on fishing or hunting by virtue of age.

Adult men and women also assume secondary legal status as owners of real property, as heirs to the property of others within the community, as members of a regulated community that provides rights to safety and comfort, as voters and potential tribal councilors, as official tribal committee members, and as jury members or witnesses. The implications of each of these legal statuses are somewhat different for men than for women.

The NICS Study

After an initial flurry of activity in creating tribal courts and training court officials in order to manage tribal assets, especially the salmon fishery, tribal leaders and community members reflected on their own prior justice practices and concepts and how these have been transmitted and transformed. This work took the form of an intertribal study, completed in 1991. The study is notable, not just for its effort to record justice ideology, but because it itself became part of the current discourse about justice between segments of the larger Coast Salish world. The

Table 2. Key legal statuses and their entitlements and restrictions

Minor (under-age individual)

Rights to participate in ceremonial life (e.g., attend funerals even if incarcerated)

Restricted from fishing, hunting, voting

Adult (adult individual; age of adulthood defined by activity; includes emancipated minors)

Rights to fish, hunt, and vote (if a tribal member)

Kinfolk (as defined independently of membership in corporate family networks)

Some restrictions on tribal officeholding by nepotism rules in some codes

Parent

Some limited rights to control of offspring

Mitigated by rights of extended family members in some codes

Household head (an emancipated youth may be a household head)

Rights to tribal resources (if a tribal member)

Community member

Rights to residence and some tribal services

Restricted from voting and holding tribal jobs

Family network member

Some rights regarding access to children

Some customary resource-use rights (e.g., for fish camp sites) in some codes

Restricted from holding a tribal office or permit by nepotism rules in some codes

Tribal member (or adult individual)

Rights to vote, hold a tribal office, and compete for tribal jobs, and to collective resources

Source: B. Miller (1994:53).

current politics of justice, then, are both reflected and altered by the NICS study, and for this reason I consider closely how justice of the past is understood in the early twenty-first century. It is interesting to note how anthropological materials produced in an earlier period have been employed in this study.

Each NICS tribe maintains its own court and its own codes and constitution. The NICS project in 1989–90 "aimed to provide a background to the tribes and their tribal court systems and how disputes were handled traditionally and how these processes and behaviors changed over time" (NICS 1991b:2). Members of three tribes, the Sauk-Suiattle (immediate northern neighbors to the Upper Skagit), the Swinomish (immediate southern, saltwater neighbors), and the Skokomish, participated in the project. At the time of this project, the Upper Skagit tribe was a member of the NICS. The project focused on "traditional dispute resolution within and between villages, and, after the creation of reservations, dispute resolution within a reservation or tribal community" (3). The research included historical research, interviews with elders and other tribal members, and observations of disputes. This research was conducted in communities with functioning tribal courts, Peacemaker programs (also known as Tribal Community Boards that developed as alternatives to formal tribal courts), and control over significant assets and tribal programs. This study was not intended, however, to provide the basis for beginning a new justice initiative, nor to substantially redirect the ones already in existence.

Here, my attention is directed to the NICS elders' reconstructions of the justice practices from an earlier period and the way NICS authors, some academics and others community members, have constructed their study. The research team included tribal researchers, a tribal Peacemaker program coordinator, two university professors, and a NICS attorney. The initial framing of the research as a study of "traditional dispute resolution" has critically shaped the direction of the work. The document reveals internal disagreement about whether to acknowledge prior conditions of difficulty and focus on the local-level resolution of small-scale disputes or to advance the notion of a harmonious prior society, or "harmony society," to borrow Nader's term (1990). This latter stance gives little attention to how real conflict was resolved. Even the focus on the local resolution of disputes underplays significant violence and social contradictions such as those imposed by the existence of social classes and slavery. Such violence shows up with great regularity in ethnographic field notes, oral traditions, community histories, and current discussions within the communities about earlier periods.

The document and, arguably, the views of contemporary elders fail to reconcile these differing viewpoints. The project summary notes, for instance, that one elder objected to the terminology of "dispute resolution" because "in pre-treaty times, people would not have focused on 'disputes' and their 'resolution'. The focus was on how to get along together to minimize the outbreak of disruptions in family and community life" (NICS 1991b:5). However, another elder caused the NICS researchers to "define resolution very broadly" by humorously and cynically observing: "Research on dispute resolution? You mean there was ever a dispute that was resolved here?" (5).

Still, the analytic focus on dispute resolution and on "patterns and values that reinforced social cohesion" (Nader 1990) casts a conservative light on Coast Salish justice. The elders' commentaries appear to reflect their publicly stated views of ideal behavior, rather than actual practice, and to present the view of a conformist community, rather than one rife with difference of opinion and of the persistent failure of intersubjective agreement that characterizes Coast Salish society. Those ethnographic materials cited in the document also reflect the conservatism inherent in ethnographic materials gathered fifty to seventy years ago (although published more recently in some cases). These materials emphasize cultural cohesion and internal consistency through descriptive, flattening, normative statements (see, as examples, the critiques of this sort of ethnographic description in Clifford 1988; Clifford and Marcus 1986). This conservatism is reflected in turn in the approach to the issues taken in the document.

In addition, the commentary is unable to reconcile its picture of conformity to cultural norms with the failure to conform or to resolve disputes, as indicated by the presence of ongoing blood feuding. The approach underplays the persistent theme of competition and struggle over resources and status within and between Coast Salish communities and individuals. Despite the conservatism of the ethnographic materials for the area, these struggles show up in descriptions of intercommunity gambling, in thinly disguised mock violence between antagonistic guests at potlatches, in episodic seizure of slaves and marriage partners, in village fissioning, in the spiritual murder of those not yet strong with their spirit powers, in "evil doctoring" (the use of spiritual gifts for malevolent purposes), and in accusations of the slave status of someone's ancestors.

The authors of the NICS report are not unaware of conflict, but they acknowledge and address the undercurrents of violence and competition with a functionalist twist, observing that "Gambling and other challenge contests and games may also have served to alleviate tensions between families and communities" (NICSa 1991:45). But this, too, reflects the intellectual predispositions of the period in which much of the ethnographic writing occurred. For instance, Marion Smith, an ethnographer who wrote in 1940 that gambling was a substitute for fighting among south Puget Salish, is cited to support the view, a thesis in line with Codere's functionalist interpretation of central Northwest Coast potlatches as a symbolic substitute for war (Codere 1950). The NICS report notes that the prestige of potlatch hosts was lost if serious trouble broke out between guests, although the literature suggests that, nonetheless, this happened, and continues to happen today. The NICS report quotes Smith's description of a *xadsitl* ("crowding against you") that occurred as guests arrived at a potlatch: "The leader or warrior sang his power song and others joined in. According to Smith, each singer was calling on his power to protect against hostile shamans and to provide protection for the women and children. This was seen as offensive rather than defensive behavior." Smith relates:

> In such situations men lined up along the landing place to receive the newcomers. These men were generally of one guest-group and the host and his followers and the other guests who might have already gathered did not participate, they watched, ready to interfere if occasion demanded. The waiting line held a pole parallel to the beach to be used in a tug-of-war with the landing group. In attempting to push each other across the goal line the contestants not only grasped the pole but tried to loosen each other's grip, cutting their opponents' hands with knives, pulling hair, etc. This contest sometimes became so serious that persons were badly wounded or killed. In any case, the losers "felt bad and they gave presents to wipe out the stain." During the struggle slaves could be taken as in warfare and these were immediately redeemed so they bore no stigma later. (Smith 1940:108–9, quoted in NICS 1991a:44–45; see also Smith 1949, 1950)

The NICS summary report concludes, however, that previously society was primarily cooperative. One passage reveals the focus of the documents on consensus and cooperative coexistence: "The way in which the pre-treaty Salish societies were organized minimized open disputing and emphasized a cooperative coexistence that was essential to the survival of the family and village. With a strong community consensus about standards of behavior, various forms of indirect social control, rather than regulations and sanctions, pressured people to control their behavior" (1991a:47–48). Other passages connected family discipline and training with group cooperation:

> The family was the most important social group. When conflict arose within a family, every effort was made to resolve the issue within the family. Dispute resolution was learned from birth. Proper attitude and behavior were taught—primarily by elders—by example, lecture, story telling and recounting of family history. Story telling, history and advice that was passed from generation to generation within the families ensured the continuity of tradition and identity.
>
> Children were trained from an early age in the qualities that led to continuity and flexibility within the communities. They learned to respect their elders and teachers, to refrain from boastfulness, and to value qualities of self-discipline, self-control, generosity, peaceful attitude and hospitality. Their training prepared them for their role in a society that was structured to minimize open expression of dispute. (NICS 1991a:4–5)

In these passages, the significant phrase is the fear of open displays of hostility or dispute, which was avoided to a degree by the use of coded, oblique language in public oratory. These passages do not treat the issue of expressions of covert hostility, such as spiritual harm done through shamanic practice or even secretive efforts to harm others. Snyder (1964), for example, notes the occasional effort to disguise aggressive actions, which could then, potentially, be found out by spiritual measures such as the use of the *skedelich* spirit boards.

The authors of the report summarized the present-day elders' views concerning pre-reservation period practices in ten propositions, which they refer to as "traditional themes," and which I paraphrase here:

1. Families are central to dispute resolution. Loyalty to family and

family privacy are strong forces affecting disputing behavior. Pressure can be applied to family members.

2. Dispute resolution was learned from birth. Elders and others taught proper behavior and attitudes that influence disputing behavior, particularly generosity, cooperation, and privacy of the individual and family.

3. Elders were key to advising about disputes. They exercise power by expressing how they see things. This power was advisory.

4. Indirect social controls (gossip, teasing, ignoring, insulting) help reduce the need to dispute.

5. Frequently, disputes are resolved by allowing time to pass. During the interim, elders' counsel and spiritual practices help things calm down. Eventually the dispute may be set aside following a large gathering over a meal.

6. Family or multifamily gatherings over meals are opportunities to set disputes aside, air concerns, restore status, and make payments to end a dispute. Elders' oratory helps bring everyone to a "common level."

7. Meetings for decision making and group disputes featured oratory, the hearing of all sides, and consensus.

8. People became leaders and were turned to for help because of age and seniority in a generation or a family, as well as character, status, and ability. Their positions were not formalized, and their authority was dependent on acceptance and respect.

9. Spiritual beliefs and practices allowed the individual great freedom and privacy that helped ease tensions created by group living. These beliefs may be associated with a non-interference or privacy ethic, which makes people reluctant to intervene directly in the disputes of others.

10. The annual cycle of fishing affects disputes because during the fishing season disputes are commonly put on hold. (NICS 1991a: 7–10)

The report's discussion makes a particular reading of the ethnographic literature concerning social class in which persistent inequality is referred to, but not disagreement over rank. Winter ceremonials are mentioned as the time for putting aside difficulties in order to "pay tribute to their relationship with their spirit power" (NICS 1991a:19). However, contests between antagonistic Spirit Dancers are not mentioned, nor the dangers that co-exist for humans in their personal and collective relationships with nonhuman beings.

Shamans are described within the benign context of "social control," a term that dismisses the sources and objects of domination. Their use of power is described as generally socially approved and operating within a "practical" ethical system that releases a shaman from blame if his "power went out of control," although, it is noted, if he caused too many deaths, he might be killed himself (NICS 1991a:23). This killing of shamans is reported widely among Coast Salish communities. This section also notes the likelihood that "violent bullies" who wronged their own family or village would "die soon" (23), although community histories reveal instances in which this did not happen and bullies continued to dominate communities that remained frightened of their physical and spiritual powers. An example of this is the story of the "Agassiz boy," noted in Duff (1952:42) and still told in various forms today. In this story, a boy killed his sister's child and subsequently attacked travelers, killing for pleasure. His relatives at Agassiz disbanded their village and moved to the south side of the river about 1840 (as summarized in J. Miller 1999:157).

NICS authors report the role of heads of families and villages as the organizers of ceremonials to settle feuds and their obligation to "maintain internal harmony in the community" (1991a:31). However, their role in arguing and competing for the interests of their own families, potentially to the point of violent conflict, is not mentioned. Likewise, those senior people who remembered family history and genealogy are said to have been useful in settling disputes, but their role in challenging claims of other families at naming ceremonies or the transference of privilege is not considered. Authority, generally, is said to be based on respect and "acceptance of established modes of conduct and behavior" (33), although it is not made clear that individual families are described in the literature as holding a variety of teachings and practices, with considerable disagreement over proper conduct.

In addition, leaders are described as emerging unscathed from the social field around the axes of birth, charisma, wealth, and ability (NICS 1991a:34), but not the politics of leadership and the undercurrents of dispute and contention that surround leaders, sometimes through their whole life or longer. Collins (1974b) reports, and community members recount, for example, that one Upper Skagit leader was murdered because of differences of opinion even though he had dominated community life. The emphasis in the ethnographic literature and in elders' discourses on "quiet" leadership and on leading by example distracts attention away from the issues of how domination works and how subordination is experienced, issues that have received critical attention in social theory (Foucault 1979). The NICS report notes, for example: "Leaders had qualities that lent them authority and caused others to call on them for help. Stern provides examples of how people chosen to represent a family, to end feuds and personal quarrels, or to mediate a quarrel between spouses, were good speakers. . . . A leader never referred to himself as wealthy or important but in fact might belittle himself. From childhood, there was the teaching that it was improper to boast" (Stern 1969:72–73 in NICSa 1991:27).

In this case, the absence of boasting and the public use of coded language to ostensibly belittle oneself is confused with the absence of the exercise of power. A better case can be made that the mastery of oratory allows one to claim the right to exercise authority—and, ultimately, the power to impose one's own viewpoint—through culturally appropriate appeals to modesty. These claims to modesty are not to be taken as literal statements of the leader's self-assessment (nor did the speaker's audience make this mistake), but, rather, they are themselves the tools of leadership and power (Duff 1952:80 implies something like this without developing it). Presentation of the self as humble left others to take precautions because "things were and never are what they seemed to be" (J. Miller 1999:146). Indeed, the report's reference to charisma disguises and naturalizes the play of power by implying that the exercise of charisma (noted on 34) is unambiguous and uncontested. Collins's commentary on the Upper Skagit "quiet leader" is cited to underscore this point: "A *sia'p* [upper class] showed that he deserved his title by behaving in a special way. He was not aggressive or disagreeably forceful. He was slow to take offense and display anger and often acted as a peacemaker within the family" (Collins 1950:334, cited in NICS 1991a:35).

A passage that cited Collins to convey the point that "people took time to consider the matter before deciding" (1950:36) instead reveals something quite different. Collins, writing about councils called to "settle differences," indirectly points to the distinction between an ideology of egalitarianism and the authoritarianism implicit in the pervasive hierarchy: "Anyone could speak for as long as he or she wished. *In actual practice only certain persons were likely to speak since there was a tradition of formal oratory in which not all persons were skilled*. These were more likely to be men than women" (Collins 1974b:112–13, cited in NICS1991a:36, emphasis mine). I do not wish to be construed to indicate that because women were less likely to be orators they lacked political clout, because this is not uniformly true (see B. Miller 1992a, 1994a); my point here relates to rank and class rather than gender.

Finally, because distinctions of rank and class are naturalized in the document, the problem of social mobility, and the irritants this presents, are not considered. Ethnographic materials suggest that social mobility was limited and that a change in status to the upper class was not ordinarily available in one's own lifetime (Suttles 1987b). The concentration of ethnographic material that shows the persistence of concern for social status suggests that issues of social hierarchy must have been significant and that limits to social mobility were deeply felt and the source of conflict. More generally, then, the issue of stratification is treated as unproblematic and from the perspective of cultural continuity rather than that of conflict, domination, and subordination. Although the NICS report indicates that there must have been conflict that was addressed by leaders and in councils, it does not purport to show the sorts of conflict or the causes and sources of conflict. The report thereby fails to reveal the ways in which those who exercised power and authority were implicated and the ways subordinated community members responded.

While the NICS report presents the view that residual justice practices can be reinforced and reestablished, it also presents standards from the past that the present-day community has little reasonable chance to meet. In addressing such circumstances, O'Nell (1996) created the concept of the "empty center," a circumstance in which indigenous peoples view their own lives as inadequate compared to those of their ancestors. According to O'Nell, this problem is partly hidden because community members assign elders the task of cultural continuity, a task for which the elders themselves feel inadequate. Since community elders do not regard themselves as equal to their ancestors, they have become aware of an "empty center," in the absence of anyone to carry the community in the way it is thought to have once been led. Such a viewpoint is frequently expressed in Coast Salish communities in both British Columbia and Washington. People report, for example, that Spirit Dancers of earlier generations had greater powers than those of today and could "Hug the stove with both arms and not get burned" or that grandparents' powers of precognition exceed those of the present elders. There is a constant sense of slippage and failure in these communities, even while monumental efforts are made to rebuild for the future. Bierwert wrote that contemporary Stó:lō elders complain of a decline in storytelling ability (1986:382), although to her, virtuosity persists. Nevertheless, the scale of loss, of many sorts, and the symbolic importance of loss are the cause of deep grief (416). This perspective is not new, however, and field notes of ethnographers of earlier generations (Snyder, for example) reveal similar feelings. The idea of slippage may simply be characteristic of societies that give authority to the past.

The Upper Skagit community faced the difficult tasks of adjusting to life after the creation of a mid-nineteenth-century treaty without a land and resource base, without compensation, and without a clearly defined government-to-government relationship with the nation-state. However, long-term efforts were undertaken to resist, to gain compensation for the land, and to create a political structure capable of helping to retain cohesion and identity. There were a range of Upper Skagit responses to imposed legal concepts and practices. Upper Skagit leaders monitored the making of the most significant legal documents, treaties, created in 1855, by attending the discussions and allowing minor leaders to sign. Later, in the 1870s and 1880s, efforts were made to repudiate the authority of the mainstream society's courts and modes of surveillance through surveying the land and regulating people's activities on it. Attempts were made to ascertain the chain of command in American political life and to make appeals for compensation based on the ideas of continuity of indigenous ownership of the land and resources. Later still, Upper Skagits took advantage of federal legislation to gain title to the land in a new way—through the American system of land tenure. Much of Upper Skagit postcontact history concerns the efforts to elude American authority by moving beyond its reach geographically and eluding its reach through continuity in cultural practice (such as Syowen). By the 1920s, however, the main impetus was to use the mainstream legal system to directly defend their resources and rights.

Finally, in the 1970s a court system was created in response to the establishment of the legal status of the Upper Skagit people as a tribal entity and clear rights to a tribal commercial salmon harvest. The court became elaborated with time, following a process of borrowing legal language from other jurisdictions and eventually tailoring it to local purposes. In establishing a legal system, the tribe created code that addressed fundamental issues of the relationship between the constituent segments of society—individuals, families, and the tribe itself. The legal processes allowed for the use of elder testimony in litigation or in sentencing. Other Coast Salish tribes of Puget Sound, however, approached the core issues somewhat differently, an indication of the extent of efforts to localize justice and to tailor imported code. The Upper Skagit people, in common with the other Puget Salish, attempted to resist the legal reach of the mainstream society and to extend their control over their own membership by writing code for major crimes and youth in incarceration in other jurisdictions, areas over which, in theory, they had no jurisdiction.

An intertribal legal consortium, the Northwest Intertribal Court System, created its own study of traditional dispute resolution in 1989–90, relying on elders and a reading of the ethnographic record. The subsequent report, rich in detail and careful in interpretation, nevertheless expressed a conservative view of tribal life that gave little attention to processes of community power and dissention, relying instead on normative, functionalist descriptions of a stable society and omitting consideration of the causes and sources of conflict.

4

The Stó:lō Nation

A Brief Political History

The circumstances surrounding justice are strikingly different for the Stó:lō under the Canadian regime than for the Upper Skagits in the United States. The Stó:lō have had less control over the institutions of justice and, as of yet, have not reestablished criminal and civil jurisdiction over members. For these reasons, their responses to intrusions of the mainstream society have not been the same. They do, however, face the same core question: namely, how to order relations between the constituent groups within their own society while managing relations with outsiders. Like the Upper Skagits, the Stó:lō are in a creative historical phase, currently working out the structure of governance and justice while contemplating earlier practices. A recurrent theme has been the relations between the bands that compose the nation and the central government, the Stó:lō Nation political apparatus, particularly in light of current negotiations with the federal and provincial governments to create a treaty and settle compensation for territory. These issues are not resolved, and the great extent of community diversity and the differences between bands in size and circumstances make resolution difficult. Current justice debates recapitulate traditional mythic concerns regarding greed, fairness, and power. The reproduction of mainstream concepts is another thread, and external influences on justice discourses, especially healing narratives, are strongly felt.

The Stó:lō are the indigenous residents of the upper Fraser Valley of the lower mainland of British Columbia. Historically speakers of a Coast Salish language known as Halkomelem, today English is the first language for the vast majority, and Halkomelem is fluently spoken only by a handful. For this reason, the justice dialogues take place predominantly, but not exclusively, in English. Occupants of the region for some ten thousand years, only over the last one hundred sixty or so years have they had regular direct contact with non-indigenous peoples. The five thousand Stó:lō people are organized under the federal Indian Act into twenty-four bands, each of which holds status as a recognized First Nation. The Stó:lō Nation is a political organization formed in 1994, as a successor to earlier groups including two immediate predecessors, the Stó:lō Nation Canada and the Stó:lō Tribal Council. Three bands within Stó:lō territories remain independent, although the number varies, and there is a regular movement of bands in and out of membership within the political body (*Sqwe'lqwel te Stó:lō* 1, no. 1 [1995]:3). A primary reason for the unification of bands under a single political umbrella was to "effectively marshal resources and present a stronger presence at the treaty table. More importantly, however, following treaty negotiations the Stó:lō anticipate increased political autonomy" (McMullen 1998:8).

A smallpox epidemic in the late eighteenth century dramatically reduced the indigenous population before direct contact with whites, killing perhaps two-thirds (Carlson 1997b:28). Shortly afterward, in 1827, the Hudson's Bay Company established Fort Langley, thereby creating the first permanent white settlement in the Stó:lō territory. Hudson's Bay Company policy initially encouraged marriage between employees and Stó:lō and other First Nations people as a means of creating good will and enhancing the economic success of the trade. However, the company also began the process of establishing an external, coercive authority in the region, even before the formal governance associated with the establishment of a colony (Harris 1997). Canadian control over the Stó:lō was not quickly established, however, and it was not until the gold rush of 1858 and the arrival of perhaps thirty thousand miners (Carlson 1997b:60), including many heavily armed miners from the California gold fields, that outside ideas of property and title began to be thoroughly imposed. Miners staked claims to territories the Stó:lō had never ceded and disrupted fishing locations on the Fraser River. By 1860 most miners had left, but the government of Canada encouraged immigration to the valley in order to maintain Canada's interest in the area in light of concerns about further American encroachment. To further this aim, the colony of British Columbia was proclaimed in 1858, and the stage was set for the implementation of policies of assimilation and removal from the land. Colonial authorities, initially under Governor James Douglas, did not negotiate treaties with the indigenous peoples, although Douglas had begun the process in a

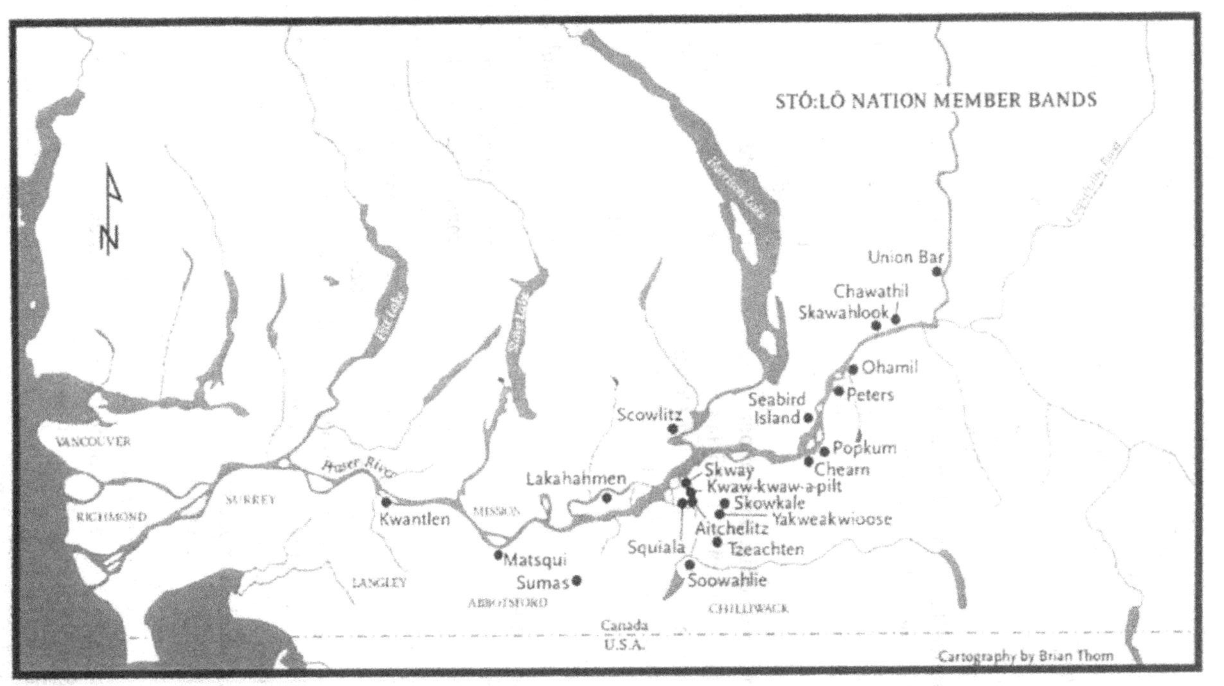
STÓ:LÔ NATION MEMBER BANDS
Union Bar
Chawathil
Skawahlook
Ohamil
Peters
Seabird Island
Scowlitz
Popkum
Chearn
Skway
Kwaw-kwaw-a-pilt
Skowkale
Yakweakwioose
Aitchelitz
Lakahahmen
Squiala
Tzeachten
Soowahlie
Kwantlen
Matsqui
Sumas
Fraser River
VANCOUVER
RICHMOND
SURREY
MISSION
LANGLEY
ABBOTSFORD
CHILLIWACK
Canada
U.S.A.
Cartography by Brian Thom

small way on Vancouver Island and intended to do so in Stó:lō territory according to Stó:lō oral traditions (67). In any case, the Canadian view, in common with American policy, was that assimilated peoples, with time, would no longer reside collectively on reserved lands and that treaties would become unnecessary. Nevertheless, land surveys were begun, but not completed, and reserves were established in 1864.

There is ample evidence of Stó:lō efforts to resist all these changes to their circumstances. Several individuals and indigenous groups attempted to subvert Hudson's Bay Company efforts to dominate the economic field by establishing themselves as intermediaries in the fur trade being conducted at Fort Langley, and leaders hoped to use strategic marriages to gain influence over company activities and to make their own economic profits. Second, there were efforts to diffuse predations by violent miners, including both armed attacks and efforts to aid and befriend the miners (Carlson 1997b:63). Later, Stó:lō leaders met with government officials, in order to represent their communities' interests. Following British Columbia's entry into the Dominion of Canada in 1871, jurisdiction over Indian affairs transferred to the federal government, and Stó:lō leaders organized a meeting of chiefs in 1874 in order to draft a petition asking for an increase in their land base, hoping for better treatment than they had received from British Columbia. In 1913, leaders appealed to a Royal Commission established to respond to undiminished indigenous complaints about the size of their reserves. However, in 1929 the federal Indian Act was amended to make it illegal for any lawyer to work for an indigenous person or group in bringing suit against the federal government, a provision that remained in force until 1951. As a consequence, later efforts focused on participation and leadership in intertribal political and cultural groups, including the Indian Rights Association of British Columbia, the Allied Tribes of British Columbia, and the Native Brotherhood of British Columbia, which had an implicit interest in band legal rights.

The first residential school in the Stó:lō territory, St. Mary's, was established in 1864 by an Oblate priest at the invitation of the colonial authorities. A Methodist residential school, Coqualeetza, was created later. The government mandated school attendance in 1884, although enforcement lagged behind. Some Stó:lō children attended public day schools with non-indigenous children, but many others were raised away from their homes in one of the two residential schools. The assimilationist school program hoped to break children's use of their language and to retrain them in a westernized, Christian worldview. Residential schools began to be closed down and children integrated into the public day-school system after First Nation dissatisfaction with the system of education became widespread in the 1950s and 1960s and the injustices became apparent to the mainstream communities.

In 1969 Prime Minister Pierre Trudeau introduced his White Paper, a document written in the hopes of directing public policy toward dissolving the Department of Indian Affairs and abolishing the federal trust relationship with First Nations, and with it, aboriginal rights. This document advocated the completion of the historic mission of assimilation, a direction rejected under U.S. policy by President Richard Nixon in 1970. Unexpectedly, this policy initiative galvanized indigenous people in Canada, along with the widespread realization that cultural identity was seriously threatened in a new way.

Soowahlie (Stó:lō) elder Wesley Sam told historian Keith Carlson that in the period before the White Paper, "No-one wanted to be a chief. It was bad enough having whites treat you differently because you were Indian. You didn't want to make matters worse by being really Indian; by being Chief" (Carlson 1997b:104). This changed quickly, and local, provincial, and national political organizations rapidly formed to push for aboriginal rights and title. Stó:lō members participated in the Union of British Columbia Indian Chiefs and, more locally, formed the Chilliwack Area Indian Council, a forerunner of the Stó:lō Nation. The area council had sixteen member bands by 1973, and nineteen in 1978. Social assistance programs were transferred to the council between 1974 and 1975, as was the Community Health Representative program in 1977. The Stó:lō Nation Canada tribal council was formed in the early 1980s, and the Chilliwack Area Indian Council assumed administrative and service delivery functions, prior to amalgamation in 1988–89. The Stó:lō Nation Tribal Council was formed in 1990, and the two councils amalgamated in 1994 as the Stó:lō Nation.

Since the merging of the two tribal councils, the Stó:lō Nation has undergone a rapid, dramatic transformation in an effort to assume governmental authority for social, health, educational, and child welfare services. The nation has gone from fewer than twenty employees in 1994 to more than two hundred in 1998. The organizational structure of the nation continues to change rapidly, but to facilitate the process

Leaders at a ceremony held 3 September 1994 in honor of the unification of the Stó:lō bands within an organization known as the Stó:lō Nation. They are wearing cedar headbands and blankets and standing on new blankets, symbolizing purity and a new beginning. The Stó:lō Nation's mandate includes the establishment of justice practices.

of self-government, organizational features of the Canadian state have been replicated. The nation is organized into "a political arm and a bureaucratic arm, much the same way the federal, provincial or municipal government is. The political arm, like the Canadian federal government consists of three branches" (Carlson, 1997b:106).

The Stó:lō political arm is composed of the Lálém Te Stó:lō Sí:yá:m, glossed as the House of Respected Stó:lō Leaders, the Lálém Te S'í:yelyó:lexwa, or House of Elders, and the House of Justice. The House of Respected Leaders is the main political body, and the membership is based on modified proportional representation, with each band holding at least one representative (some bands have as few as twenty-two members), and others with as many as three. The representatives (chiefs) elect from among their group a five-person cabinet called the Special Chiefs' Council (SCC), which consists of one representative for each bureaucratic department of the nation, known as Portfolio Chiefs. The Chiefs' Representative, who is the primary spokesperson for the

The Stó:lō longhouse, constructed at their tribal center, Coqualeetza, located in Sardis, British Columbia. The building is the site of an educational program designed to teach local elementary school children about the Stó:lō Nation and for ritual events such as First Salmon ceremonies. Such buildings were the sites of the conduct of justice in prior times.

nation and, effectively, the head of state, chairs the SCC and is directly accountable to the Stó:lō Special Chiefs.

The House of Elders is composed of elders from every member band and is designed to function in the manner of the Canadian Senate. Elders are selected for their knowledge of Stó:lō traditions and customs, so that "Stó:lō ways of knowing and understanding are well represented by the actions of the Stó:lō government" (McMullen 1998:11). Under the Stó:lō constitution, the House of Elders must approve new laws. Further, the elders are responsible for seeing that the members of the House of Respected Elders live up to their moral obligations to the Stó:lō community. The elders retain the power to remove chiefs who abuse their power or fail to live up to the title (*Sqwélqwel te Stó:lō* 1, no. 2 [1995]:1).

The third governmental branch, the House of Justice, is as of yet unformed. Carlson noted in 1997:

> This body is not yet fully functional, but will deal with justice issues

> of particular concern to the Stó:lõ people. Stó:lõ concepts of justice emphasize "rehabilitation." Many non-Aboriginal people find the thought of a separate justice system for the Stó:lõ disconcerting. Stó:lõ leaders assure people that they have nothing to fear from a parallel Stó:lõ justice system. One important function of the "House of Justice" will be to deal with justice issues that are aboriginal in nature. For the Stó:lõ, certain songs and stories are "owned" by particular individuals or families. If a Stó:lõ person were to go to a provincial court house and ask a judge to adjudicate who had a right to sing a song or tell a story, the judge would be at a loss as how to proceed. Similarly, Stó:lõ families "own" specific fishing sites along the Fraser River. These rights are based upon complex family laws and customs which the mainstream legal system is unfamiliar with. Such matters are very serious to the Stó:lõ people. Through the Stó:lõ "House of Justice," these and other culturally specific justice matters could be dealt with by Stó:lõ people within a Stó:lõ justice setting.
>
> Similarly, other justice and legal matters may one-day be dealt with by the Stó:lõ "House of Justice." Property crimes and violent crimes between Stó:lõ people may be handled more effectively within the context of the Stó:lõ justice system. (Carlson 1997b:106–7)

A quasi-legal arm of the Stó:lõ Nation, Xolmi:lh, has assumed authority for the welfare of children under a transfer of authority within the self-government process. Its program "combines traditional Stó:lõ child care techniques with social work to help recreate healthy families" (Carlson 1997b:107).

Stó:lõ Views of Indigenous Justice in the Early and Mid-Twentieth Century

Wilson Duff's (1952, n.d.) fieldwork with a small set of Stó:lõ elders in midcentury provides a brief look into then current understandings of indigenous justice. Duff's six Stó:lõ collaborators were aged from about fifty-three to over eighty, with all but two about seventy or over, putting their dates of birth from about 1870 to 1900. Their accounts appear to reflect the period of tremendous dislocation by population loss, loss of self-governance, and the endemic physical violence that these people either experienced or heard of from their parents' generation, who experienced this directly. Duff summarizes his work in two paragraphs in a published monograph, but more detail is contained in his field notes. The published account focuses on the practice of exiling, deserting, or killing those who disrupted the community harmony. Duff observes that elder E. L. "thought that large groups 'could never hang together. There were always one or two persons causing trouble, especially women' " (1952:89), a circumstance that required sending troublemakers away or for everyone to move away. Duff references two stories, one concerning a man who killed his own brother, a troublemaker, and the other, a young man who was deserted by his fellow villagers.

Duff's field notes (book 3) suggest the penalty of death or banishment ("stripped and turned loose") and the loss of one's possessions following "a law trial before a council." The notes (book 4) connect pride and the acquisition of inappropriate power with punishment by X̱á:ls in myth times or by the community in historical times. The notes (book 5, for example) reveal a number of stories about no-good people who killed "for little things," sometimes warriors who could not be trusted.

A Perspective on Contemporary Stó:lō Views

The Coast Salish people whom the University of British Columbia students and I interviewed in cooperation with the Stó:lō Nation were selected at the recommendation of Stó:lō research staff and community elders. Not all were elders themselves, but all were regarded as knowledgeable concerning aboriginal culture. Their dates of birth are from about 1915 to the early 1950s, making them from generations subsequent to those Duff interviewed. I use or obscure their names on their own choice. They framed their presentations to us in particular ways. All did not express the same viewpoint or emphasize the same issues. These elders and leaders are situated in various ways within the community—some as members of large, dominant families, and others more on the margins. Here I wish to present both their common beliefs and their divergent viewpoints. What is most striking when viewed in contrast to the South Island program materials I describe in later chapters and the discussions of Stó:lō people with ethnographers in the 1940s is that few of the elders explicitly mentioned the Transformer, X̱á:ls, other myth-time beings, or Spirit Dancing and their connections to justice, although the tribal cultural adviser did so. References to cosmology and spiritual beliefs were embedded in the frame of reference, but the discourse on justice made little immediate appeal to its primacy as a primordial gift of X̱á:ls as transmitted to elders (as the South Island elders did, as I describe in a later chapter). Unlike the Stó:lō elders of the early and mid–twentieth century who focused on murder and its consequences, today's Stó:lō focused on less striking causes of community disharmony. As Fienup-Riordan (1990a) pointed out concerning Eskimos, elders' commentaries highlighted particular social processes and values and obscured others. As with the Eskimo case, the conversations foregrounded the role of elders and partially obscured considerations of class, although these were not absent. The interactive effect between class and seniority was generally largely muted or rendered unproblematic. For example, the relative influence exercised by elders and by people from noted families in public or private (interfamily) conflict was addressed only by one person. Participants did clarify the role of senior people (sí:yá:m) in dispute resolution, in giving "advice" (formal training in spiritual and other significant matters), and in counseling those who were causing problems. The senior people in stories and examples, without exception, were described as elders.

Resolution, rather than persistent conflict, was emphasized thematically; indeed, some elders presented the view of an earlier, Edenic society devoid of conflict. In addition, there is an undercurrent in the discourse that privileges the significance of the family in justice matters as opposed to community harmony. Notably, those whose primary frame of reference is family rather than community made more reference to class and to class-based problems. Divergence in perspective can perhaps be explained by another orientation: oddly, and unlike the Puget Salish materials described in chapter 3, those who regard their task as excavating aboriginal practice and knowledge make more reference to underlying conflict than those whose task is to find a way to practice it today. I suggest this inversion reflects the yet undeveloped state of affairs in the Stó:lō world concerning justice; the realities of conducting a working system do not seem to have fully sunk in to some, unlike the Puget Salish.

Still, a cluster of ideas presented to us play on the theme of family autonomy, an important feature in a period when the relationship between families, bands, and the tribe is a major issue. People's views of how the community was constituted and the relationship between the community and the constituent families in the past and in the present do not necessarily correspond. Some view the growing institutional strength of the tribal government as threatening, or potentially threatening, to the independence of families and bands, which, ordinarily, comprise a single or a small handful of families. For example, tribal control of the delivery of child welfare services has led, in the event of the removal of children from homes, to the transference of frustration from the provincial authorities to tribal authorities. Elders emphasized that the resolution of problems lay in earlier times within the family, that only the right people, acceptable to the family and knowledgeable of the local circumstances, could be brought in to help resolve conflict in the event that it could not be done internally. In the report to the House of Justice, McMullen and I describe this as a "non-interventionist" ethos. Elders spoke further of the importance of the family name (reputation) and of protecting "Indian names," that is, ancestral names that are given primarily to youth and that are thought to have particular spiritual attributes (described in chapter 2). Since only the family itself could deal with its own reputation, and subsequent relations with other families, the family is the site of resolution of internal problems. Further discussion focused on spiritual retribution, the idea that improper behavior generates its own punishment.

Several stories depicted greedy or spiritually inappropriate people whose lives ended in disease or disaster. The consequence of this spiritual retribution was that others need not intervene and that an apparatus of law and order need not be created. Associated with this was the idea of "evil" or bad doctors, spiritual practitioners whose powers were available for good or for bad, and whose influence could explain the wrongdoing of some. As a consequence, the proper resolution in the event of harm is ordinarily not intervention by outsiders, such as members of other families, but, rather, the work of a family-appointed "Indian doctor" capable of countering the effects. All of this emphasized the autonomy of the family.

In addition, young people who act inappropriately were described as analogous to those who are ill, a concept that appears to connect to a widely circulated healing metaphor. But here, the reference is to spiritual sickness caused by the bad thoughts of an individual that result in bad actions. In this case, too, the idea of wrongdoing is embedded in a spiritual explanation, somewhat akin to psychological explanations for behavior in the mainstream society, which do not suggest resolutions in the workings of tribal authorities. Here, too, the family is seen as the site of action.

There are two other key features to the contemporary discourses of justice. These concern the role of early training to avoid difficulties and counseling in the event of problems, both activities that take place primarily, but not exclusively, within the family. Early training, or "advice," is said to produce adults who know who they are (know their appropriate place in the world) and, as a consequence, know how to act and, especially, how to treat others in a way that avoids conflict. In the event that a family member encounters problems, resolution is achieved primarily through counseling by senior family members to awaken the wrongdoers to the difficulties their kinfolk will experience as a consequence.

These constructions ask, but fail to answer, the question of how individuals and whole families without advice should be treated. An implication is that members of families said to be low class or descended from slaves will be unable to access advice and to know how to behave and avoid trouble. Stories reveal the problems for whole communities when members of such families cause problems, and they emphasize the notion that these troublemakers should conform to good sense (advice). In the absence of intersubjective agreement on who has advice and who does not, a characteristic of Coast Salish society in earlier periods, as it is today, it appears that intervention in the affairs of low-class families might be tolerated as a necessary cost of doing business, but not in the affairs of one's own, more positively valued, family.

A final twist on the theme of tribal-family relations is the focus on greed as a determinant of improper behavior. For many elders, greed is a primary issue, including the hoarding of money but, especially, hoarding of resources available to the band as a whole. Although claims of greed are sometimes made against other bands (for example, in disputes over fishing locations that are held by bands for their own members, thereby discounting claims to the locations on the basis of ancestral use-rights), more frequently they are against others who catch too many fish, live in too fine a home, or drive too nice a vehicle. While these claims are countered as examples of the "crab-in-the-bucket" syndrome (crabs that appear to be crawling out the top are "pulled down" by those below them), they are connected to supernatural sanctions and to values of reciprocity and sharing. Underscoring this is an unease with unequal access to the limited stock of jobs, patronage, and other resources controlled collectively by the band.

Finally, the interview texts reveal a tension between the spiritual dimension—spiritual causes and remedies for problems—and the human, pragmatic domain. Some see a pragmatic resolution to justice issues through social control of the lower classes, and some through a careful effort to obtain a balance of forces within society. To others, the emphasis is on healing through counseling.

The Stó:lō Interviews

The fourteen Stó:lō people we interviewed (some on many occasions and over several years) all advanced ideas that refer to preferences in aboriginal law for informal resolution and peacekeeping over formal procedures and nonintervention over confrontation. They were uniform in stating that the first stages of solving a wrong or a dispute involved a great deal of talking. A wrongdoer would be spoken to by family and friends. If the wrongdoer continued causing trouble, or if the situation escalated, more people could be brought in to help, including elders, extended family members, and even respected people from other communities. Shirley Julian said:

> At feasts there would be special people who were speakers, real good speakers, one from each place that knew the background and the history and the culture. A teaching is that when you have an argument in the family that you try to resolve it on your own. If you cannot solve it on your own then you invite your people to help you out from the neighboring [areas]. They all get together and say the same thing and then the wrongdoer understands that their parent must be right because everyone is telling them the same thing. You do not want things to be made public, you do not want other people to see your dirty laundry. They will ask someone who the elders knew that was raised with the teachings, the correct way. If it was really serious they would go to the Island and get relatives and friends and sometimes they would go east too.

Jeff Point provided an explicitly primordialist viewpoint, emphasiz-

Chief Frank Malloway (S'íyemches) of the Yeqwyeqwí:ws (Yakweakweeose) Band, Sardis, British Columbia. Chief Malloway is standing in front of the Richard Malloway Memorial Longhouse, a winter ceremonial ritual house. To the right is a carving underway.

ing the influential role of spiritual people who have been described elsewhere as "family historians" and "Indian doctors" and the power of precognition that allowed family members to know of such a person's impending birth. As is characteristic of Coast Salish society, such people had to confirm their spiritual gifts:

When a spiritual person was born, they knew it. They knew it at the time and they knew before it would happen, this man was well respected after and later on in years he was tested to see if it was real because anyone could come along and say 'I know someone is going to be born with it.' So he was tested to see if it was real or not and it was a long process, until he was 18 or 19 until he was considered he could be listened to [see McMillan 1998].

There [spiritual persons] are the ones that carry through everything that was law. You could break the law and they would be the ones who decided whether it was right or wrong. And most of the time the lady would tell her mate, but they were usually brother and sister. . . .

You see, those children would be brought up away from everybody else. . . . They are isolated from everybody, they are not allowed to talk to anybody because their elders are constantly telling them what took place 500 years ago and that has to be brought forward 500 years from that time, you cannot change anything. You see, nothing is allowed to change. I cannot build a house over there because it was not there 500 years ago and it is not going to be there 500 years ahead. . . . [The] decision-making was brought about by a council that served those two people.

Dorris Peters described another significant spiritual practice:

We had seers, everyone had seers, it is just like my great grandfather, he was a seer for a whole community because his totem or clan was the thunderbird. . . . He would, if it was a nice day with no clouds or anything, he would cause it to thunder and people knew it was him calling. He would travel by canoe, walk over the mountain over to where he was in Yale, and they would all arrive there and he would have announcements to make. Also [he would] see ahead and also it was a preventative as well.

Q: (Bruce Miller): They could also find things? Stolen items or bodies?

A: Oh, yeah. . . . They could help to find people, they help to heal people.

Elders stated that those who could "give a good talk" were valued in times of trouble. Therefore, justice depends on counseling; it can even be seen as a system of counseling. Elder Vince Stogan emphasized these healing features of justice and a more diffuse spirituality. To him, talking and counseling serve to diminish tensions and diffuse problems as they arise (see Kulchyski, McCaskill, and Newhouse 1999:458 for a published interview with Mr. Stogan).

Counseling and, relatedly, teaching started early in life when individuals were taught traditional attitudes and proper behavior through the telling of family history, lectures, and stories. Through this children learned who they were, the significance of their family, their position in society, and what was expected of them. Their family provided the foundation for a good relationship with the community. An elder said: "Each family had their own laws. A lot of families were very strong in their own laws, own family laws, well in everything; way of living, supporting, helping, teaching and even looking after the children and everything like that. I think part of your family law became community law. But it has to start with the family."

Vince Stogan explained to us the important role that all family members had in the counseling and raising of young children:

> They visit the other families and they laugh and are happy together, and so are the children. It was companionship. When they go home they're happy. . . . So, you know, they're continually guided to the goodness of a human being. . . . That is a child growing up. When they're angry at somebody and I say, "Don't talk about that child, your friend, that is your friend, don't talk about them. You'll be alright, you go on your way and don't do that." That is one of the teachings as the child grew up. So they did grow up without too much trouble, see, it's guided all the way.

During times of trouble individuals were reminded of their early teachings by those closest to them. The same elder told us: "So there's not really too much trouble, but when there was, there was a lot of sympathy. You'd sit them down and talk to them for a long time."

Many chances are given to wrongdoers to reinstate themselves in the community. Another elder stated that you have to work with people, that you cannot just forget about them: "It's through contact and counseling and supporting, and letting them know that they did something wrong."

Dorris Peters observed: "I guess the punishment for people in traditional laws were that you were always given four chances, you were taught four things, I mean you were taught four times for certain things and if you didn't get it you were reprimanded."

Shirley Julian reported a different family practice: "Law is justice. . . . Once it was said one time, that was it, you never questioned the elders, you just listened, you learned by watching and it was only shown to you once."

Jeff Point described a somewhat grimmer picture than others in the event of intrafamily difficulties:

> The young fellow who got caught stealing. Because I heard my uncle tell me about that. It was the common thing to do for anybody who broke the law to cut his ear off. And kick the family out of the home. And then nobody was allowed to take them in. And so what happened was this family turned on the boy and they ran away from him so they could be accepted to another family. . . . This young man, it must have taken a long time to decide to cut his ear off, that is the last point to do that and to excommunicate someone from the house. . . . I imagine the young man had many chances to redeem himself before they did this.
>
> I remember another uncle of mine telling me that this young fellow ran away from home, ran away from his longhouse. He disputed living that way, this was when the time was turning, so when they found him, they brought him all the way home and the ladies were collecting the wood and he had to do that. . . . He had to prove himself that he would not do it again.

Another premise of Stó:lō justice practice is a non-interventionist, non-confrontational ethos coupled with a strong belief in spiritual sanctions for wrongdoing. Elders observed that one's actions determine one's destiny or fate and that people do not necessarily have to punish a wrongdoer, as in Jeff Point's examples, because "things come around," and eventually the evil ways of the wrongdoer will catch up to him or her. One elder told us: "It might take a long time but justice is served by just your actions. . . . If you do something bad you'll get punished for it later. The people don't have to do the punishment, its our Creator, I guess, that makes sure that you don't benefit from what you've done. Maybe you'll benefit in a certain degree, but in the long run you'll suffer for it."

This premise ties in with the first premise of non-interference.

Spiritual beliefs and spiritual powers all contribute to the autonomy of the individual and the desire not to interfere, although there are limits. Angry thoughts can make others ill, and therefore there is an emphasis on self-control. Vince Stogan told us:

> This is the teaching that we got from my Grandfather: "Never hate anybody. Never get angry at anybody. If somebody's real angry at you and still wants your help, you go there and help. Don't have this feeling, 'Oh, he's mad at me, why should I help him?' No, you go there and help. Otherwise, if something happens to that person you'll feel responsible for it after. No matter how mad you get looking at him you go and help." So that's the teaching we got.

This elder's comment relates to the conception that ill-feelings can cause illness or injury in others, even when it is not consciously intended. Similarly, Shirley Julian stated that one must "Have a good mind when you give away. . . . We were taught that if you don't quit what you are doing it will happen to you. You have to be very careful each day."

Stó:lō people told us that if, in spite of repeated attempts at talking and counseling, a wrongdoer is unrepentant and continues wrongdoing, eventually the wrong ways will be reflected in his or her life. In this case, elders are referring to older people in the community, unlike the young people Jeff Point mentioned (above). The wrongdoer's past, in these narratives, will show through in the quality of relationships, health, or other aspects of life. Elders gave us examples of people who became ill, became isolated from others, or died a terrible death because of wrongdoing throughout their life. Thus, there is an imbedded analogy between the fate of evildoers and the notion that all things are eventually returned to you in a reciprocal arrangement. One elder talked about how his grandfather's wrongdoing in life was reflected in his death:

> [My grand]mother always used to accuse [my grand]father of doing something bad because my grandfather died a terrible death. . . . My grandmother always used to scold my grandfather when he was on his deathbed, "Oh you did something wrong, you did something wrong, that's why you're suffering now," because he had TB and he just went down to a skeleton. When he died my dad said there was no flesh on him at all, he was just skin and bones. . . . But my grandmother always used to scold him, "you did something wrong."

A third premise of Stó:lō justice is the view that wrongdoers hurt their families as much as they hurt themselves and their victims. A wrongdoer puts a "black mark" against the family's name, and thus the family is affected and hurt by the wrongdoer's actions. These black marks extend back through the generations as wrongdoers shame ancestral names. There is a great deal of external pressure from family (especially elders) and internal pressure to behave and put things right. One elder told us:

> If we do something wrong you're not only dirtying your name, you're dirtying our family name. So if you do something wrong you put a black mark on us too so we want you to go out there and fix it. . . . In other words you almost have to live up to why that name is given to you 'cause elders already see some traits in some young people and usually they won't give you a name until you're in your teens or late teens so at least you're developing some of the traits or characteristics of someone, maybe your father, mother, grandfather, great-grandfather, and maybe they think that maybe you deserve that name because maybe you have some of the traits of somebody in the family.

Another elder told us a story of a young person whose excessive drinking was destroying his life. An elder family member spoke to this youth to say that it was not just his life he was ruining but the lives of his parents and siblings, too. It was this realization that prompted the young person to put his life together: "He realized then that he's hurting us, not himself. That struck him in the head, 'I'm hurting Mom and I'm hurting my Dad so I better quit.' "

Stó:lō people told us that conflict resulted from several factors, but chief among these were a failure to be given proper instruction as a child, ordinarily an outcome of birth into the lower class, greed, and the action of spiritual forces. Sonny McHalsie explicitly connected class and behavior, and the implications of class in the interpretation of behavior, as Stó:lō people commonly do:

> Q: (Jane McMillen): What causes people to do wrong?
>
> A: Most people would say it is their upbringing. If you are from a lower class, you are more like to commit a wrongdoing than from an upper class.
>
> Q: If someone from a lower class does something wrong, it is less likely to be a big deal than if someone from a higher class does something wrong?
>
> A: I think so. Because the lower class actions can be easily explained

> away. I am sure some action would be taken. The higher class would be more frowned upon for sure if they did something against their name, then it would be probably taken away, but the lower class did not matter too much if they did not know about the meaning of the [ancestral] name, or did not realize the importance of the name and did something to tarnish it.

Social class in this discussion is connected to the idea of "advice," or family teachings, that provide a spiritual mooring and that enable people to know how to behave, rather than to the idea of the division of society into groups on the basis of differences in wealth reproduced over the generations. Nor does this necessarily refer to where people live; lower- and upper-class people commonly inhabited the same villages. Instead, there is the implication that anyone with proper behavior would be regarded as a member of the upper class, and in this sense, attributions of class are ways of talking about others more than a reflection of discrete groupings of people on the grounds of material differences. In this reckoning, attributions of class status are circular and personal; one identifies oneself as of the lower or higher class because of one's actions. Suttles (1987b) captured this idea with the image of an inverted pear, in contrast to the more common image of class in the shape of a pyramid, with a small upper class and large lower class. Suttles argued that relatively few Coast Salish people are lower class (although some whole villages were "low class"), and most could make claims to upper-class status, and that, consequently, discussions of class are primarily a means of commenting on the behavior of others.

Yet, there is the contradictory notion that one's class is inherited and that personal qualities are likely to persist in families; the child of a lower-class person or family was also of the lower classes (see also Glass 1998). Members of upper-class families are given important ancestral names because they are thought to embody some of the qualities of their predecessors who held that name. Acquiring the name itself is sometimes said to provide support; people attempt to live up to the name and to the social status associated with it. There are other features of the heritable nature of class in practice, as well. The difficult spiritual training undertaken by children would enable an upper-class child to potentially obtain a powerful spirit helper that could help in the achievement of prosperity and significance in the community. Those without proper advice and training would be less likely to obtain such an important spirit helper and, consequently, membership in the upper class. Coast Salish stories reflect this notion: children of the lower class eavesdrop on the teachings of upper-class families and, as a consequence, become successful. In the stories, this is contrasted with children of upper-class families who fail to heed these lessons and subsequently fail to succeed. Finally, people of very high status were, in many ways, more significant to the welfare of the community than others. They were the ones who managed relations with other communities, who managed the resource stations, and who held important responsibilities for maintaining peace and order within the community. They were expected to marry outside of the group and to have useful external connections. Consequently, their actions were more carefully scrutinized, as McHalsie's comments suggest, and they were expected to be careful not to do wrong and offend public sensibilities. In fact, procedures were in place for them to attempt to recover from mistakes. Upper-class people could (and still do) hold "shame potlatches," in which their improper actions, already public knowledge, could be acknowledged and overcome.

Greed was described as a state of alienation and the opposite of generosity; it isolates people from the community. Waste is considered to be a form of greed, and to be greedy and hoard things is wasteful. The reciprocal movement of goods and services through the community is the glue holding people together on a practical basis, both in mundane giving of food gifts to relatives or the distribution of gifts in potlatches. This system is threatened by greed and waste, and people are kept away from each other. One elder explained, "The most serious crime of our people is greed. That's what we were told by our elders, 'don't you be greedy, you share what you have and in the end it'll all come back.' "

Sonny McHalsie gave another view of the issue of greed, relating it to X̱á:ls stories and the issues of stratification, greed for power, and social control:

Many of the Transformer stories have qualities of social control values about them, the boy who stayed out after dark was turned into a stone.

Q: (Bruce Miller): What can we learn about justice and relations from the X̱exá:ls stories?

A: Some of them [chiefs] challenged him [X̱á:ls or the X̱exá:ls siblings], and some of them were just doing wrong, I guess. The one about the warrior at the Mouth of the Pitt River, he was transformed [into a stone] because he wanted to kill a X̱exá:ls. The warrior had heard he would have more power if he killed a X̱exá:ls. So he stood at the mouth of the river waiting for the X̱exá:ls. The X̱exá:ls knew he was there so he came around on land and tapped him on the shoulder and asked him what he was doing, and the warrior, not knowing this was the X̱exá:ls, told him he was waiting to kill X̱exá:ls. X̱exá:ls asked 'why?' and the warrior said so people would recognize that he had more power than X̱exá:ls. The upriver story said that X̱exá:ls transformed him into a stone; the Musqueam story says that he took the warrior's spear and broke it up into his face and transformed him into a blue heron, saying that from now on people will hunt you and use you for food.

Q: So this is a story of pride or greed or misuse of power?

A: Greed for power.

Another way of viewing wrongdoing is through the metaphor of illness. A wrongdoer is akin to someone who is in spiritual danger; the sick, those in mourning, the very old, or the very young are in a state of XeXe. Sonny McHalsie connected the issue of being exposed to too much spiritual power and the subsequent state of dislocation and disturbance: "XeXe means sacred, a place where you stay away from. A spiritual place where an Indian doctor left his power." Wrongdoers are not necessarily considered to be bad people or criminals, but rather it is thought that something has happened in the lives of wrongdoers to put them in a state of alienation from the community. Therefore, there can be a supernatural dimension to wrongdoing that can be manifested in a variety of ways.

Elders stated that bad doctors are often considered to be responsible for wrongdoing. Bad doctors are powerful, and people are wary of them. They are not often called upon to account for their actions. People avoid bad doctors; they are often in a state of informal internal banishment within the community. In one elder's words:

You don't do anything with them. They have a class by themselves. Nobody touches them, nobody does anything with them, nobody even helps them survive. They do their own fishing and hunting. Most of the old people in the villages always received help from the young

> people. They'd bring them fish or deer, or whatever. But when you are a medicine man and a bad man, you had to go on your own and that was a sort of a type of banishment, but he lived in the village or lived in the area. I don't know if you seen pictures of this . . . when my dad was a kid, his mother used to tell him "Don't you go near that house. He's a bad man." That was. . . . Yeah. He was a medicine man, he'd do bad things to you. So they just ignored him or kept away from him. That was a banishment, but he didn't go anywhere, he stayed right in the village. It's just that they ignored him and wouldn't go near him. . . . I guess the only ones who visited him were the early settlers or people in your job that were looking after the history of our people and that was a sort of a banishment that he suffered, you know. Nobody came to see him, nobody went near him. He wasn't told to leave the village, he was in the village but they just stayed away from him, and if you understand Indian doctors you really had to be careful of them, because if [you] got them mad or angry or anything they could cast spells on you and you wouldn't know what was happening to you, so they just stayed away.

Consistent with the notion that "things come around," it is thought that eventually a bad doctor's ways will catch up to him. He may become isolated and sick or die a terrible death. One elder said:

> A young man that lost two children, they died. He blamed his uncle, a granduncle, who was a medicine man, and he said that he would get even with him for doing what he did. It was something about, something that happened between them that created hard feelings, and the old man was telling his grandnephew that he was going to get even with him, you know, that he would really be hurt emotionally. When this young man's children died he blamed his granduncle. I guess when the fellow was out on the river, the old man was out on the river fishing, and the young man shot him. The canoe drifted down river to the . . . people. The . . . people found him floating down the river in his canoe. They pulled him ashore and sent a runner to Chehalis and said we found a certain person. So they sent four guys down to pick the body up, and they brought it back to Chehalis, and the guy was buried. But there was nothing done about it. You know all they felt that what the fellow received was what he deserved for doing all this bad work. It was really interesting to me because my father said nothing was said and settlement was around all ready, and he

> said the provincial police weren't even notified. It was just done in a silent way. I was thinking I guess that is Indian justice, the young man that carried out the ambush, or whatever, the people thought he was delivering a sentence that nobody else could do, and the family looked after their own problems. People came and took the body home and buried it, and no authorities were notified. He said the news just died away, people just forgot about it. In a way I guess they were going back to their old way of dealing with situations like that, when somebody committed a serious crime and the people judged that person and felt that he didn't need punishment, he was just carrying out a justice because the Indian people all say if you do something bad to hurt people, it will come around in a circle and you will be dealt with. You know when that dealing comes through, when that justice is served, nobody questions it. I guess in a way that's what the people thought about this murder, or ambush, or whatever it was. They felt that justice was served, and that's why it just quietly went away and nobody talked about it anymore.

This story appears to reflect a measure of community cohesion; people apparently did not disagree with the means by which this problem was resolved and were willing to conceal this episode from the outside community. More than reflecting uniformity in beliefs, however, the story reveals a disinclination to intervene in the affairs of other families and to draw the mainstream society into internal affairs.

The influence of spiritual forces, induced by bad doctors, is a possible explanation for the behavior of chronic offenders. If someone comes from a good family and has advice, there is often no other reason for repeated bad behavior. One elder explained,

> They look at a person and say, "Well we know you were brought up with your uncle and your grandmother and your grandfather . . . and your parents are good people, so what happened?" . . . People will say maybe bad spirits. . . . A long time ago we had a lot of medicine people, good and bad, and they could inflict, even to this day, maybe not as powerful as before, but it's still being done, to this day. You know put something bad on you to make you maybe, more than likely, to this day its mostly because of jealousy. Maybe, if what you are doing is good, or they are jealous because you are doing well at something or your family is *smalash*, you're above the others and you're doing well, they'll probably be jealous and they'll go grab this person and put something

on you or do something to you or part of the family or someone else. . . . So it happens, you read about it. . . . When it come to the courthouse thing and that person couldn't be reconciled by counseling so they'd bring him maybe to a healer to find out maybe if there's something else besides or why to make him go that way. . . . Maybe the person looks normal maybe, but we'll work on them just to make sure that—and again usually you can't work on anybody that doesn't want to be worked on, so that person has to agree. And more often that not, a lot of times the person themselves didn't know why they were doing this, or maybe something was troubling that person they weren't even aware of. Like I say, its happening to this day. . . . Again sometimes its kind of a last resort, if people know if there's some wrong, you know like they say nowadays, "The devil made me do it," okay, well, then let's do something about it if you really believe that.

A primary goal of traditional Stó:lō justice practice, according to the accounts we heard, is to reinstate wrongdoers into the community, solve the immediate problem, and restore right relationships with people. The restoration of the community is more important than punishing the wrongdoer, although these might overlap. Jeff Point described the significance of gambling, *slahal*, in disputes, although he did not describe it as a form of dispute resolution:

Now this game [*slahal*] came in three or four different ways. . . . If it was a way of playing, when they say a dispute, now that is an English word for two people who don't agree. A long time ago when there was a disagreement among people it was not a game. The game did not see if you are right and I am wrong. The game brought us to thinking both of us are okay and we can forget about it.

Q: (Jane McMillen): To forget about the dispute?

A: Yeah, it did not resolve it. Let's say if you owned the jacket and I said, "No, that is mine," they would play the game and never mind the jacket.

Q: So it was like a diversion away from the disagreement?

A: Yeah.

Q: That would resolve the bad feelings toward one another?

A: That's right. You see, the dispute was over what, just forget about it. The game brings balance out.

Q: So the game is to remind people of the teachings?

A: That's right. Now you're getting it.

In interfamily disputes often the heads of the families would meet to discuss the problem so that things may be made right again through the exchange of gifts. Wrongdoers did not present their own case because they could not mediate. Sonny McHalsie noted the connections between the underlying logic of ceremonial life generally and dispute management:

> It would be someone from their family rather than themselves because it ties in, even when you are doing your own ceremonies you cannot speak on your own behalf, you have to get a speaker from somewhere else to do your work for you. . . . What chance do you have to speak on your own behalf if you are the wrongdoer? The person that would probably be better to mediate the difference would be the *sí:yá:m* of the family because the respect he'd have from other community members.

Frank Malloway described how families might settle problems between them:

> I think most of it was done through the head of the family. The head of the families would meet and they would discuss the crime, or whatever it was, and they'd reach a consensus. I've never really heard about what the sentences were. They'd say, "Well, we had a family meeting with this family, and they decided on what had to be done," but you never really hear about the punishment itself and how the families reach that verdict, or whatever you'd call it. . . . If you did something wrong the family would take the resposibility and make an offering. They call it an offering. Some of the things in the old days were canoes, because they were like cars today, "Ah, I'll give you my car if you forget about this." But it was canoes in those days. I don't think it was really food because food was so plentiful that it wasn't expensive. Later on, my dad was saying, when it was settlement time, it was horses. They took the place of canoes. He talked about people bringing horses right into the longhouse to distribute to somebody.

The families are brought together through this gift exchange, and the reciprocal relationship is ongoing. The restitution further cements community relations in a manner analogous to marriage and other gift-exchanging events. This reciprocal exchange of goods was described as an exchange of "good feelings." In this sense, the procedures for the resolution of interfamily conflict are described as conforming to a larger cultural pattern of interchange. One elder said that gift giving "brings the good feelings back"; it means, "we're not mad at you anymore." Elders stated the importance of resolving interfamily problems as the community must be held together and must get along together. One elder said, "you can't have a good community if your families aren't together."

This relatively unproblematic view of community conflict can be contrasted to another that accounts for difference in status and the implicit possibility for ongoing problems within ritualized exchange. Sonny McHalsie connected conflict to its social class implications:

> There is a word for stepping on people. Class and status wise. You know how you are always giving [as in potlatches] to elevate your status, and if someone comes along from the lower class and starts trying to build themselves up to the upper class by giving all of these things away. Well, you know how when someone gives you something you are obliged to give it back, an upper-class family would, to discourage someone from moving up by giving them so much resources and wealth that they could never fulfill the obligation to return it, thus stepping on it.

Another, quite different, although not contradictory, view is that the generosity expressed through the reciprocal exchange of gifts means that the families are no longer alienated from each other. One elder explained it this way, "I think if they, the family, agree that this person is sorry and really trying to pay back by doing different things they'll agree, 'okay, maybe you've done enough.' Maybe then they'll have a little ceremony to say, 'okay, we'll agree with that family and this family,' do it publicly in a feast or potlach or something. . . . Of course they agree to it first." The elder explained that the public ceremony was also a way for the family who was wronged to publicly state to the family of the wrongdoer, "We're not going to be angry with you, we're not going to bring you down, we're not going to say anything. We understand you're sorry, okay, we'll agree to that, we think you did enough to say, or show, you are. Okay, we'll get together, we'll do it publicly where we'll let the public know the thing's been resolved. Let's get on with living together, sharing and helping."

Vince Stogan stated that law and justice are a

> right relationship, a good relationship. . . . I guess our people are always talking about getting along. I guess maybe that's justice. But a

> good relationship, not only with your family but with everybody, and not only people, with mother earth, the birds, the fish, the animals the plants, the grass. It's a relationship with everything, everything on this planet. . . . Take care not only [of] yourself but anything and everything whether it's human, or even the rocks, even the rocks are alive. Take care, and that way you take care not only of yourself and everything will be okay, be balanced.

Law and justice in these discourses can be thought of as directly associated with proper conduct. It is thought that people who have been raised in the community, who have advice, and who live in the community should know the rules and abide by them. It is in this sense, then, that Stó:lō justice is not procedural and legalistic. However, legal procedures do exist and are considered next.

Even in the absence of intent by wrongdoers, restitution must still be given to the families of the wronged. The community must be restored. In this sense wrongdoers might have no intent, or no conscious or controllable intent (although there might be uncontrollable intentions). Wrongdoers are responsible for their actions, however, whether they intended to commit a wrong or not. This holds true even in the case of an accident, injury, or death. There do appear to be some differences in how accidental injury and intentional injury are regarded, however, and some differences in what should be done about them. An elder described for us the events that occurred between the families of two young friends after one friend was accidentally shot and killed by the other.

> What that family done that shot that young fella, they put up a big feast and invited a lot of people to witness how sorry he was, that is hurting him, he's not gonna get over it, but we want your people to help us solve that feeling that we have. . . . The families are talking today, they're not mad at one another because he apologized for shooting his partner. . . . He apologized right there, "I'm sorry, I'll never get over it—that he was my good friend, yet I was the one that—and that's why he's not here today." His family, the one that was shot, his family got up and said, "We forgive you because we want to be your friend, too. We look at it as an accident, but that won't bring back my son, but we're not mad at you anymore." The two families are working together again.

A significant feature of Stó:lō justice is the employment of appropriate personnel. Only the proper people must be drawn into the resolution and only at the right time. Ill feelings arise when people involve themselves in other people's problems and when those who should be taking care of the problem do not. This is especially true when issues cross family boundaries. An elder gave us an example of an individual stepping in and apprehending his daughter's children. The elder felt it appropriate to do this work himself because he is the grandparent, and the children are his responsibility. There is a strong preference for settling intrafamily disputes within the family. There is also a preference for settling disputes within as narrow a circle of disputants as possible, even in cases involving nonfamily.

Depending on the nature and severity of the conflict, however, outside *sí:yá:m* can be drawn in to resolve the problem. These are widely recognized and respected people, but they do not necessarily occupy a formal position, although formal councils are noted in the late nineteenth and early twentieth centuries in several Coast Salish communities. Counseling from *sí:yá:m* was taken seriously, and they often had the final say on a dispute. Frank Malloway gave an example of a *sí:yá:m* coming in to settle a land boundary dispute between two farmers.

> So they called in Chief Harry Stewart . . . and I remember that because my dad used to babysit me when my mother was busy, he'd take me with him. I was about four or five years old. It's like a dream, I remember walking back here with my dad and the old man with two canes, that was Chief Stewart. So, he heard both sides of the story and looked the site over and then he said, . . . "You're taking his land, but you're half way to the ditch with your fence. I'm not going to tell you to take your fence down and move it. What you do is you go across and cut your lot off." So if you go back there today I think there's a fence still up there. It goes towards the ditch and then stops and goes across to the Scowkale cemetery and that was done maybe about fifty years ago, I guess. And that was the only incident where I've seen outside *sí:yá:m* coming in to decide on an issue and that was Chief Harry Stewart. . . . He heard both sides of the story and then he made his decision. . . . The old respected chiefs, Billy Sepas and Harry Stewart and Billy Hall, their decisions were honoured by the other people even if they didn't come from this reserve. They held high positions as leaders. Whatever they decided, you respected their decisions. So [the farmers], they agreed on it and they never brought it up again.

Harry Stewart was noted by another elder for his ability to settle disputes: "If this community had troubles correcting some families or children or whatever, they would call upon another chief from down in Chilliwack. His name was Harry Stewart. He was one of the greatest . . . and he used to come up here and talk to the people and give them a good talk." There is a strong preference to settle problems within the family, and outside *sí:yá:m* were brought in only for significant, longstanding, unresolved disputes.

Family feasting is a commonly referenced feature of Stó:lō justice practices. Feasting can act as both a means to resolve and to prevent problems, through the act of generosity and the establishment or reestablishment of exchange relations between families. Feasting brings families together and provides a public forum for discussion, and resolution is achieved, if it is to be achieved, through consensus. Payments may be made to end a dispute, and this was witnessed in the public setting of the feast. Sonny McHalsie pointed out the role of witnesses, called to speak at the feast, to affirm generally held values and comment on the specifics of a problem: "I think this is the role witnesses play. Because that is what they always say, that is what they always start with, it is almost repetitive. This is the opportunity they have to remind everyone at the gathering of what the teachings are. They start with the positive stuff and end with what was done wrong, like 'next time you should do this.' "

However, there was no rule of closure, and so in instances where there were deeply divergent views it was possible that the forum could continue for a very long time and that no decisions would be made. Even in such a case there was a benefit, we were told, for in the end, everything could be brought out in the open, and everyone knew where others stood.

Some communities had community courts established in the early reservation period that served as a site for formal public dispute resolution. Headmen or orators presided over these courts. The court was not a forum for determining guilt, and elders observed that if something was serious enough to be heard in the courthouse, then the details of the situation and the parties involved were known to most people in the community: "Well, first of all word gets around and people begin to know, and if they didn't know then you have a runner to go around if you want certain people to come." The wrongdoer was brought before elders and community members who discussed the problem publicly. Any people brought in from outside the community were given the details of the situation beforehand through a runner. Elders also summarized the problem in the court at the beginning of the proceedings so that everyone would know why they were there. One elder described his memories of the community court house:

> When I was younger, before I was ten years old, our old village site was just back here. There's a church that burned down now. The church was up on the hill and right below was our court house. Our court house, as it was called then, was used for, I guess, it was used as court houses are used today. I was quite young then and I wasn't even sure of exactly what was going on, but I knew by the time I was ten that people that did something wrong were brought to the courthouse, and if it was something that was not really serious then the offender and the victim, people put them in the center and people would sit around. They had benches all the way around, parents and some of the elders would sit around and talk to that person and try to resolve the situation between the offender and the victim. As the offense or crime got more serious, the more people were brought in, like the chief and some members and some elders, and when it got a little more serious then they'd bring other chiefs in from the surrounding area. Elders that had knowledge of some of the things to help resolve the matter. I guess it was more of a reconciliation between the groups. . . . I'm not sure how it really came about. The people at that time used to get together and help one another and share and maybe build it themselves. It was an old building, it looked old with cedar siding, and there were benches all the way around where people could sit down. There were chairs in the middle where the offender and the victim would sit down.

Another elder stated, "More often than not they know what's happened. And I guess with the pressure from the family, you know, talking about the name thing, that person will say, 'Yes, I did it,' and now what are you going to do now? What do you intend to do, and of course then you'd hear views from all sides, and the person more often will say they did it, and if not then the session will go all night."

The court system relied on the cooperation and participation of the wrongdoer. The wrongdoer had to agree to appear before the court, endure public shaming, and then agree to the terms for amending the wrong. One elder told us that family pressure provided a strong incentive for the wrongdoer to cooperate: "I think when something like that happened they had no choice but to come, and they were almost made to come by their own family, otherwise it's kind of a disgrace. . . . I would think to somewhat degree peer pressure but mostly the elders in the family. They were really strict that way at that time."

Public shaming could involve a public talking-to from members of the community, elders, and visiting participants. It was also possible that those wronged could stand up and make a statement to the participants. Shaming also involved support for the wrongdoers to change their ways. One elder stated, "As the crime gets more serious, then you have more people, and you can really talk to that person and of course let them know that what they've done is wrong, and it's not in our tradition that we do this and about the family thing—how you're damaging the family, family breakdown, and maybe say, like, 'Well, if you keep doing this maybe you won't even be allowed into anybody else's territory.' "

One Stó:lō elder said the public setting of the court proceedings and the prospect of public shaming served as a deterrent for others witnessing the events. "Quite often most of the village would be there whether they were part of it or not. But they'd be there to see what's going on, and they'll know, and I'll guess they'll pass the word on like, 'If you don't behave, you'll know what will happen.' "

Elders told us that restitution (sometimes expressed in that language) was the most common way to settle a dispute. As mentioned before, gift exchanges sorted out problems between families and brought them together in a reciprocal relationship. Restitution may have also included service to the family and community as a way for individuals to reinstate themselves in the community. Vince Stogan described the notion of service:

> To this day I call it a win-win situation, not like the other type of system where its win-lose; you did something wrong so you're the loser, you're going to pay for it by going to jail or something else. But our system at the time was what I call win-win, where it's you did something wrong, let's try to resolve it. Either through restitution or even go live with that person to help them. At that time things were kind of a matter of survival, you had to get wood, you had to go fishing,

> you had to go hunting, because there was no such thing as welfare, so it's a matter of survival.

Vince Stogan and others described healing as a key feature in aboriginal dispute settling. From this viewpoint, it was generally thought best to settle problems right away. However, when disputes were particularly heated and emotions were running high, sometimes it was best to settle the problem after people had calmed down. When disputes are set aside for a while, both parties practice avoidance. Elders' advice and spiritual practice help to calm people down.

Several elders stated that sometimes disputes could not be settled, or wrongdoers would not listen to the teachings of their family and community members or would continue wrongdoing in spite of talking to or shaming in the courthouse. In these extreme cases where problems could not be resolved, a sentence of exile could be imposed by the community. Elders made the distinction between two types of exile, internal and external. The concept of internal exile has been discussed above in relation to bad doctors. Internal exile relates to a state of internal alienation. The wrongdoers still live in the community but are not a part of the community. People practice avoidance of the wrongdoers, who live their lives alienated and alone. Internal alienation can sometimes be taken to extreme ends.

External exile was a formal banishment of wrongdoers from the community. This type of punishment occurred for extreme offenses such as incest and murder. An elder gave us an example:

> Another banishment was if you married somebody too close to you, if you fell in love with somebody that was in your family and it was too close a relationship, you were asked to leave. There's a lot of stories about one fellow falling in love with his sister. When they say sister it could be your first or second cousin because the Indian people for three generations they were your sisters or brothers so when you hear stories like that from the elders you don't know how really close related they are. Today your sister is the same father and mother or same mother, but they were banished too, told to leave the village if they started a family together, they were asked to leave the village. They usually moved away, in those days it wasn't hard to survive because there was so much around you that you needed, you didn't suffer any, but just lack

of companionship with other people and not participating in your village functions. I guess that was banishment enough, lonely people.

External exile apparently was rare, and the practice was ordinarily not to isolate wrongdoers but to restore them into the community and heal wounded relationships. It appears that the purpose of external exile was not to starve or kill wrongdoers but to isolate them from their family and community. The sentence nonetheless led to loneliness and isolation, creating a desire for an individual to be restored to community life. In some instances an exiled person could be reinstated. One elder told us how a banished individual could be brought back into the village: "We had banishment, too, but that was the last resort. Banishment isn't, say, 'So long and we don't see you any more' if they sent you away, and again it depends on how serious it is. If the person mends their ways and does better and helps and gives restitution and [does] all those sorts of things, then maybe they'll be allowed to come back. But again, it depends on how serious it is."

Another elder described the banishment process this way: "The stories I heard was that they accepted the second generation back, the children were accepted back, eventually, but I've never heard anything about the people that were banished being accepted back. Like today, people do violent crimes, and you sentence them to five years, and then they come back to your village or come back out. Well, they've never taken their stories that far where the person is forgiven for the things that they've done. It probably happened, but I never hear the elders talk about it." One elder told us that new communities could be formed by people who were externally exiled. "Some of the ones that were sent out away from the community here they started their own little communities . . . that's how a lot of the smaller communities began."

Formal exile was the most serious community sanction for wrongdoing. Formal execution of wrongdoers carried out by the community does not appear to have occurred. However, elders told us that individuals carried out executions of wrongdoers on their own initiative, such as the young man who killed his granduncle for causing the death of his two young children.

Official Discourse, Community Questions

By the late 1990s, the Stó:lō efforts at conceptualizing and acting on justice issues remained broad and unfocused, tied to a uncertain treaty process that was the target of widespread criticism across the province for its slow pace. In the early 1990s, an effort was made to consult the tribal membership concerning fisheries and aboriginal fisheries law (Glavin 1993). The Stó:lō Nation, under the direction of a retired officer of the Royal Canadian Mounted Police (RCMP), undertook a policing study through the Aboriginal Rights and Title department during the period of the formation of the House of Elders and before the creation of the House of Justice. Questionnaires were distributed through the communities in 1995, and staff conducted additional surveys. Meanwhile, Robert Phillips, then a Stó:lō Nation justice worker, organized a major justice conference to broaden the debate concerning the future of Stó:lō involvement in corrections, aboriginal justice, and policing. The Stó:lō Justice Conference of 30–31 October 1996 drew representatives of the federal, provincial, and municipal governments, as well as First Nations from around Canada. In his opening address to this meeting, Chief Steven Point, Chief's Representative of the Stó:lō Nation, raised a series of questions central to Stó:lō justice: What should Stó:lō justice look like? Should it include police, jails, and other institutional trappings? Should the Stó:lō take responsibility for offenders in their communities? (McMullen 1998:12).

Internal and outside forces, meanwhile, pushed for the immediate deployment of an already packaged, widely publicized, and purportedly proven program from the Maori of New Zealand (see Olsen, Maxwell, and Morris 1995 for a description of this program). The program had the advantage of a set of media materials to sell it, including a video and a variety of well-placed supporters ready to talk it up, and could, in theory, set the Stó:lō on the way to taking over part of the youth justice program. For the purposes of the tribal government, the New Zealand program would mitigate accusations of inactivity on the part of community members. Furthermore, the federal government was in support of the program and willing to provide funding. Martin Suo, an officer of the federal Aboriginal Justice Directorate, Justice Canada, who serves the British Columbia–Yukon region, made a presentation concerning Family Group Conferencing (FGC), indicating federal support for adaptation of the program within indigenous communities of Canada. In subsequent discussions, the FGC program was compared favorably to the South Island Justice Project and was said to have "greater community involvement" than the elders council of the South Island Project. In addition, FGC would "find appropriate people" rather than rely on pre-identified elders. Kathy Louis of the National Parole Board, however, observed that the FGC model left out the spiritual component of wellness and healing within a restorative model (conference notes taken by author, 30 October 1996).

The Stó:lō Traditional Justice Project was initiated in the spring of 1996, and Stó:lō leaders stressed the value of incorporating important aspects of Stó:lō indigenous justice into the contemporary practice of the House of Justice. Stó:lō elders and chiefs were presented with information concerning a variety of programs in operation within First Nations of Canada, particularly in the Prairie provinces of Manitoba, Saskatchewan, and Alberta. The federal government continued to promote the Family Group Conferencing model for Canadian indigenous communities. The Navajo Peacemaker Court approach was promoted by James Zion, counsel for the Navajo court and a speaker at a variety of international gatherings, including a seminar entitled "Policy Forum on Non-Judicial Family Dispute Resolution in Aboriginal Communities," held in Vancouver in April 1996. Meanwhile, provincial legislation aimed at the British Columbia Ministry of Child and Family Services made provision for implementation of FGC, and the Ministry of Social Services promoted the idea (McMullen 1998:22). As a result, the Stó:lō Nation acted to implement FGC in a small way into the House of Justice family and youth service programs, and a small number of cases were carried out under the provisions of FGC, beginning in 1996. Implementation proved to be difficult, and complications arose, particularly the failure of cooperation of parents and RCMP officers. The justice worker in charge gave an account in a Justice Committee meeting of March 1997:

> It's not going according to plan. I figured it would come together much sooner than it has. . . . I still haven't received the report from the RCMP—the incident report. . . . So I got the run-around from the Mission RCMP! . . . I think it will work much better once we get a

> position for this, or, and I should say, the Stó:lō Peace and Security Service, because then we'll be dealing with our own people and then there will be a line of accountability to our own people and by our own people. (Quoted in McMullen 1998:24)

Family Group Conferencing achieved some limited successes by 1998. However, the Stó:lō justice worker found federal and provincial government agencies to be focused on policy and procedure and to thwart creativity in planning.

At one "traditional justice" planning meeting one Stó:lō leader observed, "We don't want to know what others are doing; we want to know what we did" (quoted in McMullen 1998:15). The dilemma of creating a highly localized system and importing existing, easily fundable models from outside persisted, however, although plans for a Stó:lō Healing Centre were outlined at the Stó:lō People of the River Conference in 1997. In this program, envisioned under the terms of Section 81 of the federal Conditional Release Act, First Nations offenders could be released to the custody of First Nations to finish out their sentences. The Stó:lō House of Justice would broaden its service to include other indigenous people, with the possibility of a financial benefit. This development was critiqued by community leaders, including one who pointed that "the reason the federal government gets rid of facilities is because they are losing money" (paraphrased in McMullen 1998:42 n.15). Others, observing that the offenders were guilty of serious crimes, did not wish them to remain in Stó:lō territory.

A second Stó:lō Justice Conference was held two years later, on 29–30 October 1998. The Stó:lō Nation convened the World Indigenous Corrections Symposium on 23–25 March 1999, in Chilliwack. The Stó:lō Nation's newspaper reported that "Many of the presenters spoke of a history of oppression; prevention of the practicing of their culture, language and traditions, the residential experience etceteras [sic]. The result of all of the above was, high rates of drug and alcohol addiction, incarceration, and suicide" (*Sqwélqwels ye Stó:lō* 2, no. 3 [May 1999]: 40).

In 1999, the Stó:lō Nation began a new stage of development of their justice program by hiring summer intern Kate Blomfield, a non-indigenous law student, to begin the process of producing a statement of Stó:lō legal principles to be presented to chiefs and elders and, subsequently, a draft of legal procedures and tribal code. Blomfield's work was under the direction of the nation's Aboriginal Rights and Title department. As part of her orientation to the Stó:lō Nation, a connection between justice and landscape was established. Blomfield accompanied Sonny McHalsie, tribal culture adviser, on a tour of the territory emphasizing locations that reveal the work of the Transformer, X̱á:ls, are connected to place-names, and are associated with histories of conflicts and outcomes. Additionally, Blomfield took a boat tour of Stó:lō waterways—reflecting Stó:lō preferences for water travel in earlier periods and the existence of petroglyphs, pictographs, and other cultural markers, which were created to be seen by water rather than by land.

Blomfield's work was to focus on resource rights (ownership, access, use, and guidelines for transmission), traditional territory and relations with non-Stó:lō, heritage and sacred site protocol and protection, methods and procedures of conflict resolution, child and family welfare, and obligations and rights of individuals to family and society (Blomfield 1999a:2, 1999b, 1999c). Blomfield's job was to "serve as a record of the inherent and perpetual principles and values of the Stó:lō legal tradition. . . . Ultimately, the codification of traditional laws will better enable Stó:lō legal principles to form the foundation of Stó:lō self-government and the resolution of disputes with the Stó:lō Nation or those that involve Stó:lō people, territory, rights, or resources" (1999a:2). Blomfield added to her tasks a consideration of the desirability of a Bill of Rights and Obligations (personal communication, 1 June 1999). She continued her work in the summer of 2000.

Meanwhile, the Stó:lō Nation's newspaper, *Sqwélqwels ye Stó:lō* (formerly known as *Sqwelqwel* and spelled several ways over the years) provided semi-official summaries of the tribal government's views. In the June 1999 issue, the appointment of a new justice worker was announced, along with the statement that alternative justice initiatives were underway for the Stó:lō Nation Justice Program, including a new try at Family Group Conferencing, (FGC), which was explained in these terms: "Rather than relying solely on the mainstream system as a means of settling disputes and conflicts, FGC offers an alternative that is more culturally appropriate. Rather than focusing on punishment, FGC aims to restore balance and harmony for both the person who has done the harm and the person harmed, as well as for the families and communities involved" (2, no. 4:29).

The FGC program was the outcome of an agreement between the Province of British Columbia, the Ministry of Child and Family Services, BC Corrections, the federal Aboriginal Justice Directorate, and the Stó:lō Nation. The plan was to start small, beginning with first-time youth offenders who admit guilt, and to include the victim, offender, families, friends, and community members in the FGC meetings. A call for facilitators was put out to the community members through the Stó:lō Nation's newspaper. At the Stó:lō: People of the River Conference in October 1999, justice worker Donna Moon reported that the Stó:lō program, begun by Robert Phillips, had "settled on the Maori model" because research and surveys showed that "this is what Stó:lō people had practiced in the past" (Moon 1999). A Halkomelem word glossed as "Family Group Counseling" was applied to the program (Moon 1999), and funding was provided through the Aboriginal Justice Directorate.

An Aboriginal Justice Advisory Board was sworn in on 19 June 1998, composed of RCMP officials, a member of the federal Aboriginal Justice Directorate, a Crown counsel, justice employees of the Stó:lō Nation, and the Chief's Representative, among others. The committee was formed to allow for Stó:lō and professionals in the criminal justice system to regularly talk together and for the committee to meet with Stó:lō community members to discuss alternative justice programs (*Sqwélqwels ye Stó:lō* 1, nos. 7–8 [1998]: 37).

A carefully constructed special issue of *Sqwélqwels ye Stó:lō* in fall 1998, entitled *Xyolhemeylh* (or Xolhmi:lh, both the name of the tribal health and family services program and a reference to respecting and caring for children), addressed criticism of the Stó:lō Nation's health and family services program while describing a reorganization and centralization of tribal service delivery. The special issue also advanced the idea of "listening to the Nation's elders," several of whom were quoted in support of restructuring as a form of "working together." A program of "runners" was announced to facilitate the delivery of information from the tribal headquarters to the bands in order to replicate the aboriginal practice of sending messengers to announce potlatches and other major events. This followed a major disruption of community services that arose, in part, over the issue of whether service delivery should be centralized in Chilliwack or decentralized with regional offices. The special issue contained feature articles that described traditional life; culture, law, and the role of elders; and how this was accommodated within the current and revised government structure. Meanwhile, privately, an elder who had served on the House of Justice corrections feasibility study questioned whether justice initiatives should occur at the level of the tribal nation or at the level of individual bands (McMullen 1998:25).

The special issue provided a two-page statement of "traditional law," which I summarize here. The headline, in bold print, reads "Traditional Stó:lō People Conduct Their Lives According to the Seven Laws of Life: Health, Humility, Happiness, Understanding, Generations, Forgiveness, Generosity" (6). Cultural traits said to be shared with many other native cultures are detailed: (1) Spirituality—"reflected in direct communications with the Creator"; (2) Respect; (3) Sharing of knowledge; (4) Old Ways—"reflected in practices such as custom adoptions"; (5) Listening, with the notation that "What is meant for you, it will stay with you." The accompanying text describes the Stó:lō concept of "doing things in a good way" (actions that are conscientious, polite, kind, respectful) and notes that the Elder or helper assists couples to resolve family conflict by

> speaking the truth to both members of the family without offending the feelings of either of them. The Elder or helper in this case will carefully balance the harsh truth (crude reality) with a softer version of the same truth (perceived reality) while still maintaining the integrity of the truth.
>
> In traditional ways, conflict resolution and problem solving is achieved by assisting two or more parties to talk to each other and to listen to each other until an understanding and consensus is built . . . the traditional helper will focus on containing the level of anxiety, animosity, and anger from all parties so that each person can gradually see each other's position. The traditional process may also include STORYTELLING . . . the story told by the helper resembles the conflict experienced by the listeners and the listeners clearly see their own conflicts being unfolded in front of them [caps and emphasis in original].
>
> Often, the traditional helper will use his/her own life experience as an example so as to assist the "clients" to feel more comfortable with the helping experience . . . the traditional helper [thereby] acknowledges his/her own humanity including faults in character. . . . The

> words selected by the helper are usually spoken from the heart rather than from the mind. Compassionate words carry the unequivocal message of care, allow the listener to become relaxed and more open to the healing words of the speaker. (7)

This presentation introduced the idea of a "traditional helper" as a central figure and paired this with a profile of a "Cultural Worker", Herbie Joe, who was selected by significant elders and who works with elders in the Stó:lō Nation's health and family services program. The presentation of "traditional law" was couched within the consensus-healing discourse and overlaps with the "wellness" language of social services. A *Xyolhemeylh* editorial in the July 1998 edition of *Sqwélqwels ye Stó:lō* (1, no. 5: 16), for example, presents Maslow's hierarchy of human needs in explaining the process of healing. Significantly, the presentation emphasizes the role of story telling and of the use of elders' personal narratives as examples. This account of aboriginal justice infuses ideology, including twentieth-century Western healing rhetoric, with the realities of prior indigenous practice and has significant implications for the real world, particularly the community debates about justice.

In common with other Coast Salish peoples, the ancestors of the present-day Stó:lō members suffered through the loss of population due to episodic epidemic, the loss of political autonomy, the loss of lands and resources, and language loss through government efforts at assimilation. The Stó:lō responded with various efforts at using the dominant society's court system through petitions aimed at political leaders and by finding their way into the new economy through attempts to control the trade of the Hudson's Bay Company and, later, through wage laboring. Eventually, indigenous political organizations, including the present-day Stó:lō Nation, were created to advance Stó:lō interests.

By the end of 1999, Stó:lō justice initiatives were driven by a variety of ideas coming from within the communities that compose the Stó:lō Nation and from outside. Some community members were fearful of the consolidation of authority within the nation. The nation paradoxically advocated Stó:lō traditional practices while importing systems from New Zealand with federal government encouragement and contemplating ideas from the Canadian Prairies. An institutional structure had been established, with Houses of Elders and Justice, but justice practices were not institutionalized. Justice narratives and practices moved toward an explicit link to tribal social services through the Family and Child Services branch of tribal government. Some community members spoke from within the language of consensus, healing, and wellness. Others articulated a more conflictual stance based on real-world problems of relations between families.

5

An Intertribal Justice Discussion

The differences in experiences of the Coast Salish nations on opposite sides of the international border are sufficiently great that there are sizeable gaps in knowledge and differences in viewpoint. This is true even though there is commonality in traditional culture, intermarriage, and persistent patterns of mutual participation in ceremonial life. I have spoken at a number of Stó:lō gatherings about my views of what has transpired in the court systems of neighboring Coast Salish communities of Washington State. I spoke at two lunchtime gatherings of tribal employees and chiefs in 1996 and circulated copies of my own published work about tribal courts. Later, I spoke for an hour at a more formal national conference of tribal and federal justice dignitaries sponsored by the Stó:lō Nation on 31 October 1997. This was followed by a visit to the House of Justice and a talk at the multidisciplinary People of the River Conference, also sponsored by the Stó:lō Nation. I spoke privately to a number of Stó:lō people about the issue of justice. My theme at these gatherings was consistent: U.S. Coast Salish people had already begun to conduct their own justice affairs and could reasonably be expected to do so on the British Columbia side of the border. My experiences in Washington State had convinced me that the emphasis in much of the indigenous literature on dichotomous differentiation between Western, adversarial systems of justice and non-adversarial, healing indigenous practices was both misleading and unnecessary. Further, at various talks in British Columbia I found it difficult to get listeners to understand that American tribes actually held a meaningful measure of jurisdiction. Questions to me persistently returned to diversionary systems, rather than freestanding ones.

I felt that the experiences of the Coast Salish communities of Washington State ought to be part of the debate among Coast Salish peoples of

British Columbia; that their efforts, both successful and failed, ought to be examined; and that the ways the Washington State codes and constitutions approached the critical issues of relations between families, the use of elders, and the role of folk law ought to be debated. Keith Carlson, head of the research wing of the Stó:lō Nation, agreed that it was worth considering, and he expressed his opinion to Clarence (Kat) Pennier, a Grand Chief and executive officer of the Rights and Title branch of tribal government. According to Carlson's account, Chief Pennier held the view that the tribal courts of Puget Sound were dominated by the state and were likely not worth considering. These views seem to embed in them characteristic problems in American-Canadian relations and the curious partial disconnection between adjacent populations.

Despite Chief Pennier's initial reservations, and with his subsequent approval and participation, a meeting was convened on 16 September 1998 between representatives of the Upper Skagit Council and the Stó:lō Nation. I drove down to the Upper Skagit reservation in Sedro-Woolley, Washington, from my home in Vancouver, and Kat Pennier, tribal cultural expert Sonny McHalsie, justice worker Donna Moon, and Keith Carlson came down from Chilliwack, British Columbia, arriving at about ten in the morning. The Upper Skagit reservation is nestled in the foothills of the Cascade Mountains and is located along Route 20 of the U.S. highway system, a designated "Scenic Highway." The seventy-six-acre reserve is a few miles from the Skagit River and is surrounded by flat farmland, a derelict mental hospital used during an earlier era, and scattered houses and service stations. A few miles away is the small town of Sedro-Woolley, which is, incongruously for a largely rural area, the location of an abandoned steel mill. The tribal headquarters are housed in an angular, modernist wooden building constructed in the 1980s and thought by the architects to reflect Coast Salish traditions of construction.

A striking feature within the tribal center is the relative absence of male employees and the presence of female employees. One of the particular features of contemporary Upper Skagit life is the significant participation of women in tribal political life, including a regular majority on the tribal council. This emerging role reflects women's central contributions to family income as wage earners and their work as brokers with the outside world; women have assumed many responsibilities and have obtained training in education, health, and social services (B.

Miller 1990, 1992a). Women have played pivotal roles in the development and management of the justice system.

I arrived first among the visitors and met Michele Robbins, the Upper Skagit court clerk and administrative assistant, and shortly thereafter greeted Cindy McMullen, a former research assistant. Floyd Williams, the longtime tribal chair, was seated in the council chambers. Michele Robbins expressed concern that councilor Doreen Maloney, an expert in tribal courts and the one who was to make the major presentation, was apparently distracted by her other duties and was not yet present. Robbins provided coffee and pastries and convened the meeting while the chiefs and assistants, uncertain about what the other might offer, sounded each other out. Members of Canadian bands have no clear view of the nature of Washington State tribal government, and the converse also holds. Initial comments suggested that the Coast Salish people of British Columbia, as nonsignatory tribes, were thought to have little self-governance and, perhaps, leadership functions not on a par with their own. Some nineteenth-century treaty signers enjoy near-legendary status among members of the treaty tribes of western Washington, and descent from them confers a measure of pride and status. In an effort to signal the significance of the current situation and the present Stó:lō leaders, I observed to Chief Williams, the descendant of a treaty signer, that Chief Pennier of the Stó:lō Nation might perform that task himself in the near future.

Robbins, making her own position clear on the issue of the relative maturity of tribal government, observed that the Upper Skagit government is "in early adulthood" and that the tribe had "asked other tribes for codes to get what is best for us. So you don't reinvent the wheel." She noted further that Upper Skagits participated in a consortium of judicial services (the Northwest Intertribal Court System, or NICS), which "worked for a while until the tribe matured."

Doreen Maloney arrived and made her own effort to create connections with her guests. Maloney commented on shared Stó:lō–Upper Skagit territories at Chittenden Meadows, a place where managed fires were used to enhance berry growth, and on relations with the Thompson tribe, a neighbor in common. Although the tribes were enemies in the past (and were said to have killed each other on sight when encountered in lands used by both groups), they are cooperating in U.S.-Canadian national park issues and in relations with Seattle City Light, a utility company that generates much of its power from rivers in the joint Thompson–Upper Skagit area. The territory of the Thompson tribe, now known as the N'lakapamux Nation, borders the land of the Stó:lō, with whom they intermarried and had generally, but not always, peaceful relations.

The conversation quickly moved to the problem of managing relations between the constituent families composing the tribe and the potential for the failure of tribal governance. Maloney provided a précis of the Upper Skagit situation. She remarked that the Upper Skagit community, though not as large as the Stó:lō Nation, had "politics [that] were identical." She commented that in order to avoid political fragmentation and paralysis,

> We have four major families. . . . Tribes to the north and west are almost paralyzed by [family] politics. We look around for the representatives of groups within families to share the responsibilities in order not to take all of the power. Each unit needs representation—taking part of the blame and responsibility. We identify these people. I came from the biggest family, but we know we should have x positions. The group is made up of the whole. With that solidarity we've moved forward. At times we've had too many reps in one family—and they took themselves off [the council]. Floyd [a member of another large family] will chair until he retires. The young guys will have to learn how to do it. We owe that to elders.

Carlson followed out the discussion of the disruption of community-level politics due to differences in family teachings and in orientation to folk law:

CARLSON: Can you incorporate Salish customs?

MALONEY: Yes, make the code broad enough, so you can also do community services. Or, coordinate with the court clerk on another reservation to satisfy that they did the service.

CARLSON: Is there a way to address the balance between families [in the justice process]?

MALONEY: Yes, do they participate in the outcomes? The other family may come in and say . . .

ROBBINS: (interrupting): Especially with alcohol—the family may comment on their own member.

MALONEY: You can take impact [testimony] from anyone about what will work. Formal or informal.

Maloney emphasized her position that, as a government, the Upper Skagit tribe had cause and the obligation to act on community problems, even at the risk of offending families and stirring up problems between them. Major issues in regulating the community and managing relations between families arise over access to resources owned collectively by the tribe as treaty reserves or otherwise, control over children, and exclusion of sex offenders and others. The following exchange captures the sense of the interrelationship of these issues:

CARLSON: Are there laws for extradition [to other First Nations]?

MALONEY: No, but there are laws for exclusion. Member or non-member. But you can't deny access to some services. The Lummi [tribe] is moving on this in sex crimes.

CARLSON: Banishment?

ROBBINS: Yes, otherwise, resources are spent on these people.

In response to a discussion of the possibility of allowing member bands within the Stó:lō Nation to develop their own codes, Maloney made analogy between the Stó:lō situation (of a composite tribal council composed of separate bands) and the existence of separate codes for each of the Puget Sound tribes.

MALONEY: Tribes can have code, but local communities can modify this.

MILLER: Then you could have Stó:lō law and variation within this for the bands?

CARLSON: Local bands [of the Stó:lō Nation] want their own jurisdiction.

MCMULLEN: What do you do about criminals on the reserve who flee?

MALONEY: You contact the other jurisdictions to return them.

MOON: How do you deal with youth crime?

MALONEY: We look for behavioral change; the alternative is deferred prosecution. Use incentives to get the youth under control for a while. Youth find jail to be okay, so figure out what matters to them.

MOON: You use an informal process? Family group counseling with influential people?

MALONEY: With the breakdown of the family law structure we find that parents must participate in the behavior of their kids. Some believe kids can do whatever they want. Then we kick them out of [tribal] housing at some point—only when it's critical. But, often, the informant [about youth crime] may be a close family member, for example, theft from a grandmother. The issue is how to deal with this effectively without tearing apart the community. You need someone to go to without tearing up the family.

ROBBINS: Parents sometimes ask the court to take on the jurisdiction [for children]. Extended family members speak to the court. The court helps enforce parenting.

MALONEY: Neglect is destructive to the community, and there is some willingness on the part of the community to step in, even though some get mad. Referrals are often made from family members.

MOON: You have referrals for kids?

MALONEY: If there is no family member; the interests of the child is first. It must be an acceptable family member [who intervenes for the child]. There is a case of a child with multiple disabilities who was taken out of the tribe to place where [care can be received]. If there is no stability in the home, no regular home and so on. If the parent's role is identified as the kid's problem and the kids are subjected to crazy things . . . [the child may be removed].

PENNIER: Do you force people to quit going to bingo if they neglect their kids?

MALONEY: Yes, it's neglect.

A second critical exchange concerned relations with other indigenous people resident within one's own territory.

CARLSON: A majority of [non-Stó:lō] Indians in the Fraser Valley want to bring their own rights . . .

MALONEY: No! Inherent powers come from property and territory.

CARLSON: Most prisons in Western Canada are in the Fraser Valley—and therefore there are lots of non-Stó:lō Natives here. They want Prairie traditions . . .

MALONEY: The sort-down [the process of channeling the case into the tribal legal system] will cause heartache. Push for recognition of bands and traditions of the bands there! You can internally recognize the Prairie, but not externally. The basis of authority of the people—the point of the argument about aboriginal title—is not based on a mixture of people's rights. When we go to Makah [tribe], that is Makah. Arguments are based on populations there, that is inherent.

PENNIER: We used to allow other Indians to fish if they were licensed. About 1992 we stopped that. Some married in.

The dialogue led to a consideration of the context of justice initiatives, including difficult relations with the federal governments. Chief Pennier informed the Upper Skagits of his view that with a changeover in community leaders, the Stó:lō, like the Skagits, "have to go back and educate about prehistory." Further, the 1991 *Delgamuukw* decision of the Supreme Court of Canada indicates that aboriginal title is part of the federal treaty process, not the provincial responsibility, and that "it isn't business as usual any more—it will be direct action." Maloney responded that it is "the same here; it still came to civil disobedience, even with title."

Maloney provided a history of the tribal court in her community (see the introduction to this book) and emphasized the "flexibility [in the system] to make it a peoples' forum."

Subsequently, on 23 September, I summarized the meeting for the Stó:lō Nation in a brief, edited portions of which I present below:

Brief Presented to Stó:lō Nation

SUMMARY OF ISSUES IN UPPER SKAGIT-STÓ:LŌ JUSTICE DISCUSSION

Background

There are several background differences between the circumstances at Upper Skagit and the Stó:lō Nation. First, Upper Skagit has a smaller population (750 vs. about 5,000). Second, Upper Skagit maintains jurisdiction over tribal members and community residents uncontested by the state or federal governments, with some exceptions. Third, Upper Skagit is a confederated tribe—that is, eleven bands long since confederated. The constituent bands never held federal recognition; this has been held by the tribe alone. The Upper Skagit now participate in the Boldt fishery (50 percent) for tribes and operate a multi-million dollar gaming operation. The communities are alike in cultural background (Coast Salish, Shaker Church, Syowen, Christian worship); in history of oppression by the mainstream (loss of lands, fishing rights, residential schools, and so on). Both operate a range of social, health, and educational services. The Upper Skagit have a single residential reservation and therefore are more compact on the landscape. The Upper Skagit tribal court arose as a response to the need to prosecute offenders after regaining fishing rights under the Boldt decision; that is, the court began its life linked to the management of resources and has grown from there.

System Flexibility

Upper Skagit councilor Doreen Maloney presented what seemed to me to be a model of community justice with built-in flexibility at several levels. She emphasized that the delivery of justice in her community seeks to avoid violating due process for any member. She observed that this is a difficult standard to maintain because of the overlap of roles of tribal members who are also implicated as family members, and who may have information concerning an issue in one capacity as a tribal employee that they ought not have in some other capacity. Doreen emphasized the issue of asserting tribal good over family benefit. To achieve this, she noted that tribal leaders look for representatives of each of the major families to share authority and responsibility.

Concerning the issue of flexibility: Doreen Maloney hoped that the court was "a people's forum." Constituent groups in the community have been called on to suggest appropriate code for the tribal system. An example provided concerned the problem of "snatching" of people for initiation into the Smokehouse. Health concerns for the babies [initiates into Winter Dancing] and accusations of kidnapping were addressed by allowing the Smokehouse leaders (Smokehouse Association) to suggest resolutions whereby the tribal government's legal obligations and liabilities concerning health and safety could be met and cultural activities maintained. The Smokehouse Association now provides release of liability forms, physical exams, and so on.

Doreen observed that they can "take input from anyone about what will work. Formal or informal." It is a "People's Forum" ("sort-down").

"Sort-Down"

The Upper Skagit system of justice appears to rely heavily on a method described as a "sort-down" in which court officials help individuals and family members through the justice process. This takes the form of letting people blow off steam and tell their stories or file official complaints, which are sometimes never signed and acted on. Sometimes, no on wishes to testify after filing charges. Court staff in the sort-down process determine where particular issues go; and at this point in the process, or later on, individuals, families, or groups may suggest a wide range of paths to the resolution of disputes. In some cases, these are highly traditional (such as feasting or service by wrongdoers to the offended family). In other cases, the dispute or wrongdoing can proceed to the court itself and be conducted in the English common-law adversarial system. The system is both flexible and informal in nature, while maintaining a more formal court system for cases that cannot be resolved otherwise. Elders and tribal culture experts can participate in the system through providing advice and interpretations, either in the body of the trial or in sentencing or alternatives to sentencing. The actions of this system reveal that (restorative justice) systems and Western adversarial justice are not opposites; they can overlap in many ways. They appear to do so in the Upper Skagit system. In fact, it appears to be an advantage to have a variety of possibilities within a single system. The current academic literature is beginning to point out the problem of posing these systems as mutually exclusive.

This sort-down process relies on a small set of skilled, assertive tribal employees who are knowledgeable about the community, family relations, cultural values, and so on. This may not be a disadvantage, however. Wherever tribal justice systems work well, reliance on key personnel seems to be the case.

Jurisdiction

Doreen Maloney observed that the Upper Skagit court sometimes prosecutes cases outside its jurisdiction when the federal system fails to act (re: Major Crimes Act). In anticipating this eventuality, tribal code has been adopted so that prosecution can go forward. The tribe has also adopted legal language allowing them to employ legal language from the federal, state, or municipal systems or from tribal traditional practice. These may be set in priority. This measure is taken to allow the tribe to assume jurisdiction when they wish and to stand in conformity with outside legal requirements. The tribe, on the other hand, has chosen not to exercise its jurisdiction in some areas because of what was described as "local volatility." The tribe emphatically denies the application of customary law from any other tribe or cultural group, arguing that the legal jurisdiction itself relies on the specificity of Upper Skagit and Coast Salish practice and control over its own territory (i.e., law is specific to a location). The tribe does, however, borrow code or concepts from other Coast Salish communities. The tribe wishes extraterritorial jurisdiction in order to enforce its law on its own people, even off-territory.

Code-Writing Process

The code-writing process depends on staff members who have (1) detailed practical knowledge of the issues involved (such as fishing technology) and (2) know the interface with outside government. These are not always the same person. These staff make the first pass on creating ordinances and code. These drafts are then shown to tribal committees, such as the natural resources committee, and then to the council. (Alternatively, suggestions may come from the annual general meeting of the tribal members). Earlier in the history of the tribal court, staff relied on outside code writers, who created drafts to be amended and revised, and borrowed prototype code from other jurisdictions, including tribes and municipal, state, and federal governments. The present tribal system seeks to act cooperatively with surrounding governments through the lease of jail space and through reliance on the state to return people to the tribal court.

Fisheries code is written so that it suits tribal members but is clear enough for the state government. The process of producing this code has been gradual, over several years. The current code allows for the use of elders councils, or individual elders to testify or to make recommendations on sentencing, but does not require this. The trial judge may also use his or her own understanding of Upper Skagit cultural practice in the body of the trial or in sentencing. In this sense, the code itself is not absolute.

The membership of the tribe may, at the annual general meeting, direct the council to draft or amend code for any given issue.

Resource Code

Doreen Maloney notes that the Upper Skagit view is that equal fish harvest cannot be guaranteed, but opportunity can. The Upper Skagit tribe does not restrict drift netting—families can drift where they wish. Elders can designate family members to hunt, fish, or clam on their behalf for home use or sale. The tribe retains the right to inspect fish tickets to see that others purporting to act on their behalf do not abuse elders.

Family Law

Doreen Maloney noted that with the decline of practice of family law, "we find that parents must participate in the behavior of their kids. Some believe kids can do whatever they want." Parents who will not participate may be kicked out of reservation housing at some point, but only when the situation is critical. Several methods are used to create behavioral change: deferred prosecution or incarceration "to get kids under control for a little while so we can figure out what is the matter with them." But youth find jail "okay," so this is of limited use. Also, parents sometimes ask the court to take over jurisdiction of children. Extended family members speak to the court; the court can help enforce parenting in these cases. In the event of neglect, because this is destructive to the community as a whole, the court must step in, often with referrals from family members. Maloney noted that the tribal government has an obligation to act in the interest of the community, even though some heartache is created. On the whole, the community supports intervention. Family members who wish to take a child must be found acceptable. The interest of the child is placed ahead of family in the event of unsuitability.

A question was posed concerning whether people would be forced to quit going to bingo if their kids were neglected. Doreen responded, "Yes, it's neglect." She observed that "it's good to have someone in the community who knows the details. Get someone on the bench who knows how it works."

Selection of Court Officers

Court officers are not elected but rather are selected based on skills. The court may have judges for different components of law (family, resource, and so on). They are appointed by council, with provisions for impeachment. Judges must (1) know the community—families, values;

(2) know provincial law—and evidentiary rules; (3) and be able to balance the two. They need not have a law degree.

Because the system generally does not rely on a "full-out adversarial system," prosecutors must have training in dispute resolution and be able to work with other jurisdictions.

Tribal Custom

Doreen Maloney noted that code must be broad enough to incorporate tribal law, for example, incorporating community service as a type of sentence. She noted that the court clerk coordinates with other reservations to certify that someone sentenced to perform their community service has done so.

6

The South Island Justice Project

In the 1980s and 1990s, a third group of Coast Salish communities engaged in an attempt at diversionary justice. Under the authority of the mainstream judicial system, a limited number of criminal cases were diverted to a local indigenous system of justice. The now-defunct South Island Justice Project (SIJP) differed from those at Upper Skagit and at Stó:lō on many grounds; SIJP was not a freestanding system with its own jurisdiction (rather, jurisdiction was delegated provisionally and temporarily); it was not directed by a tribal government; it was not connected with treaty negotiations, as at Stó:lō; and it was not connected directly to the creation of governance in a larger sense. The very organization of the project reveals the depth of the difficulties in arranging legal relations between the constituent groups of society, issues addressed directly by the Upper Skagits and Stó:lō, and in providing justice to a community diverse in religious practices, wealth, and education and marked by distinctions between generations and genders. The problems the SIJP encountered also reveal the difficulties members of the mainstream society have in comprehending the difficulties faced by indigenous communities as a result of contact and colonialism and the ways in which this incomprehension itself creates new problems. In many ways, the underlying perception within the mainstream society of indigenous culture, and therefore the practice of justice, as wholly intact and merely traditional, bound by custom, and homogenous, became an obstacle. The contemporary politics of nation-state–indigenous relations pushed community leaders into reinforcing these misperceptions.

The southeastern tip of Vancouver Island, British Columbia, is the homeland of Central Coast Salish peoples who are historically speakers of Island Halkomelem and Northern Straits languages, both within the Coast Salish language family. In the mid–nineteenth century the speakers of Island Halkomelem were divided into several "tribes": the Nanoose, Nanaimo, Chemainus, Penelekuts, Cowichan, and Malahat, most consisting of more than one named group (Suttles 1990:455). The

Northern Straits people of the period were composed of the T'Soũke (previously Sooke), Songhees, Saanich, Semiahmoo, Lummi, and Samish. The successor group to the Lummi and Samish live today in the United States, and the Semiahmoo are located on the mainland. Successors to the others, however, today make up the First Nations of South Island Tribal Council (SITC). In common with other Coast Salish peoples, the South Island people were organized into households composed of cooperative families related through both males and females. In stronger households, the core group of blood relatives composed a functioning "house" with heritable rights to resource stations, names, and ritual prerogatives under the direction of an elite. Society was divided into worthy or upper-class people, known as *sí:yá:m*, "worthless" people, and slaves. Suttles (465) observed that conflict was common within and between villages. Injury or death, whether accidental or intentional, created the grounds for demanding compensation or became the cause of conflict, if compensation was not forthcoming quickly enough. Within a village, ongoing conflict was resolved by payments from the stronger party to the weaker party or the relocation of the weaker party. Conflict between people from different villages could lead to raiding led by professional warriors with spirit helpers (465). In common with other Coast Salish peoples, the smallpox epidemic of the late eighteenth century reduced the indigenous population, and Lekwiltok (Kwakwaka'wakw) raiders and slavers further reduced the population in the latter half of the century.

The contact history of these communities is distinct from that of the other Coast Salish peoples. In 1846 the Treaty of Oregon split central Coast Salish territory into British and American sections, thereby placing the residents under separate administrative schemes. On the British (now Canadian) side, every large village was classified administratively as a band, unlike the policy of aggregation practiced in the United States. Following his appointment to the governorship of Vancouver Island in 1850, James Douglas began negotiations with nearby indigenous communities and concluded fourteen treaties with tribes near Victoria by 1854 (Kew 1990a:159). One incentive to make agreements was the discovery of coals near the town of Nanaimo. The indigenous people were paid in goods in exchange for relinquishing rights to all of their lands except their villages and fields, and they retained rights to hunt and fish on unoccupied lands (159). Douglas purchased T'Soũke, Songhees,

Saanich, Vancouver Island Clallam, and Nanaimo lands in 1850 and 1854, but no other titles were extinguished. Although the costs of negotiating the settlements were very small, the British government and the colonial assembly were unwilling to allocate more funds for treaties. However, Douglas continued to establish reserve lands in the hope of making treaties when funds became available (159). Meanwhile, settlement of the area continued, and the adjacent mainland was made a colony in 1858. After Douglas's retirement in 1864, Joseph Trutch was appointed the chief commissioner of land and works. Trutch held the view that "the Indians have really no rights to the lands they claim, nor are they of any actual value or utility to them; and I cannot see why they should either retain these lands to the prejudice of the general interests of the Colony, or be allowed to make a market of them either to Government of to individuals" (cited in Kew 1990a:160). Following the entry of British Columbia into Canada in 1871, Trutch continued his policies of limiting the size and location of future reserves as lieutenant governor. No further treaties or formal surrenders of land were completed. The process of creating reserves was not completed until the 1880s (Suttles 1990:471). The Songhees reserve in the city of Victoria was ceded for cash in 1910.

The Oblate order moved its headquarters from Puget Sound to Vancouver Island in 1858. Methodists were active among the Songhees and Nanaimos in the 1860s, and Anglicans among the Nanaimos. Fort Langley, a Hudson's Bay Company operation, was established on the Fraser River in 1827, attracting some interest from Vancouver Island people. By the 1860s, many south Vancouver Island indigenous people found employment as loggers, as mill hands, and in other enterprises, and others sold foodstuffs to whites. By the 1870s, men were employed in the fishing fleet and women in canneries, and there were successful farmers by the 1880s (Knight 1978; Suttles 1954). Many worked in hop and berry fields in the Fraser Valley and Puget Sound.

Despite these changes to the economy, important features of cultural life persisted. A Saanich potlatch held in 1876 attracted some three thousand indigenous people, and goods valued at $15,000 were distributed (Suttles 1990:471). Even after the prohibition of the potlatch, activity continued, and large potlatches were held on Vancouver Island until around 1912 (472). However, the early twentieth century was a difficult time for indigenous people of south Vancouver Island. Economic op-

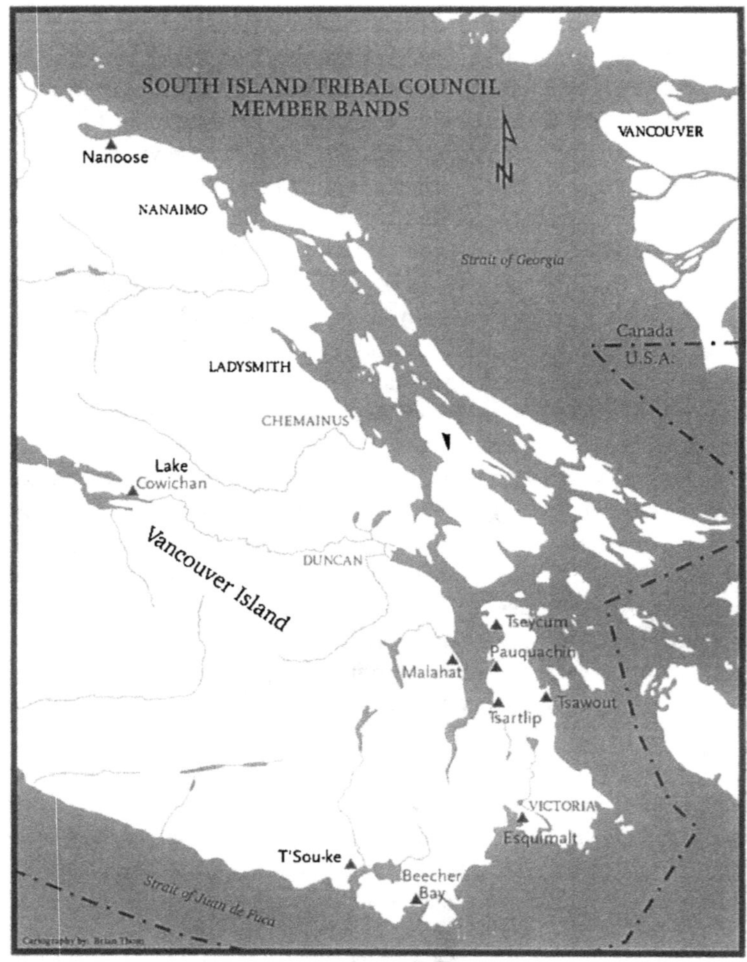

portunities dried up, and indigenous language use declined as a result of official repression, especially in schools. However, the Shaker Indian Church spread into the region, and Syowen (Spirit Dancing) experienced a revival with the incorporation of features of the potlatch (472).

With the creation of four major Indian agencies for British Columbia by 1886, the Coast Salish communities of Vancouver Island were assigned to the Cowichan Agency. Indigenous people of British Columbia, including the Coast Salish, came under the provisions of the federal Indian Act after confederation in 1871, an act amended in 1884 to prohibit the major indigenous ceremonies, including the potlatch and Winter Dancing. Provincial laws restricted indigenous people from homesteading and from the provincial franchise until 1949. The province treated indigenous people as noncitizens whose care was the responsibility of the federal government; provincial public services were not extended to reserves, and indigenous children were excluded from public schools. When federal funds for the indigenous children in public schools became available, there was increasing school integration and, following World War II, integration of provincial services generally. Although the Indian Act had extended the federal franchise (citizenship) to war veterans and their wives who chose to waive their tax exemptions, this right was not extended generally to registered Indians, those with special legal status and of federal concern, until 1960.

Starting in the mid-1970s, bands began to organize themselves into regional organizations known as tribal councils in order to collectively focus on such issues as land claims, political lobbying, and the efficient provision of services to members. Among these regional groupings is the First Nations of South Island Tribal Council.

The Preamble

In 1988, immediately prior to the establishment of the South Island Justice Project, the SITC was involved in a precedent-setting child custody case that was subsequently cited as "a good illustration of Aboriginal dispute resolution (Michael Jackson, cited in Royal Commission 1996:210). Jackson gives the following facts of the case (I summarize): The case concerned the custody of a child whose mother had died and who had previously requested that the child be brought up by her sister, a member of the Nuu-chah-nulth Nation (not a Coast Salish people), in order that the child learn family traditions and assume an appropriate position in the community. The boy's father, a member of a Coast Salish nation, wanted custody for similar reasons. The case went to provincial court, and the question before the court concerned whether the court should recognize the importance of early instruction to achieving high status, and, if so, whether the mother's family was more important than the father's. The SITC obtained intervener status in provincial court hearings and asked that a council of elders mediate the dispute. Terms of reference for mediation were agreed to by both parties, including establishing a council of elders agreeable to both families and chaired by the intervener, the chair of the tribal council; having the mediation occur in a neutral bighouse; and holding the meeting on Coast Salish territory. The families could call speakers and elders, and others could act as witnesses to the proceedings. The right to legal counsel as observers was retained, and the mediation would not be binding (Royal Commission 210).

A council of elders met with the parties; in Jackson's words, "The case history and the precedents in Coast Salish Aboriginal law were discussed," and the parties agreed to proposed resolution (Royal Commission 1996:211). A formal agreement was made up awarding custody to the father and acknowledging the role, advice, and influence of the grandparents on both sides and the special interest of the aunt. Further, the child was to be raised in respect to "customs and traditions of both families and cultures" (211). Access and visitations by relatives were provided for in the agreement.

The judge of the provincial family court was presented with a consent order giving the father custody, which was affirmed. Jackson concludes why this case was successful: "The parties were able to accept the recommendations of the Council of Elders because they have legitimacy as lawgivers; the forum—The Big House—in which deliberations regarding the law and its application took place reflected the interconnectedness of Coast Salish families and its carving . . . encapsulates their shared history; the procedures in the Big House, the making of speeches which are listened to with respect and without interruption in the search for a consensus, draw upon time honored traditions of Coast Salish decision making" (Jackson, cited in Royal Commission 1996:213).

But, as I argue next, this case did not turn out to be a blueprint for indigenous justice. Instead, the analysis of the case reflects an Edenic view of a society without a past in which serious conflict arose. Consensus, again, is treated unproblematically, and the idea of precedent in aboriginal law is given without clarification (the concept arose later in representations of the SIJP). Nor is there any consideration of who the elders were, how they were selected, or what the relations of power or the existing state of relationship was between them and the litigants, issues that later came to haunt the SIJP. Elders, instead, are treated as an undifferentiated commodity. Finally, what is contested and political within a society (in this case the disposition of a child) is treated by outsiders as merely cultural (see LaRocque's discussion of the analogous process of the "culturalization of rape," 1997:89).

This case is of interest here for two reasons: it helped pave the way for the South Island Justice Project, and this case and the SIJP are tied together through the central role of Chief Tom Sampson, then chair of the SITC. Justice Edward O'Donnell, in his "Reasons for Judgement" (1988a), writes, "Through the leadership of Chief Sampson, the Tribal Council offered to the court and to the parties, to convene a Council of Elders to attempt to find a solution. . . . It is my understanding that the institution of the Council of Elders had not been convened since possibly the 1920s in Southern Vancouver Island."

Justice O'Donnell (1988b) subsequently wrote Chief Justice I. B. Josephson of the Provincial Court of British Columbia to report on the success of the case, to describe the role of Chief Sampson and the Council of Elders, and to offer Chief Sampson as a liaison concerning "any questions as to Native Institutions and Concerns." Further, O'Donnell expressed his expectation that the report would be circulated to the provincial court judiciary. Seen retrospectively, the issues that were not attended to in this relatively simple case were precisely the ones that became most difficult for the SIJP. Secondly, the naive response of the judiciary and legal analysis in presuming an intact and consensual approach to justice on the part of the deeply divided and distraught present-day Coast Salish people facilitated the creation of a subsequent program that advanced a particular viewpoint without accounting for others.

The Project

The SITC was composed of the membership of nine (ten at one time) of the nineteen Vancouver Island Coast Salish bands. In 1992 membership came primarily from bands in the South Island area (Beecher Bay, Esquimault, Malahat, Pauquachin, T'Soũke, Tsartlip, Tseycum, and Tsawout) and included two nearby bands (Nanoose and Lake Cowichan). These small bands varied in size from 11 to 492 members and totaled just over 2,000 within an urban region of some 389,000 (a.m. Research 1996:2). The SITC represented "the majority of bands and the majority of the aboriginal population in the south Island" and was one of the oldest tribal councils in the province, founded in the early 1960s (Tennant 1992:5).

In the mid 1980s the SITC joined with the provincial justice ministry to explore ways to apply Coast Salish indigenous practices in the search for solutions to the problem of youth criminal behavior and to avoid their entanglement in the mainstream justice system (a.m. Research 1995). The circumstances were favorable for this. The report of the British Columbia Justice Reform Committee, *Access to Justice*, 1988, encouraged the provincial justice ministries (then known as the Ministries of Attorney General and Solicitor General) to make indigenous issues a priority. Local advisory councils, with indigenous representatives, were formed to examine the circumstances facing indigenous people as they encountered criminal justice in the province. The institute responsible for training provincial court judges for the four western provinces and two territories, the Western Judicial Education Centre (WJEC), and members of the University of British Columbia faculty, focused on indigenous issues (see UBC *Law Review* 1992). By the late 1980s, diversionary programs, funded by the province, were in place in British Columbia indigenous organizations, including elders groups, and oversaw the limited administration of justice in these programs. In one noteworthy case, considered above, a provincial court judge recognized the right of an elders council to rule on a child custody case. In 1989, following an annual workshop on indigenous issues sponsored by the WJEC, representatives of the WJEC and the SITC and other indigenous leaders on Vancouver Island made a commitment to bring together elders and justice system officials. University of British Columbia political scientist Paul Tennant, who participated in the program and wrote an evaluation, observed that the resulting Project "had its origins in 1989 in the thinking of three persons: Tom Sampson, the Chair of the First Nations of South Island Tribal Council; B.C. Provincial Court Judge Douglas Campbell, the director of the Western Judicial Education Centre; and Sam Stevens, the Director of the University of British Columbia's Native Law Program" (1992:1). Judge Campbell, program facilitator during the years 1988–94, observed that the project needed visionary leadership, and "Tom Sampson had the vision" (telephone interview, 26 November 1998).

A proposal, submitted on behalf of the SITC, was funded by the federal Department of Secretary of State for a cross-cultural education pilot project. Other moneys came from the provincial Ministry of Attorney

General. The cross-cultural education program forwarded the idea of a project to build on the partnership between the elders and the mainstream justice system. At the annual assembly of the SITC in July 1990, consent was given to seek formal approval for this plan. This followed on band resolutions in 1988 from nine bands interested in enhancing their communities' role in the practice of justice.

Additional funding proposals were drafted on behalf of the SITC, calling for further education sessions and a diversion program. The diversion program involved the creation of an Elders Council "to receive referrals from the community, police, Crown, corrections and the Court, and would recommend and supervise action to be taken within the traditional community in individual criminal and family law cases" (a.m. Research 1995:5). In March of 1991, the Education Committee combined both components, education and judicial, to be called the South Vancouver Island Justice Education Project (SVIJEP). Funding for eighteen months was received from the federal Department of Justice, the provincial Ministry of Aboriginal Affairs, the federal Department of Multiculturalism and Citizenship, and the British Columbia Law Foundation. Candidates for the diversion program came primarily from bands in the greater Victoria area, but other bands, particularly the Cowichan, were involved through participation of their elders on the Elders Council.

The SIJP proposed a series of project objectives, including using both Canadian and First Nations justice systems; improving the mainstream system's response to indigenous people; improved delivery of justice to indigenous people on south Vancouver Island; the integration of the Elders Council in each stage of justice delivery to indigenous people in criminal, youth, and family cases; the reduction of incarceration rates of indigenous people; the application of indigenous justice practices to alternative measures, diversion, dispute resolution, and family counseling; the promotion of cross-cultural education for justice systems professionals and indigenous peoples; and support of reform of justice delivery (a.m. Research 1995:6).

A small administrative and reporting structure was established. One part handled financial issues, and the Education Committee served as the administrative body. Two representatives on the board, the SITC chairperson and the regional Crown counsel, were key decision makers concerning the direction of the project (a.m. Research 1995:28). No formal reporting or accountability system was established to inform the SIJP sponsors, communities, or the justice community of the project developments. Instead, a process of "talking to one another" and the informal building of trust was relied on, and the authority of elders as "custodians of traditional First Nations' knowledge, custom, and law was recognized and accepted by the Committee" (28). Tennant notes that "the key initial players regarded maintaining the process as the way to achieve eventual agreement between the two cultures [indigenous and the mainstream culture of law] on specific goals and objectives. . . . In this sense a plan was not part of the plan . . . the strategy was 'first relationships, then trust, then action' " (Tennant 1992:27).

Those selected to be project elders were a group of influential senior people who headed complex corporate multigenerational families (or family networks) and whose standing is recognized by the term S'ul *Hwen* (sometimes given as *sí:yá:m* in Stó:lō territory and *Siep* in Puget Sound). This group, including six prominent elders "who participated fully and continually in the Project," was invited by Tom Sampson in March of 1990 to the first meeting. Sampson, although himself a S'ul Hwen, did not serve in that capacity for the project but rather acted within his tribal council role (Tennant 1992:2). The home areas of the six project S'ul Hwen covered the whole of the Island Salish territory. The S'ul Hwen and their supporters sought to "continue and re-empower the traditional Salish teachings," although they were hesitant to allow discussion of teachings in English and in the bighouse with justice officials present (5).

A fundamental issue that confronted SIJP participants is the relationship between the elected band councils and the authority of family leaders and elders and, less directly, the role of the tribal council. The SITC and supporters, in Tennant's words, saw the SITC as "an advocate of tradition and as speaking for interests, values, and goals, not commonly or necessarily represented by Indian Act band councils" (Tennant 1992:6). The objective of the SITC leadership during the initiation and development of the project was to act as "agents of, and communication channels for, the S'ul *Hwen*," and then to withdraw from the project, to be replaced by the Council of S'ul Hwen, which would become the "aboriginal voice and authority for the Project" (6). Significantly, neither reserve populations nor band councils were consulted in the process of creating the project because of negative perceptions by key indigenous project participants of Indian Act reserves, bands, and band councils. Nor were off-reserve band members or "front-line workers" (band staff engaged in projects aimed at aiding community members) included in the project design. The project was underscored by the view that "the only legitimate aboriginal communities are the traditional families, for whom the *S'ul Hwen* themselves, are, by definition, the only legitimate spokesperson" (6). Tennant concludes, "The S'ul *Hwen* and the leadership of the SITC are passionately concerned about the state of their peoples and view the Project as one important means of remedy. They see the traditional teachings not as ends in themselves, but as practical means of bringing guidance, meaning, and morality in place of anger, frustration, an suffering that is now so prevalent" (7).

There were two significant positions taken by SIJP members. Key indigenous project participants "explicitly disavowed" any idea of the creation of a separate indigenous justice system and even though the indigenous system was thought of as autonomous and freestanding, "the goal was to have it function in partnership with the justice system" (Tennant 1992:27). Second, an implicit strategy was to have the mainstream judges and courts serve as the agents of change and the WJEC act as the conduit for extending partnership principles to other communities (27).

Texts

The texts generated by the South Island Justice Project view justice as derived from the primordial teachings of Hals, or the Creator, which were given to humans during the myth time and which have persisted as underlying cultural values and as defining characteristics of Coast Salish peoples. "This hereditary system . . . acted as guidelines" (First Nations 1990:3). These teachings create a moral space, and abridgment of them is thought to diminish justice and offend the relations between members of the moral community. A committee of elders spent several years, beginning in 1987, codifying these orally transmitted teachings and created an intellectual framework for capturing central ideas and connecting to mainstream legal constructs. As is the case with other examples of codification of traditional law, this framework renders what were once fluid and localized processes of justice into a discourse suitable to advancing the viewpoint and, ostensibly, the political purposes of present-day elders. The framework privileged some elders and indigenous language speakers' position in their communities. The process also simplified the social and cultural reality of the community into a form that was accessible by mainstream community members and justice officials.

The elders expressed several concerns. Chief among these was that it was inappropriate for elected tribal council members to represent cultural values connected to justice to the mainstream legal system. Tom Sampson, one of the organizers and prime movers of the project, observed that "The elders weren't happy with our own leadership—they were more like the government, the DIA [Department of Indian Affairs]" (Sampson, interview). The extended family, rather than the tribe, was identified as the core of the community, and elected tribal or band leaders were seen as usurping the authority of family elders and leaders. Tennant writes: "In the view of those oriented towards tradition and towards the *S'ul Hwen*, the basic units among the Salish of the Island are not the 19 bands but the many extended families. In this view, it is the *S'ul Hwen*, not the band councils, who are the legitimate representatives of the Island Salish concerning all fundamental questions. Sampson and the Project S'ul Hwen consider there to be some 80 traditional families whose *S'ul Hwen* live in the south Island" (1992:6). This viewpoint finds support in Coast Salish ethnography. Suttles (1987b:8) described fundamental ideas, values, practices, and knowledge of magic, genealogy, and proper behavior as "advice," which is passed along within families exclusively, and which varied in its details.

Elders involved in the project were further concerned that speakers of Halkomelem, the local Coast Salish language, conduct the project, a view based on the idea that justice concepts were directly embedded in language and not easily translatable, if at all. They expressed grave concerns about the alienation of land, the reduction of game and fish stocks, the imposition of outside law, Canadian law, the loss of control over youth in trouble, and the influence of families without proper instruction in Coast Salish practices. In general terms, elders were concerned for the decline of cultural practice, which was linked to the ability to use the productive capacity of the land. The elders' role as teachers of respect and proper behavior was itself connected to justice and regulation (Sampson, interview). Tennant summarizes the situation this way: "The *S'ul Hwen* and the leadership of the SITC are passionately concerned about the state of their peoples and view the Project as one important means of remedy. They see the traditional teachings not as ends in themselves, but as practical means of bringing guidance, meaning, and morality in place of the anger, frustration, and suffering that is now so prevalent (1992:7). Other, more particularistic issues concerned elders, including "justice system [mainstream] involvement in traditional native activities," including Syowen (13).

In their briefing notes entitled "Introduction to Aboriginal Justice and the Function of an Elders Council," the authors note that "Aboriginal Justice is the standards and regulations pertaining to behavior and community; orally preserved and handed down through centuries since time immemorial" (First Nations 1990:2). At the heart of justice was family law, which is said to "govern the people and regulate family and community" (2). Judicial authority, by extension from the Creator, is given to the most powerful interpreters of the Creator's law and "centers around the 'Longhouse and our Elders' " (2). Sampson referred to the process of codifying law as "describing spirituality" (interview). Further, he stated, "We take the holistic approach. Our laws are not separate from spiritual healing and discipline. Everything fits together, all in one. We hold the Bighouse as paramount over all other things that we do." The South Island elders project documents describe justice as "addressing standards of behavior. Our traditional laws are not based upon punishment. The Aboriginal Common Laws of our land focus upon reconciliation, rehabilitation, and education" (Sampson, quoted in Tennant 1992:4).

The family law itself is composed of three domains: spiritual issues (teachings), conservation (traditional), and economics (value) (First Nations 1987). For example, law concerning fisheries has spiritual, conservation, and economic components. Under the rubric of spiritual law, the documents report that "Thanks are given to salmon 'for the life it gives to our survival.' " Salmon is shared first with elders, then family, and then the community. "Later, salmon is shared with ancestors via the spiritual burning of food 'in respect of those gone before us so they would not harm us and in return they would help us in not having difficulty in harvesting our food for they are with *Hals* (Creator)' " (8).

Conservation law dictates that "We always allow a first run by for spawning"; "We harvest enough for family and community need or until Elders say we have enough"; "We move to different locations to avoid depleting stock as well as to acquire species not available in our area." In addition, conservation law regulates human-nonhuman interaction. "Widows, widowers and new Indian dancers stay away from fish habitat for one to four years depending on Tribal customs" in order to avoid the salmon being repulsed by humans and leaving an area (First Nations 1987:8). Conservation law also provides specifics concerning equipment used for harvesting, for instance, where weirs, dip nets, spears and gaffs or reef nets may be used."

Finally, there is an economic law concerning fisheries, a category that overlaps considerably with the conservation law but that incorporates the teaching "Do not waste any part of fish." "We preserve, smoke, half smoke, sun dry and salt salmon" (First Nations 1987:8).

The summary of the elders' presentation of tribal law indicates the following:

> These laws that have been past on to us by our parents and elders are law from Hals (Creator) and not made by man. They are held sacred by our people. These laws are for our survival and for protection of all our resources.
>
> These laws are received from Hals (Creator) after a purification period or a retreat of months or years of daily bathing in cold water, in streams or lakes and living with nature during this period. Laws would come after Hals (Creator) feels that you are pure enough, then he would give you the law through one of the resources or through a vision. It is through total commitment, concentration and fasting of an individual that he is able to receive these laws from Hals (Creator).
>
> When one received a law from Hals (Creator) he would further bath and fast to give thanks for the law or vision he has received. He must show his thanks for what he received for it should be for the survival of his family, the community, and the resources. Once this law is in place it is the responsibility of parents and Elders to uphold this law and pass them onto their children and their children's children.
>
> When these laws are upheld by individuals, families, and community, Hals (Creator) gives us bountiful resources. We do not show greed towards our resources but share with those in need. It is a way of saying thanks to Hals (Creator) for the laws he has given us for our survival and for the bountiful resources.

In the view of the South Island elders, the sacred law creates a charter for the ongoing social organization of the community:

> Indian Government Family Law, tradition and culture are dealt with, taught and developed in our traditional bighouse. At these gatherings all members are involved in decision making. If they have a proposal for action or questions, they would use their family spokesman and call upon several witnesses in support of their proposal or questions. Elders are always involved in decisions. (First Nations 1987:1)

A particular social role for elders is created because of their "knowledge of law given to us by Hals . . . [and] their knowledge of customs" (First Nations 1987:1). They held the opinion that "The elders are today and have been traditionally 'the Teacher, the Lawyer, and the Counsellor' " (First Nations 1990:4). The elders pointed to their own role in describing "Local and Private Matters (Disciplinary and Social)" "which involve elders in decisions made . . . because of their "wisdom and knowledge of the laws and customs" (5). Further, law enforcement also falls into the domain of elders (together with parents), as does economics. The elders wrote, "In bartering for some of our resources our Elders and parents are the ones to decide what resources and how much to be bartered for" (5).

In addition, the elders described two other social roles that would support their own. One is spokespersons: "These persons are used, at the assembly, to voice the opinions or wishes of the general membership or family. . . . These spokespersons must be knowledgeable of Tribal Affairs and Customs that have been given to them by the Elders" (First Nations 1990:5). A third social role, which derives from the teachings of Hals, is that of witnesses who are

> persons . . . called upon when the membership want to voice their opinions at a gathering. They must be reliable because, when called upon at a later time, they must be able to recollect what was discussed and be able to relate that to a gathering. They must be able to thank those for their help or payback, and encourage others to carry and pass on this teaching to their children. Witnesses must have the respect of the Elders and general membership, and they must be knowledgeable of Tribal Affairs and Customs. (5)

Concerning the administration of justice, the elders recorded that "Justice is handled by the Elders of the community because of their wisdom and knowledge of the laws given to us by Hals (Creator). They are the ones to decide on discipline, depending on the seriousness of the violation." Further, "Parents and Elders are the ones to enforce laws given to us by Hals (Creator). Should it be decided that further action be taken in the enforcement of law, it can be done at a gathering, where a number of people are called upon to further advise the offender of the law he had broken" (First Nations 1990:4).

There is a pervasive sense that wrongdoing (my word) is primarily associated with children and youth, the pliable and teachable, and that aboriginal law, then, is directed toward them. Tennant notes that the S'ul Hwen declined to accept cases concerning older people accused of major or violent crimes because they "won't listen to anyone" (1992:21). The exercise of justice lies with elders, who decide on discipline, sometimes in association with parents, and the system of authority is top-down, with communications flowing from elders to parents to children. "Aboriginal Common Law" is viewed primarily as a system of counseling with reconciliation, rehabilitation, and education as the major goals. There is no direct acknowledgment of the possibility of wrongdoing on the part of elders or other senior community members, despite the rich oral traditions that speak of dangerous warriors and even abuse by elders of grandchildren in their charge (see Snyder 1964). Indeed, there may be a connection between the intractability of problems of wife abuse and rape, clearly identified by women who objected to the project for its failure to protect them (a point I develop later), and the association made between justice and youth.

The South Island Justice Project, then, developed these features: the conception of law was "elder-driven," rather than linked to conceptions of rank and class that characterize Salish society. In this sense, age and seniority, rather than family status and personal achievement, were advanced. The laws themselves, although equated with common law, which is historical and changeable in its conception, were held to be primordial and unchanging in fundamental features. There is a twist, however. These laws are thought to be revealed to elders following a process of personal purification and later taught to family members. In this sense, tribal law is not Mosaic, that is, revealed to the society as a whole at one time and for all times. Rather, tribal law pertains to a particular family and, although this is not clarified in the documents, could in theory continue to be revealed to elders who could then proclaim tribal law that is both new and primordial (derived from X̲á:ls in the myth time).

The system of justice, then, is directly connected through a specific spiritual tradition, Syowen, which was thought to embed both the core spiritual concepts and the training and discipline that support moral behavior. The articulating model of justice that connected to the mainstream society discourses was that of restorative justice, with an emphasis on rehabilitation and reconciliation. In this case, reconciliation referred to a process whereby individuals acquiesced to the authority of current guardians of traditional law. Further, although the extended family was advanced as the basis of knowledge and authority, a composite group of elders stood in for family leaders in adjudication. The emphasis on rehabilitation placed the model squarely within the current "justice as healing" metaphor, which itself conjoins Western psychological and judicial concepts and indigenous social practice. Conley and O'Barr (1998) note, for example, that in the mainstream legal system, three discourses predominate, including healing, legal, and rehabilitative. In a similar vein, LaRocque (1997:85) queries whether the Hollow Water, Manitoba, mediation program had "fallen prey to contemporary, white, leftist/liberal, Christian and even New Age notions of 'healing,' 'forgiveness,' and offender 'rehabilitation.' "

Despite these unexplored connections to Western discourses, the aim of the project was to restore traditional life and the primacy of traditional values through the rejection of mainstream values and community elective leadership. However, explicit connections were also drawn to mainstream concepts. A fascinating development was the reference to indigenous law-and-order practices and personnel thought to parallel those of the mainstream society but not described in ethnographic literature as characteristic of Coast Salish life. Specifically, aboriginal Coast Salish law was described as "common law," "natural law," and "conservation law," and the death penalty was said to be extinguished and violators controlled by police. One sentence implicitly connects Coast Salish aboriginal practices and Western legal concepts by employing terms (*advocate*, *witness*, *clerk*) for Western court officials: "They [elders] deliberate over problem [sic] arising from causing offence to or violation of the community standards of behavior. The Elders are assisted by 'Spokesmen': who act as advocates. The affair is observed by 'Witnesses' whose function is to relate the events and proceedings to the families and communities. They act as clerk of the court and as our historians in this regard" (First Nations 1990:4).

Further, the justice process itself is described in a way that emphasizes overlap, making reference to an "appeal process" with stages, going first to an Assembly in Council of the Chiefs and Elders and then to an Assembly in Council of families and membership (4).

Project material advances the argument that Coast Salish traditional culture overlaps with contemporary progressive Western practice in several other significant ways as well. Here a paradox arises out of claims of difference and efforts to base authority on traditional practice and the connections drawn to Western legal categories. "An Introduction" states that:

> Many of the safeguards included in your legislation of recent decades have been significant in our traditional practices for centuries. 1. The Death Penalty: was extinguished as a form of punishment, centuries ago. 2. Inter-Tribal Warfare: As a means of political force was outlawed a century ago. *Violators could be addressed and dispatched by the police forces of our nations.* (First Nations 1990:5; emphasis mine)

However, First Nations ethnonationalist rhetoric frequently contrasts the absence of coercive authority and personnel associated with centralized power within First Nations and their presence in white society. Further, ethnographic notes from interviews with elders of the early and middle twentieth century make explicit mention of the execution of serious troublemakers within Coast Salish society in earlier periods, as described earlier.

Family law is, by inference, said to be "Indian Common Law" (First Nations 1990:5). Here, the term *family law* ought not to be confused with the idea of family law in the mainstream society, namely law that applies to family matters. Rather, the term refers to the primacy of the family in Coast Salish society and the idea that there is, in effect, no teaching that is not derived from family knowledge. Family law is further associated with *natural laws*, or "laws tied/based with nature" (3). The laws, however, were said to be "general" in that they apply to individuals and the community, not to families (Sampson, interview). "No one interferes with other families' teachings," and therefore the elders recorded what "all can agree on." In this sense, the laws were composite laws, or "laws of the lowest common denominator," in Sampson's terms.

Finally, the construction of "aboriginal common law" as revolving around "traditional conservation" as one of the three fundamental domains creates an explicit connection to current Western political thought and builds on perceptions of indigenous peoples, in contrast to Western peoples, in Fienup-Riordan's terms, as "original ecologists" (1990b:167).

Cases

Once a structure was created, the South Island Justice Project was in a position to begin to accept cases diverted from the mainstream justice system. The expectation was that counseling and dispute resolution functions were to arise from self-selection by clients and by a process of identification by the S'ul Hwen. The assistant Crown counsel and the regional Crown counsel were to identify candidates for consideration of the Council of S'ul Hwen, excluding non–Coast Salish and older people accused of major or violent crimes. The council would then decide whether to proceed with a case, and candidates and victims (both of whom had to consent to the diversion before it could occur) would be contacted prior to the production of a signed agreement between the candidate, SIJP coordinator, and Crown counsel. Clients would then be placed under the supervision of one or more S'ul Hwen, who would teach and counsel, supervise any community work, and arrange and witness apologies or restitution. The hope was that the relationship established or reestablished between client and victim would continue, thereby allowing the S'ul Hwen to monitor clients after the diversion process was complete (Tennant 1992:29).

Knowledge of an offender's or victim's family or family situation was the most important factor in the decision to accept or reject a candidate for diversion or sentencing intervention (a.m. Research 1995:43). Of a total of 184 cases brought forward, 26 offenders were selected for the project. The average age of the offenders diverted was twenty-six; there were 6 physical assault cases, 9 theft cases, 2 mischief cases, and one breach of probation. Diversion contracts called for community service in 13 cases, apologies in 11 cases, counseling in 11 cases, and abstinence from alcohol in 4 cases. All cases called for meeting with the program coordinator (49).

Among those selected, one candidate declined to participate, four candidates received warning letters, and, in a program review, three files could not be located (a.m. Research 1995:89). Three of the offenders (to use program terminology) agreed to be interviewed by program reviewers, who found quite varied responses. In one case, a 32-year-old man, charged with spousal assault, reported that he was asked to do community work service in the Smokehouse (*Syowen* House), which he disliked because he already had respect for the elders and saw no need for Smokehouse intervention. However, he entered into a contract to complete his community work service, but there was no follow-up. This man told reviewers that traditional justice is "not the Smokehouse" and questioned how elders who do not know the offender could provide help (90–92). In another case, an aboriginal RCMP officer referred a second man, aged forty-one and charged with impaired driving, to the project. He met with a community elder who assigned him yard work. He enjoyed his regular discussions with the elder, who counseled him on a variety of topics. The program, this man believes, gave him a chance to straighten out and become sober (92–93). A third offender, a twenty-three-year-old man, was charged with auto theft and breaking and entering. He heard about the program while incarcerated and was released to meet with a group of elders. He was assigned and carried out tasks but did not find them relevant to his personal situation; nor did he find the experience with the project beneficial because, for him, "Nothing happened" (93–94). Legal scholar Mary Ellen Turpel, who visited indigenous justice programs across Canada in 1993, reported on a fourth offender in the SIJP, a twenty-eight-year-old man arrested for assault stemming from an episode of drinking. The man had left the reserve at age ten and had become an alcoholic at any early age. After being diverted to the SIJP he worked with elders for over a year, and according to Turpel's account of him (rather than self-accounts as reported in the project study), he had learned his place in the community and had developed responsibilities. Turpel concluded that "Through their compassion, teaching, and family reintegration, the elders have assisted this young man to gain control of his life. . . . What happened was nothing short of a miracle" (Turpel, in Royal Commission 1996:105–6).

Reaction: The Issues

No victims could be identified and interviewed by the team of federally appointed reviewers of the South Island Justice Program, but interviews with a range of participants and community members were conducted. In all, seventy individuals were interviewed, two group interviews were held, and eighty-three case files were examined. Twenty-four respondents were "key participants" from various provincial and federal agencies; ten were service deliverers (such as social workers and health providers); eight were chiefs; eight were elders; and twenty-eight were community members from ten communities (Royal Commission 1996: 10–11). Respondents agreed unanimously that the goals of the project to improve relations between the mainstream justice system and the Coast Salish peoples, to make services more culturally sensitive, and to increase the capacity for the indigenous people to carry this out were valid and necessary. However, participants described the program as employing a "top-down" approach that did not adequately involve community members and front-line workers nor consider the variety of needs within the separate communities. Most (59 percent) felt that their expectations of the project's impact on Coast Salish communities and the criminal justice system were not met (a.m. Research 1995:S-3).

A number of issues emerged that related to the larger themes of the lack of agreement within the Coast Salish world and the orientation to family, as opposed to community, leadership. The respondents to the SIJP evaluation pointed out a number of community and criminal justice issues overlooked by the project. Among the most significant was that the project's "traditional" approach failed to adequately account for the current justice ideologies of the broad range of community members, some of whom are "without traditional values" (A.m. Research 1995: S-4). Respondents recommended a more extensive consultation with the community, including grassroots involvement. Community participation should have been sought out in the process of selection of project leadership and elders (S-6). Respondents emphasized that the justice services should be administered by a nonpolitical organization and operated according to the principles adhered to in the various communities in order that responses to the needs of the victims, offenders, and community members all be localized (S-7). One of the few respondents who believed that the project objectives were not obtainable gave as a reason "the lack of consensus among community members regarding the credibility of individuals providing service" and also mentioned "the lack of consensus within Coast Salish communities respecting justice matters" (22).

The program review noted that the terms of reference for the project in two instances gave responsibility to the "First Nations Community," but the tasks of appointing the elders council and project liaison worker were instead carried out by the chair of the SITC. The evaluators wrote that "Two primary factors emerge from the responses which indicate that time and 'politics' significantly complicated and interfered with Project results" (a.m. Research 1995:32), noting that the specific objectives and administration of the project had not received band support in the form of council resolutions. The "credibility and objectivity" of the project elders were controversial to respondents and, more broadly, within the communities. Respondents reported that "Elders were selected on a case-by-case basis for the objectivity and experience they could offer in a specific case; and Elders were hand-picked by SITC personnel on the basis of inter-personal relationships" (46).

The project review uncovered no instances of S'ul Hwen making sentencing recommendations to the court. However, "service providers and other community members mention inappropriate interventions by SITC representatives and Salish Elders in certain criminal matters involving Coast Salish citizens." The reviewers concluded that "real or perceived conflicts of interest and abuses of power by Project authorities at the critical stage of the Project's initiation devastated community members and undermined the likelihood of Project success" (a.m. Research 1995:52). A case, not connected to the project, was given by respondents as an example of inappropriate intervention. The case concerned the attempts by some members of the SITC and some elders (some of whom were associated with the project) to intervene in the prosecution of a family member. The intervention took the form of a challenge to the court's jurisdiction over the matter at a preliminary hearing. The challenge failed, and the matter proceeded through the mainstream system. The project evaluators note:

> It is said that at the time of this event, significant pressure was placed upon the victim(s), family and other community members to unite in the effort to have this matter treated in a traditional way. This suggestion and the proposed outcomes were perceived by many to be unacceptable. It failed to address the critical needs of the victim(s) while raising the alleged offender to "preferred justice" status. The serious nature of the alleged offense (i.e. sexual assault with multiple

> victims), the lack of resources to ensure public safety, and the lack of any defined principles or practices of the proposed "Tribal Justice" system, increased the concern among citizens.
>
> In addition, others point out that the event was a totally inappropriate forum for the exertion of political pressure respecting Aboriginal justice issues. This specific case and its surrounding events sparked a community concern that the driving force behind "the Project" was the [participant's] desire to intervene in justice on behalf of a family member. (52–53)

A group of eight elders who responded in round-table discussion affirmed that the intent of the project was to "make an offender within the community a better person, not to find guilt." They reported that a number of people within Coast Salish communities spoke out against the project, and they attributed this to "misunderstanding" the project and to the inadequacies of those outside the Syowen tradition, who did not understand the teachings. Further, those who complained, in the elders' view, did so because of participation in the mainstream education system and their failure to receive "cultural education" (a.m. Research 1995:71). The consequence of this approach is that the program had a built-in limitation: only culturally well-groomed offenders need apply. In effect, there were implicit qualifying standards for participation, and one had to be good enough to be bad, to be an offender. In addition, a very limited conception of "tradition" was advanced: practitioners of religious traditions outside of the Syowen longhouse, such as members of the Indian Shaker Church, were thought to not qualify. In this view, no provisions were made for the vast majority of Coast Salish people who chose to attend school.

Other project respondents spoke of power relations, including generational rifts and abuse of power by families (a.m. Research 1995:58). Elders, on the other hand, reported their preference not to have political affiliations and their wish to be able to help everyone (72). This viewpoint seems sadly out of step with the reality of interfamily politics and the problems reported within the program. A study of a tribal mental health program showed the significance of interfamily politics in community members' disinclination to share information with therapists across family lines (see Miller and Pylypa 1995). In addition, other studies show the inclination of community members to vote in tribal elections and to access community resources along family lines (B. Miller 1992a).

A perhaps even greater difficulty for the project was what some critics felt were the implications for women. The project reviewers observed that "Pressure exerted by family or other community members regarding justice issues is consistently reported to have disturbed community members and service providers. Victims and offenders were likewise caught in the web of persuasion to deal with matters within the community" (a.m. Research 1995:97). They noted that some victims did not come forward because they presumed that the offenders would simply be "counseled" by elders and remain in the community, perhaps as neighbors. "In some instances, women were reluctant to approach certain Elders who were convicted sex offenders, as the women felt their concerns would not be addressed" (97). Further, the project review included a passage from an official report made during a preliminary review:

> In conversation with community members, problems in the project arose during the phase in which victims were contacted to give their consent. Despite the highly confidential nature of the information shared at the diversion take-in meetings, allegations have been made that women who made disclosures of abuse to the police were subsequently approached by Elders who would try to persuade them not to use the criminal justice system. Apparently, this was often done by emotional blackmail, or "guilt trips." . . . In one instance, the victim was approached by a male Elder and was advised to "just put this behind her" and get on with her life.
>
> It was alleged that victims who persisted were sometimes bribed or visited by spiritual representatives who again tried to "persuade" them to drop the matter, sometimes through the use of "bad medicine." If the victims continued to persist [sic], we were told that the victim's abuser might be sent to intimidate them. (98)

A *Vancouver Sun* (31 July 1992:B4) headline read "Indians fear justice experiment will hush sex abuse charges," and the associated reportage provided more detail than the subsequent project review four years later, relying on reports from female community members. Women reported the cover-up of sex-abuse charges and the use of intimidation tactics. One woman told of "several cases where powerful families pressured women to use the alternative system, which involves the band's [sic] council of elders, rather than bring sexual assault charges to court." The newspaper account concluded, "But some native women wonder about how the council can handle cases of sexual assault given the history of denial by some elders."

Critiques by urban Coast Salish women, in addition to those coming from the reserve populations, eroded the viability of the program to the point that "detractors became bold and believed the Justice Ministry was on their side," in the words of Judge Douglas Campbell, and they "won the war [ended the program] by not fighting a battle" (Campbell, interview). Sharon McIvor, a lawyer and spokesperson for the Native Women's Association of Canada, for example, noted that "the nightmare for abused native women proves native men are not ready for self-government" (*Vancouver Sun*, 31 July 1992, B4, original in paraphrase). Project operations ended in February 1993, and the final report concerning the project was filed two years later.

In this chapter I considered the "preamble," a much-publicized case of diversionary justice that was described in the academic literature and in justice circles as an example of indigenous justice at its best and that purported to show the facility with which elders councils could operate and deliver aboriginal justice. This case set the stage for the creation of an education project designed to teach mainstream justice officials about Coast Salish concepts, and this was followed by a diversionary justice project, the South Island Justice Project. The project, however, foundered through its failure to account for variability in beliefs and practices, for generational differences, for interfamilial suspicions and the consequent issues of confidentiality, and for the failure of intersubjective agreement about who belongs to the category of honored elder. In addition, the relations between band governments and tribal council were treated unproblematically. The outcome of the project renders unclear whether the "lowest common denominator" approach—taking only mutually agreeable concepts from the "law" of various families—is workable as a basis for a justice program.

Conclusion

This tour of aboriginal justice in Coast Salish communities of Washington State and British Columbia is constructed around the idea that colonial processes have transformed and distorted the politics of indigenous communities, including the ways in which community members understand their own prior practices of justice. Rather than providing a primordialist account of justice, I show the ways in which these understandings have changed historically and some of the consequences for the development of community-level justice. In particular, I point to the analytic value in treating the developments in indigenous justice as linked to the rise of the international ethnonationalist movements that effectively emphasize the moral claims to self-governance and appeals to retributive justice by minority ethnic groups. These claims are made in repudiation of European-derived centralized, rationalistic, bureaucratic, territorial, and universalistic nation-states. In addition, I employ the related concepts of resistance and accommodation within indigenous communities fractured by colonialism and domination and characterized by changing forms of internal differentiation and internal conflict.

Much of the debate within communities takes place at the level of claims to tradition and the sacred, cultural conceptions that remain invaluable as guides to community members and useful in managing relations with the outside world. Such debates, however, are less helpful in managing relations inside and in helping to create a justice forum in which community members as a whole may feel that their views are heard and that they have had what they feel to be an appropriate "day in court." The Coast Salish communities, with their own forms of internal differentiation in the period before contact, have been fractured in new ways, with new practices of internal domination. At the beginning of the twenty-first century, the problems of self-governance, particularly the management of justice systems that both promote and symbolize internal control, are exacerbated by these internal struggles and by the continuing pressures on indigenous communities imposed by the mainstream societies. A widely shared response among indigenous communities of both the United States and Canada has been to reorganize politically around the rhetoric of rejection of mainstream society's values and organizational practices with the hope of restoring the practices and values of earlier periods. But it is the act of rejection that has led away from the careful consideration of class, status, wealth, and power differences, features of life that are wrongly said to characterize only mainstream society, in promoting justice practices instead organized around concepts of elderhood, healing, restoration, primordiality, and spiritual purity. Much of the discourse about elders (but not necessarily by elders) and about healing reflects reactions to the imposition by the outside world rather than the way life was lived at one time. The use of elders as a means to buffer communities from external influences has misrepresented their family roles and drawn attention away from working through the difficult problems of how families might relate to one another and how individuals relate to the community. I have not argued that discourses of health and restorative justice are destructive but, rather, that consensus cannot be assumed concerning what direction to head and that a fuller debate about these fundamental local issues is needed in creating valued systems of justice. Substantial agreement within communities will not arise from unchallengeable and didactic claims to authority through particular understandings of tradition. Instead, tradition remains a seductive trap.

Because justice and law are not simply spiritual in nature, but rather are political as well, they concern defining crime and providing or denying access to legal processes. Disguising the workings of power and authority, I have argued, undermines the capacity of the new justice systems to achieve legitimization in the eyes of community members and to provide a real forum for the identification and resolution of problems. Much of the current discourse about justice is built on faulty notions, or at least public claims, of an earlier, Edenic society that cannot be emulated; such discourse is ultimately unnecessary and self-defeating. I have further argued that the present-day discourses obscure much of what might be of value from earlier Coast Salish concepts and practices of justice, particularly the ways in which landscape and ancestral names have been connected to thinking through problems and promoting resolution. These concepts are not forgotten by community members, however, and remain a significant resource for emergent formal systems. In fact, as I write this conclusion, a Stó:lō transformer rock near the Fraser River was inadvertently destroyed by the Canadian Pacific Railroad, and commentary by Sonny McHalsie and elders published in the *Vancouver Sun* in August 1999 emphasized the importance of the rock as a reminder to "do good."

In addition, the discourses I have described further contribute to a simplification and distortion of prior social and cultural practice that indigenous communities have been forced to undertake in order to establish legal authority, negotiate treaties, and claim lands. These self-representations potentially create problems for the future by becoming fixed in print and legally established but unable to meet the requirements of unforeseen legal battles. They create problems in the present by obscuring more subtle, less easily described, cultural practices that are central to Coast Salish thought and that give richness, flexibility, and strength, but that have little or no overlap with the conceptions of the mainstream society.

The importation of nonlocal alternative dispute resolution models of aboriginal justice, promoted by the state as an effective means of quickly and cheaply diverting a portion of the problems of justice to aboriginal communities, remains a threat to communities developing their own programs. These models are not attuned to subtle local concepts of power and are premised on the concept that indigenous communities are fundamentally the same. Nader (1990; see also Nader and Ou 1998) has pointed to related problems: the models divert attention from systemic, endemic problems by identifying the struggles as localized and encapsulated and necessarily amenable to mediation or similar processes. Further, these models disguise differences of power, a significant problem for families struggling to maintain good relations and vigilant in watching that others do not gain an unfair advantage. The widely promoted Navajo Peacemaker program, perhaps unlike the Family Group Conferencing model, differs from the Western-style alternative dispute resolution system in the reliance on prayer, on lay rather than professional support people, in the use of a peacemaker who is not chosen on the criteria of neutrality, and in the seeking for consensus rather than the imposition of judgment by an arbiter (Nielsen 1998). But this program shares features with alternative dispute resolution in that it is aimed at a limited range of localized, personalized problems between individuals who can, ultimately, find common ground (referred to as consensus), rather than systemic issues or between groups and individuals who disagree in their fundamental understandings of justice (Yazzie and Zion 1995, 1996; Nielsen 1998). This Navajo system provides limited guidance for the creation of a more comprehensive system.

In short, Canadian indigenous communities have been pushed into making inadequate, reified claims about their own prior practices to meet the demands of contemporary politics with the nation-state. Discourses have arisen that misrepresent ways in which indigenous practices overlap with Western legal categories and Western psychological thought and that boil the ambiguity and consequent flexibility out of the system. Further, by placing much of the discourse out of the way of open debate by employing the language of primordiality and sacredness, the ways in which the new justice initiatives advantage one group within society and place others at risk remain unexamined. A consequence of all of this is that tribal political movements concerned with removing indigenous communities from the coercive power of the state have come to rely on radically conservative (mis)representations. A comparative examination of the justice practices of neighboring Coast Salish communities of Washington State, which have considerably different political circumstances, reveals that misleading oppositions between Western and indigenous justice need not be the starting point for developments in British Columbia. Instead, features of both systems of justice can be incorporated into indigenous systems in a manner that can potentially accommodate the diverse interests and viewpoints of community members.

More specifically, I point to a series of justice issues that contemporary Coast Salish communities in two countries approach dramatically differently. Although much of this variation can be explained on historical grounds and by differences in national public policy, the variation is also an outcome of the personal conviction of community leaders such as those featured in chapter 5. These fundamental issues continue to be debated everywhere in the Coast Salish world. The first of the issues concerns the authority by which tribal justice systems are created and operate and, by extension, the independence of their operation. Typically, the will of the community as a whole and tribal sovereignty are given as the source of judicial authority, backed by ancestral and spiritual sanctions. In this case, tribal government can incorporate the views of chiefs (elected or hereditary), elders, tribal bureaucrats and administrators, tribal members, and tribal justice officials. But the South Island debacle suggests the limitations of the extreme approach to justice that separates elders and elected tribal governments by placing sole authority in the hands of individual elders and elders councils as interpreters of traditional law and as judges and agents of restorative justice. Indeed, the former chief of the Cowichan band specified that the major failing of the SIJP was this division between elders and elected band councils (Alphonse, interview).

A second, profoundly difficult issue is the legal relationship between the competing constituent families that make up bands and tribes. Since families typically attempt to resolve internal difficulties without outside intervention, interfamily issues remain the greatest puzzle to be encountered in the administration of justice. In a broad sense, the relations between families cannot be resolved simply by dispute resolution practices (such as the Navajo Peacemaker program), which conceive of problems as personal, low level, and amenable to the creation of consensus between wronged parties and wrongdoers. The Navajo Peacemaker program specifies that crime be identified as between individuals, not between the individual and the state, as in Western justice, a frequently made claim concerning the nature of indigenous justice. But because tribal justice systems are an arm of governance by a sovereign or semi-sovereign entity (the only grounds on which tribes might actually have justice systems, as Doreen Maloney of Upper Skagit pointed out in her discussion with the Stó:lō), larger, more comprehensive issues must be incorporated within the scheme of justice. While indigenous justice may well once have been the sum of the total of the law as articulated by the separate families, as it was conceptualized in the South Island Justice Project, this sort of family law does not address the big issues of the day. The present-day relations between families include fundamental concerns such as the problems of domination of the tribal council by large, powerful families; access to tribal jobs and services; access to tribal land and houses; and, more generally, how to define nepotism. In this sense, then, one can identify two entities: a corporate tribe (which is a creation of contact and was not a legal entity in earlier periods) and the various families. Families, in the current world, relate to one another not simply directly, but through the tribal structure of governance. It is this three-sided relationship that must be worked out and that cannot be addressed, as the south island case shows, by the creation of a third body, elders, which is thought to unproblematically stand outside of family politics. The Upper Skagit system, and potentially the Stó:lō approach, allow for the incorporation of elders as culture bearers and interpreters of history and law, without requiring or foregrounding this elder role.

A third issue is the conception of justice employed in tribal justice programs. A program strictly arranged around the metaphors of healing and restoration appears to be needlessly limiting and to have arisen from the rejection of Western justice. The more incorporative Upper Skagit approach, which allows for restitution and rehabilitation, as well as punishment, creates a wider range of ways to engage the justice system, as is appropriate to a diverse community.

A fourth issue is the association of tribal justice with a particular approach to culture and spirituality. If one regards the community as diverse, as I have done here, then the protection of diversity appears critical to the creation of a community where all have access to justice. At Upper Skagit, religious practitioners participate in code creation concerning areas of special interest to themselves and may be called in as culture experts at trial; likely something similar may emerge at Stó:lō. The case of the SIJP demonstrates that associating justice with a particular spiritual practice limits the numbers able to participate in a justice system, as wrongdoers and as participants of other sorts, and disenfranchises many. In this way, the justice system marginalizes itself and cuts out the possibility for a broad construction of justice.

The three cases show a variety of paths to the creation of law and the role of elders. Resolution by tribal council is one path to the creation of code. Another path, the use of "boilerplate" from other jurisdictions, has been criticized because it is said to erode traditional practices and to reduce tribal judicial independence (Brandfon 1991). The material from the several Coast Salish tribes of Puget Sound, however, reveals how a process of tailoring code to fit local needs and viewpoints occurs. A study of tribal courts nationwide found that "Indian judges inevitably draw upon their own sense of justice and fairness in deciding cases and interpreting legislation, so their decisions reflect custom and tradition" (Cooter and Fikentscher 1992:562). As a consequence, "*Tribal law is distinctly more Indian as applied than written*" (563, emphasis mine; see also Tso 1989; Vincenti 1995). The Puget Salish materials show other useful routes to code creation as well. Tribal justice committees can suggest particular needs that can be put on paper by legal advisers. At Upper Skagit, particular constituent groups have been consulted concerning legislation affecting them directly. This system allows the direct participation of elders on justice committees and as members of the tribal general council (all enrolled members) who can advance law at annual general meetings. Further, case law, although limited at present, provides a further location for elders to provide direction (as a group, as court-certified elders, or as called in on a case-by-case basis). The multiplicity of sources for code allows for community diversity and for continued debate.

At Stó:lō, the code-writing process is still rudimentary and conducted largely at the level of the "nation," that is, chiefs and senior officials working with tribal bureaucracy. Broad community consultation has not yet occurred, although efforts have been made. The *Sqwélqwels ye Stó:lō* (2, no. 6 [August 1999]: 14) called for suggestions for renaming Family Group Conferencing to reflect Stó:lō "ownership," and in March 2000 a "naming ceremony" was held in order that the alternative justice program receive an "official Halq emeylem name: *Qwi:qwelstom*," a term that "means to live in harmony, help one another to survive, to care and share amongst all people, if there are any disputes or conflicts it is resolved amongst family, elders, friends" (*Sqwelqwels ye Stó:lō* 3, no. 5 [May 2000]: 1). Community workshops have been held to "develop policies and procedures that are specific to the Stó:lō people." The SIJP, on the other hand, avoided broad consultation and relied instead on the elders committee to articulate the law.

There are three final issues, which I presented in chapter 1: the manner in which the systems articulate with the outside world, the related issue of the "reach" of the system, and, perhaps most significantly, the way in which internal problems and critiques are addressed. I present them here together because I have claimed that some efforts at justice are derailed by their attention to managing relations with the outside world (while, ironically, emphasizing their primordial nature), thereby eroding their capacity to come to grips with local issues of power and the critiques of constituents.

All three systems described here developed their own formal and informal strategies for dealing with the dominant mainstream society. This is perhaps easiest for the Upper Skagit and other tribes of Puget Sound that employ their own police, judges, and other justice personnel and that have entered into various agreements with other jurisdictions. These tribes have strengthened their jurisdiction by other means as well, including the creation of code in criminal areas in which they appear not to have jurisdiction under the Major Crimes Act. Perhaps most significantly, the codes and constitutions of the Upper Skagit and other tribes allow for the importation of federal, state, and other tribal law as they see fit, thereby helping to fend off the long arm of the federal justice system in those cases in which the tribal court would otherwise appear to have no remedy available. These two strategies have both extended the reach of the tribal courts and defended their systems from encroachment, but both strategies depend on deploying legal language that does not appear to be "traditional" in nature. Unlike the approach of the South Island Justice Program, these strategies of resistance do not rely on emphasizing differences with the mainstream law in content, in claims to moral priority, and in paradoxical and weak claims to parity through demonstrating comparability of Coast Salish and mainstream legal personnel and concepts. Instead, direct measures are made that rely on the realpolitik of understanding the loopholes in mainstream legal concepts and local and national politics. One might say that the outside world must be contended with, but not at the risk of ignoring the local.

Now, finally, what of the efforts to address internal critiques? The South Island Justice Project was tied to a construct, the primordial law as interpreted by elders, that placed itself above reproach. As a consequence, women's complaints about being coerced and complaints from both men and women of irrelevance were not effectively addressed. By seeking to remove itself from band politics, which was dismissed as merely hand in hand with the mainstream system, the SIJP instead ensured that local power politics would subvert the system.

In developing its own infrastructure, especially in the areas of child custody and the management of youth, the Stó:lō Nation is struggling to find ways to respond to the demands for local band authority and the demands by families for privacy and family autonomy over its own members. While the Stó:lō Nation promotes a particular view of justice, other voices are not dismissed and may well be accounted for in the imagined future of Stó:lō governance. Indeed, concrete actions have already been taken by some of the constituent bands that have altered the method of selecting band councilors by moving from an elected system to a system of designated family leaders that is said to reflect earlier practices. These changes have been directed to the problems of power generally and specifically to the domination of elections by large families and the effective exclusion of small ones. Significant debate has arisen over the issue of the centralization versus regionalization of service delivery, a problem that gets at the issues of inclusion, equity, and the balance of power between large and small bands. Developments such as these reflect a willingness to address fundamental issues of justice, seen as the appropriate relations between constituent social units. It is not yet clear whether a means will develop for these debates to occur directly in the process of governance and the delivery of justice, and whether Stó:lō people will have direct means to critique Stó:lō central policy. The current ideology holds that all Stó:lō leaders serve to reflect the wishes of their band members, particularly elders. Those who fail to do so stand to be recalled from office. This view gives an inadequate accounting for community diversity, however, or of the play of power, central themes in this book.

As is the case with the Stó:lō, the Upper Skagit system allows for the removal of councilors who fail to meet the expectations of constituents at the time of elections. Groups within the tribe can participate in redrafting code directly affecting them. Those convicted in tribal court can appeal to a superior court within Indian country, but not at Upper Skagit. But there are limitations to the handling of internal critique. Although U.S. tribal courts have failed to create a "balance of powers" and to conduct judicial review of the legislation and executive orders of tribal government (Brandfon 1991), Upper Skagit allows its court to rule on tribal law produced by the council or through other routes. This avenue might develop further with time.

The implications of the debates about justice in Coast Salish territory are far-reaching and suggestive. They are far-reaching in that they concern fundamental questions of social reorganization in communities and nations around the world that have reassumed some measures of autonomy and whose citizens have shifted in jural status from colonial subject to national citizen. Worby and Rutherford (1997:65), writing about contemporary Africa, ask, "What kind of identities and what arenas of actions 'has the law'—in both its colonial and postcolonial manifestations—made it possible for subjects and citizens to imagine?" The Coast Salish are far from alone in their struggles with tradition and their efforts to imagine their own changing identities under state law and tribal law. The debates about justice are suggestive for other debates in indigenous communities in British Columbia, Washington State, and elsewhere, including those about efforts to transfer authority over education and health services from the state to tribes. Here, too, claims to authority by tradition mix with efforts to imagine a new, larger-scale, reconfigured society.

Series Editors' Afterword

The "indigenous" is no longer tourism or artisanry, but rather the struggle against poverty and for dignity.—Subcomandante Insurgente Marcos, *Masks and Silences*

Few people working in native communities in North America at virtually any time in the last two decades, on reservations and beyond, have been able to avoid lengthy discussions of native justice systems. Where broad community mobilization and confrontation captured the headlines in the Red Power era of the 1960s and 1970s, indigenous justice systems have quietly but pervasively emerged in the 1980s and 1990s as alternatives to past efforts. Native courts are now, and for some time have been, a central focus of pragmatic efforts at reestablishing native "autonomy"—at mobilizing and deploying a form of sovereignty that combines grassroots strategies of organizing with a view of what surrounding states are willing to tolerate, condone, and support. The stakes seem smaller in the current debates: semi-autonomous institutions largely framed and limited by external authorities, but which, nevertheless, seek and gain some control over the social life of their own communities. Yet in ways that are not always obvious, native court systems strike at the same issues and reflect the same tensions—issues and tensions of poverty and dignity—as did past projects, despite differences in form and scale. This is certainly the case in the communities discussed by Bruce Miller in *The Problem of Justice*—an insightful title and a work that points to the fact that notions of justice are often a problematic element, a hurdle as it were, in people's efforts to mobilize courts for larger community projects.

As the events discussed in *The Problem of Justice* make clear, issues of justice and the study of native courts take us to the heart of characteristic, widespread situations and struggles in native communities over poverty and dignity (especially in North America, but we suspect elsewhere as well), and beyond these, to more abstract but in some ways far more relevant issues of power—how a community or group lives with, avoids, and, in some instances, gains power in ways that are substantially different from those around them. A discussion of these topics—poverty, dignity, and power, respectively—quickly points us to some widely shared reasons that native courts are both central to contemporary strategies of native sovereignty, and why these courts are simultaneously so difficult to sustain over the long term.

Poverty in native communities, to begin, ordinarily has different causes, some different consequences, and, especially, substantially different remedies or potential remedies among native people and for native communities than elsewhere in the surrounding society.

Recently, the political right—taking the historical products of its own long-term racism as the result of "natural" processes—has begun to ask whether indigenous people are characteristically different from any other victim of prejudice, any other object of current discrimination, including (inevitably) poor whites? The traditional left has, likewise, posed what seems a different question, but one that is in the end very closely related. Pointing out that all peoples who are the objects of prejudice and discrimination are, as a socially and culturally constructed category of people, internally differentiated into rich and poor, employed and unemployed, politically connected and powerless—to invoke just the simplistic polar differences, they ask: are the characteristic relations between the poor and the powerful among indigenous people really any different than they are among any other peoples?

To start with a simplification: the answer to both questions is, most often, yes, despite the fact that both questions are posed in ways meant to ensure negative responses. And the reasons for answering yes, and hence the importance of *The Problem of Justice*, have to do with the fact that native peoples in the United States and Canada form communities with a too-small, but still significant, amount of sovereignty, particularly over their own people and some of their own resources. Further, it turns out that by lumping native individuals into very general categories, such as "Indian" or "persons of color," the dominant society binds native individuals to their own communities in particularly poignant ways. For if, by way of example, an African American moves away from a small town in the South and goes to Chicago, he or she is usually still an African American once in Chicago. A Cherokee, Tewa, or Papago in Chicago usually becomes, socially and culturally, simply "Indian"; and in New York City he or she is often lumped in with that all-purpose category of color, "Puerto Rican." In sum, when natives move away, the result is not just to leave a way of life but often an entire collective identity. And the collective identity that matters in such communities is rarely as abstract as what is meant in the wider society by "Indian," but something much more specific—and often also, simultaneously, something much broader: something like "human being," an identity that is hard to effectively claim in a prejudiced society, yet one that can be simply lived among one's own, where, indeed, the most salient identities are wrapped around and through one's own personal name and interpersonal connections.

An individual's name, connection, and place are for many the most meaningful sources of individual *dignity* they know as well. And, as it turns out, they together form a kind of dignity that is largely immobile.

The sovereignty that native political communities can claim, combined with the ties that bind people to these communities, gives the community as a political entity (and thus those who control it) an unusual amount of power over the lives of its own people. It is a complicated kind of power, deeply mixed with very ordinary forms of powerlessness and intimately linked with issues of internal differentiation. All political power depends on powerlessness, but Native American sovereignty raises special issues within native communities. For an introductory example: the Navajo tribal council can, in ways they could not in almost any other community in the country, allow multinational corporations such as Peabody Coal to pursue uranium or coal mining on their reservation in a manner that poisons their own land and water—and thus in ways that are particularly harmful to the poorer Navajos who live from and on the land—and then use a portion of the mining royalties to fully subsidize college scholarships for "all" Navajo children, that is, primarily those who grew up speaking English, who could finish high school, who did not need to tend their grandmother's sheep and cut her firewood so she would not starve or freeze in the winter. Critically, part of what allows them to do this—part, that is, of what prompts Navajo people themselves to permit this—is the fact that Navajo people derive a fundamental and equally pervasive form of dignity from a way of life that is, at its base, caught up with being Navajo, and not simply Indian. And this dignity is necessarily linked to understanding oneself as a part of the community, part of the subject that acts as community, even when these actions violate one's own body, future, or family. For, as Eric Wolf points out, before one can be an agent in one's own history, one must first be the subject of one's own history (1999:21–67; see also Smith 1989). Simplistic notions of poverty or even internal difference inevitably miss this point. For Native Americans in North America, this links dignity—in its most basic form, the sense and consequence of knowing that one matters—with being part of a community. As Kirk Dombrowski notes in a previous book in this series, this is what makes such communities appear to those outside them as hopelessly factionalized, while to those within, they more usually appear as simply a community in search of itself (Dombrowski 2001).

For this reason, poverty and oppression play out very differently on reservations than off, and this difference takes us to courts in indigenous communities and to power more generally.

In subtle and direct fashion, Bruce Miller, in this exceptionally well-drawn, descriptive analysis of Coast Salish community courts, has provided us with a study of power *in, and over, one place*. The importance of this notion is often overlooked by both Native Americans and those from outside who work with them, though for different reasons. Power in a single place is at once so familiar to Native Americans and so foreign to those outside that it often passes without comment from within and without notice from without. Indeed, from Miller's description it is clear that, however new the form and process of native courts may be in this region, this aspect of their history runs very deep. We can find a revealing analogy when we look at the North American indigenous political form of "Beloved Elder," widespread during the period of early contact in Southeastern North America (see Sider 1993). With Beloved Elders we find a form of power and influence that was, like Salish courts, exquisitely local: Beloved Elders' influence and their capacity to shape events extended only as far as the reach of their personal respect, and thus rarely beyond their town.

The importance of this notion is difficult to grasp, as we have only recently come to grips with the idea that power, in the ways we know it best (state power, class power, colonialism, gender, race), is always constituted over, and more accurately through, difference (Sider 1987). Indeed political, economic, and cultural power all take their structure and dynamic force, their various anatomies and physiologies, their forms and lives, from the precise ways they combine, articulate, and differentiate people and places. Strategies of power are thus ordinarily fluid, fragile, and deeply situational, such that power has always to reform itself over the waste it leaves behind. Yet it does so most effectively when it is able to mobilize or even manufacture novel forms of difference in the scorched earth of its own past, forms of difference that make no mention of the pasts it overlays—as when Beloved Elders disappeared and were replaced with "chiefs" in the cauldron of colonialism (Gearing 1962); or as, for example, in the United States, where differences of race have given way to differences in citizenship status (which is, ostensibly, "race" free) in the transition to post-Fordist production and the attendant increasing use of "illegal aliens" in the mainstream American economy. Like electrical power, the most fitting root metaphor for power in its human forms, political-economic-cultural power comes into being only through resistance, only through the existence of the poles it marks. Absent these, power seems to disappear. Put another way, what makes power *power* is its capacity to produce unequal difference, not just within but between specific locations, locales, in ever-new, ever-reforming, and ever-ahistorical fashion.

Power in one place is, from this perspective, a strange creature—at its core, fragile, easily broken, easily captured, easily changed. It is also dangerous to those who hold it, for it is relatively easily harnessed to serve external ends. This is so because, however much power in a place may dominate those within its sphere of influence, by being restricted to one sphere of influence it is fundamentally compromised by having to live with its own past. The control and influence it exercises within its own community, over its own poor and vulnerable, measures its weakness and its limits, not just its strength. This is the lesson of the Navajo example.

Yet, given what was said above, about dignity as well as poverty, native courts hold out a special hopefulness for individuals in these same communities, the hope that their own desire for dignity can assume institutional form. This is why, given the obvious (by this time) perils of native courts and justice systems—perils both detailed and qualified in *The Problem of Justice*—native communities continue to invest such projects with interest and with deep and sincere emotions. For what is at stake in each of the three court projects discussed by Miller is the possibility of placing issues of dignity at the center of local efforts to reclaim lost sovereignty and autonomy.

This is what makes a justice a problem, not an answer, but which nevertheless makes courts the seat of hope and promise, almost regardless of form, context, or who sits on them. What we see implicitly, then, throughout this perceptive case study, we might suggest (and really only suggest, for consideration and debate) directly: native power must, we believe, develop pan-native ties that claim and mobilize relations between diverse communities—even antagonistic and unequal relations—if native power, control, and influence over their own are to move from frequently self-destructive to usually life-building. The development of new, and newly effective, relations between native communities is not simply a matter of good will within and between native communities but a proper topic for the internal organization, procedures, standards, and, ultimately, co-involvement of native community courts with one another. Yet in and through these efforts, the subtext of dignity must itself become more explicit and must also become a part of the process of linking one community with another. Put another way, social justice, perhaps more than legal, procedural, historical, or local justice, must come to the forefront of native justice—for this is the central hope that inspires the search for alternative forms of power and dignity, even as hope is formed to both recognize and struggle against the limits of alternative forms of power.

Kirk Dombrowski Gerald M. Sider

REFERENCES

Dombrowski, Kirk. 2001. *Against Culture: Development, Politics, and Religion in Indian Alaska*. Lincoln: University of Nebraska Press.

Gearing, Fred. 1962. *Priests and Warriors: Social Structures for Cherokee Politics in the 18th Century*. American Anthropological Association Memoir 93. Menasha WI: American Anthropological Association. First published in *American Anthropologist* 64(5), part 2 (October 1962).

Sider, Gerald. 1987. "When Parrots Learn to Talk and Why They Can't: Domination, Deception, and Self-Deception in Indian-White Relations." *Comparative Studies in Society and History* 29(1): 3–23.

———. 1993. *Lumbee Indian Histories*. New York: Cambridge University Press.

Smith, Gavin. 1989. *Livelihood and Resistance: Peasants and the Politics of Land in Peru*. Berkeley: University of California Press.

Wolf, Eric. 1999. *Envisioning Power: Ideologies of Dominance and Crisis*. Berkeley: University of California Press.

References

INTERVIEWS

Aleck, Joe, Stó:lō elder, member of the House of Elders, 22 July 1996.

Alphonse, Dennis, Cowichan elder and former chief, 19 November 1998.

Blomfield, Kate, Stó:lō code writer, 1 June 1999.

Campbell, Judge Douglas, 26 November 1998 (by phone).

Carlson, Keith, Stó:lō historian, 29 December 1998, 19 June 1999.

Commodore, Margaret, Stó:lō elder, former Yukon minister of justice, 4 June 1998.

Coochise, Elbridge, NICS head judge, 5 April 1995.

George, Rosaleen, Stó:lō elder, 9 June 1998.

Gutirrez, Allen, Stó:lō elder, 23 May 1996.

Gutirrez, Tilly, Stó:lō elder, 23 May 1996.

Herrling, Elizabeth, Stó:lō elder, 9 June 1998.

Julian, Shirley, Stó:lō elder, Language Development Center, Stó:lō Nation, 9 June 1998.

Kelly, Hugh, Stó:lo elder, 26 May 1998.

McHalsie, Albert "Sonny," Stó:lō cultural adviser, 26 May 1998, 29 June 1998.

Malloway, Frank, Stó:lō elder, 3 and 14 June 1998.

Maloney, Doreen, Upper Skagit counselor, 16 September 1998.

Maloney, Jim, First Nations Tribal Justice Institute, 1 June 1998.

Peters, Dorris, Stó:lō elder, 21 and 24 May 1998.

Point, Jeff, culture specialist and educator, interview with Jane McMillan, 2 June 1998.

Sampson, Tom, elder and former chair of the South Island Justice Project, 18 November 1998.

Stogan, Vince, Musqueam elder, 28 June 1996.

Suo, Martin, Justice Department, 29 January 1999.

Tennant, Paul, professor of political science, University of British Columbia, and South Island Justice Project participant, 12 February 1999.

ADDITIONAL REFERENCES

Abel, Richard L. 1981. Conservative Conflict and the Reproduction of Capitalism: The Role of Informal Justice. *International Journal of the Sociology of Law* 9 (3): 245–67.

Aboriginal Justice. 1992. Special issue. UBC *Law Review*.

Albers, Patricia, and Beatrice Medicine. 1983. *The Hidden Half: Studies in Plains Indian Women*. Lanham MD: University Press of America.

Alfred, Taiaiake. 1999. *Peace, Power, Righteousness: An Indigenous Manifesto*. Oxford: Oxford University Press.

a.m. Research Services, Sheila Clark and Associates, Valerie Lannon and Associates, Inc. 1995. *Building the Bridge: A Review of the South Vancouver Island Justice Education Project*. Final Report. Victoria BC: Ministry of Attorney General, Department of Justice Canada, and Solicitor General of Canada.

Amoss, Pamela T. 1977. The Power of Secrecy among the Coast Salish. In *The Anthropology of Power: Ethnographic Studies from Asia, Oceania, and the New World*, ed. Raymond D. Fogelson and Richard N. Adams, 131–40. New York: Academic Press.

———. 1978. *Coast Salish Spirit Dancing: The Survival of an Ancestral Religion*. Seattle: University of Washington Press.

Arcand, Chief Stanley. 1999. Clobbering the First Nations with a New "Frontier Thesis." *Globe and Mail* (Toronto), 10 May, A13.

Asch, Michael. 1997. Introduction. *Aboriginal and Treaty Rights in Canada: Essays on Law, Equality, and Respect for Difference*, ed. Michael Asch, ix–xv. Vancouver: University of British Columbia Press.

Asher, Brad. 1993. "They Are Satisfied If a Few Could Be Hung": Indian Legal Consciousness and White Law on Puget Sound, 1875–1889. Paper presented at the annual meeting of the American Society for Ethnohistory.

———. 1994–95. A Shaman-Killing Case on Puget Sound, 1873–74. *Pacific Northwest Quarterly* 86–87:17–24.

———. 1999. *Beyond the Reservation: Indians, Settlers, and the Law in Washington Territory, 1853–1889*. Norman: University of Oklahoma Press.

Barnett, Homer. 1955. *The Coast Salish of British Columbia*. Eugene: University of Oregon Press.

———. N.d. Field Notebooks. Special Collections and University Archives, University of British Columbia.

Barsh, Russel L., and James Youngblood Henderson. 1980. *The Road: Indian Tribes and Political Liberty*. Berkeley: University of California Press.

Basso, Keith H. 1996. *Wisdom Sits in Places*. Albuquerque: University of New Mexico Press.

Bell, Diane. 1988. Aboriginal Women and the Recognition of Customary Law in Australia. In *Indigenous Law and the State*, ed. Bradford W. Morse and Gordon R. Woodman, 297–313. Providence RI: Foris.

Bennett, Lee A. 1972. *Effect of White Contact on the Lower Skagit Indians*. Washington Archaeological Society Occasional Paper no. 3. Seattle: Washington Archaeological Society.

Bierwert, Crisca. 1986. Tracery in the Mistlines: Semiotic Readings of Stó:lō Culture. Ph.D. diss., Department of Anthropology, University of Washington.

———, ed. 1996. *Lushootseed Texts: An Introduction to Puget Salish Narrative Aesthetics*. Lincoln: University of Nebraska Press.

———. 1999. *Brushed by Cedar, Living by the River: Coast Salish Figures of Power*. Tucson: University of Arizona Press.

Blomfield, Kate. 1999a. Work Prospectus: Stó:lō Nation Legal Researcher. Manuscript.

———. 1999b. Common Law and Aboriginal Conceptualization of Property. Manuscript prepared for Stó:lō Nation Aboriginal Rights and Title.

———. 1999c. Recording Stó:lō Legal Principles: Options and Issues. Draft manuscript. 30 August.

Boas, Franz. 1894. The Indian Tribes of the Lower Fraser River. In *64th Report of the British Association for the Advancement of Science for 1890*, 454–63. London.

Borneman, John. 1997. *Settling Accounts: Violence, Justice, and Accountability in Postsocialist Europe*. Princeton: Princeton University Press.

Boxberger, Daniel L. 1987. The Dispossessed: Indian Homesteaders in the Sauk-Suiattle River Valley. Paper presented at the annual meeting of the American Society for Ethnohistory, Oakland CA.

———. 1989. *To Fish in Common: The Ethnohistory of Lummi Indian Salmon Fishing*. Lincoln: University of Nebraska Press.

Boyd, Robert. 1990. Demographic History, 1774–1874. In *The Handbook of North American Indians*, vol. 7, ed. Wayne Suttles, 135–48. Washington DC: Smithsonian Institution Press.

Brakel, Samuel J. 1979. *American Indian Tribal Courts: The Costs of Separate Justice*. Chicago: American Bar Association.

Brandfon, Fredric. 1991. Tradition and Judicial Review in the American Indian Tribal Court System. UCLA *Law Review* 38 (4): 991–1018.

Brown, Michael F. 1991. Beyond Resistance: A Comparative Study of Utopian Renewal in Amazonia. *Ethnohistory* 38 (4): 388–413.

Burnett, Donald L., Jr. 1972. An Historical Analysis of the 1968 "Indian Civil Rights" Act. *Harvard Journal on Legislation* 9: 556–626.

Carlson, Keith Thor. 1996. The Lynching of Louie Sam. *BC Studies* 109:63–79.

———. 1997a. Stó:lō Exchange Dynamics. *Native Studies Review* 11 (1): 5–48.

———, ed. 1997b. *You Are Asked to Witness: The Stó:lō in Canada's Pacific Coast History*. Chilliwack BC: Stó:lō Heritage Trust.

Clairmont, Don. 1998. Developing and Evaluating Justice Projects in Aboriginal Communities: A Review of the Literature. Manuscript, Ministry of the Solicitor General of Canada.

Clifford, James. 1988. *The Predicament of Culture: Twentieth Century Ethnography, Literature and Art*. Cambridge: Harvard University Press.

Clifford, James, and George E. Marcus, eds. 1986. *Writing Culture: The Poetics and Politics of Ethnography*. Berkeley: University of California Press.

Codere, Helen. 1950. *Fighting with Property*. Monographs of the American Ethnological Society, no. 18. New York: American Ethnological Society.

Collins, June McCormick. 1949. John Fornsby: The Personal Document of a Coast Salish Indian. In *Indians of the Urban Northwest*, ed. Marion W. Smith, 287–341. New York: Columbia University Press.

———. 1950. The Growth of Class Distinctions and Political Authority among the Skagit Indians during the Contact Period. *American Anthropologist* 70:331–42.

———. 1974a. A Study of Religious Change among the Skagit Indians of Western Washington. In *Coast Salish and Western Washington Indians*, vol. 4. New York: Garland.

———. 1974b. *Valley of the Spirits: The Upper Skagit Indians of Western Washington*. Seattle: University of Washington Press.

Comaroff, John L. 1996. Ethnicity, Nationalism, and the Politics of Difference in an Age of Revolution. In *The Politics of Difference: Ethnic Premises in a World of Power*, ed. Edwin N. Wilmsen and Patrick McAllister, 162–84. Chicago: University of Chicago Press.

Comaroff, John, and Jean Comaroff. 1991. *Of Revelation and Revolution: Christianity, Colonialism, and Consciousness in South Africa*. Vol. 1. Chicago: University of Chicago Press.

Conley, John, and William O'Barr. 1998. *Just Words: Law, Language and Power.* Chicago: University of Chicago Press.

Connor, Walker. 1994. *Ethnonationalism: The Quest for Understanding.* Princeton: Princeton University Press.

Cooter, Robert D., and Wolfgang Fikentscher. 1992. Is There Indian Common Law? The Role of Custom in American Indian Tribal Courts, Part 2. *Center for the Study of Law and Society* 46 (3): 509–80.

Cruikshank, Julie. 1998. *The Social Life of Stories: Narrative and Knowledge in the Yukon Territory.* Lincoln: University of Nebraska Press.

Culhane [Speck], Dara. 1987. *An Error in Judgement: The Politics of Medical Care in an Indian/White Community.* Vancouver: Talonbooks.

———. 1995. Justice and Healing: Aboriginal Peoples in Canada. *Journal of Human Justice* 6 (2): 141–60.

———. 1998. *The Pleasure of the Crown: Anthropology, Law and First Nations.* Burnaby BC: Talonbooks.

Darnell, Regna. 1998. Towards a History of Anthropology in Canadian Departments of Anthropology: Retrospect, Prospect, and Common Cause. *Anthropologica* 30 (2): 153–68.

Deloria, Vine, Jr., and Clifford Lytle. 1984. *The Nations Within: The Past and Future of American Indian Sovereignty.* New York: Pantheon Books.

Denis, Claude. 1997. *We Are Not You: First Nations and Canadian Modernity.* Peterborough ON: Broadview Press.

Depew, Robert. 1996. Popular Justice and Aboriginal Communities. *Journal of Legal Pluralism and Unofficial Law* 36:21–67.

Dewhirst, John. 1976. Coast Salish Summer Festivals: Rituals for Upgrading Social Identity. *Anthropologica* 18 (2): 231–73.

Donaldson, Laurie C. 1985. Change in Economic Roles of Suquamish Men and Women: An Ethnohistoric Analysis. Master's thesis, Department of Anthropology, Western Washington University.

Duff, Wilson. 1952. *The Upper Stalo Indians of the Fraser Valley, British Columbia.* Anthropology in British Columbia Memoir no. 1. Victoria: British Columbia Provincial Museum.

———. 1964. *The Indian History of British Columbia.* Vol. 1: *The Impact of the White Man.* Anthropology in British Columbia Memoir no. 5. Victoria: British Columbia Provincial Museum.

———. N.d. Field Notebooks. British Columbia Archives, Collection GR-2809. Wilson Duff Papers, HAL-W-001/7.

Dyck, Noel. 1993. Telling It Like It Is: Some Dilemmas of Fourth World

Ethnography and Advocacy. In *Anthropology, Public Policy and Native Peoples in Canada*, ed. Noel Dyck and James B. Waldram, 192–212. Montreal: McGill-Queens University Press.

Dyck, Noel, and James B. Waldram, eds. 1993. *Anthropology, Public Policy and Native Peoples in Canada*. Montreal: McGill-Queens University Press.

Elmendorf, William. 1993. *Twana Narratives: Native Historical Accounts of a Coast Salish Culture*. Seattle: University of Washington Press.

Everson, Andrew Frank. 2000. Renegotiating the Past: Contemporary Tradition and Identity of the Comox First Nation. Master's thesis, Department of Anthropology and Sociology, University of British Columbia.

Fienup-Riordan, Ann. 1990a. The Yupiit Nation: Eskimo Law and Order. In *Essays: Yup'ik Lives and How We See Them*, ed. Ann Fienup-Riordan, 192–220. New Brunswick NJ: Rutgers University Press.

———. 1990b. Original Ecologists? The Relationship between Yup'ik Eskimos and Animals. In *Essays: Yup'ik Lives and How We See Them*, ed. Anne Fienup-Riordan, 167–91. New Brunswick NJ: Rutgers University Press.

Finnegan, R. 1988. *Literacy and Orality: Studies in the Technology of Communication*. Oxford: Oxford University Press.

First Nations of South Island Tribal Council. 1987. Aboriginal Self Determination, Indian Family Law, Tribal Indian Governments. Manuscript.

———. 1990. Briefing Notes: An Introduction to Aboriginal Justice and the Function of an Elders Council. A Presentation to Cross-Cultural Awareness Workshop, Parksville/Nanoose, BC, 9–11 March. Manuscript.

Fisher, Robin. 1992. *Contact and Conflict: Indian-European Relations in British Columbia, 1774–1890*. 2d ed. Vancouver: University of British Columbia Press. Original ed., 1977.

Fiske, Jo-Anne. 1993. Child of the State, Mother of the Nation: Aboriginal Women and the Ideology of Motherhood. *Culture* 13 (1): 17–35.

———. 1995. The Supreme Law and the Grand Law: Changing Significance of Aboriginal Law for Aboriginal Women of British Columbia. *BC Studies* 105–6: 183–200.

———. 1996. The Womb Is to the Nation as the Heart Is to the Body: Ethnopolitical Discourses of the Canadian Indigenous Women's Movement. *Studies in Political Economy* 51: 65–95.

———. 1997–98. From Customary Law to Oral Tradition: Discursive

Formation of Plural Legalisms in Northern British Columbia, 1857–1993. BC *Studies* 115–16: 267–88.

Fiske, Jo-Anne, and Patty J. Ginn. 1998. Discourse and Defiance: Law, Healing and Implications of Communities in Resistance. Manuscript.

Fitzpatrick, P. 1992. The Impossibility of Popular Justice. *Social and Legal Studies* 1 (2): 199–215.

Fleras, Augie, and Jean Leonard Elliott. 1992. *The Nations Within: Aboriginal State Relations in Canada, the United States, and New Zealand*. Toronto: Oxford University Press.

Foucault, Michel. 1979. *Discipline and Punish: The Birth of the Prison*. New York: Vantage Books.

Fournier, Suzanne, and Ernie Crey. 1997. *Stolen from Our Embrace: The Abduction of First Nations Children and the Rebuilding of Aboriginal Communities*. Vancouver: Douglas and McIntryre.

Galaway, Burt, and Joe Hudson. 1996. *Restorative Justice: International Perspectives*. Monsey NY: Criminal Justice Press.

Ginn, Patty. 1998. Stó:lō Housing: Report for the Stó:lō Nation and UBC Ethnographic Field School.

Glass, Aaron. 1998. Stó:lō Slavery: Report for the Stó:lō Nation and UBC Ethnographic Field School.

Glavin, Terry. 1993. Rebuilding Stó:lo Fisheries Law: Report of the Community Consultation Process. Parts 1 and 2. Manuscript.

Gledhill, John. 1994. *Power and Its Disguises: Anthropological Perspectives on Politics*. London: Pluto Press.

Glenn, H. Patrick. 1997. The Capture, Reconstruction, and Marginalization of Culture. *American Journal of Comparative Law* 45 (3): 513–620.

Gordon, Robert J. 1989. The White Man's Burden: Ersatz Customary Law and Internal Pacification in South Africa. *Journal of Historical Sociology* 2: 41–65.

Grant, Peter R. 1982. Role of Traditional Law in Customary Cases. In Native People and Justice in Canada. Special issue 2. *Canadian Legal Aid Bulletin* 5 (2–3): 107–10.

Green, Ross Gordon. 1998. *Justice in Aboriginal Communities: Sentencing Alternatives*. Saskatoon SK: Purich.

Griffiths, Curt Taylor, and Charlene Belleau. 1995. Addressing Aboriginal Crime and Victimization in Canada: Revitalizing Communities, Cultures and Traditions. In *Popular Justice and Community Regeneration: Pathways of Indigenous Reform*, ed. Kayleen M. Hazelhurt, 165–86. Westport CT: Praeger.

Griffiths, Curt Taylor, and Ron Hamilton. 1996. Sanctioning and Healing: Restorative Justice in Canadian Aboriginal Communities. In *Restorative Justice: International Perspectives*, ed. Burt Galaway and Joe Judson, 175–91. Monsey NY: Criminal Justice Press.

Guilmet, George M., Robert T. Boyd, David L. Whited, and Nile Thompson. 1991. The Legacy of Introduced Disease: The Southern Coast Salish. *American Indian Culture and Research Journal* 15: 1–32.

Haberfeld, Steven, and Jon Townsend. 1993. Power and Dispute Resolution in Indian Country. *Mediation Quarterly* 10:405–22.

Hamilton, Ron. 1994. Implications of Alternative Justice on Community Healing. Talk given at Indian Health Awareness Days, University of British Columbia, 10 February.

Harkin, Michael. 1997. A Tradition of Invention: Modern Ceremonialism on the Northwest Coast. In *Past Is Present: Some Use of Tradition in Native Society*, ed. Marie Mauze, 97–112. Lanham MD: University Press of America.

Harmon, Alexandra. 1998. *Indians in the Making: Ethnic Relations and Indian Identities around Puget Sound*. Berkeley: University of California Press.

Harring, Sidney L. 1994. *Crow Dog's Case: American Indian Sovereignty, Tribal Law, and the United States Law in the Nineteenth Century*. Cambridge: Cambridge University Press.

Harris, Cole. 1997. *The Resettlement of British Columbia: Essays on Colonialism and Geographical Change*. Vancouver: University of British Columbia Press.

Havemann, Paul. 1988. The Indigenization of Social Control in Canada. In *Indigenous Law and the State*, ed. Bradford W. More and Gordon R. Woodman, 71–100. Providence RI: Foris.

Hazelhurst, Kayleen M., ed. 1995. *Popular Justice and Community Regeneration: Pathways of Indigenous Reform*. Westport CT: Praeger.

Hedican, Edward J. 1995. *Applied Anthropology in Canada: Understanding Aboriginal Issues*. Toronto: University of Toronto Press.

Hill-Tout, Charles. 1978. *The Salish People: The Local Contribution of Charles* Hill-Tout. Vol. 3: *The Mainland Halkomelem*, ed. Ralph Maud. Vancouver: Talonbooks.

Hoebel, E. Adamson. 1967. Law Ways of the Comanche Indians. In *Law and Warfare*, ed. Paul Bohannon, 183–294. New York: National History Press.

Holden, Madronna. 1976. Making All Crooked Ways Straight. *Journal of American Folklore* 89 (July): 271–93.

Hornborg, Alf. 1994. Environmentalism, Ethnicity, and Sacred Places: Reflections on Modernity, Discourse, and Power. *Canadian Review of Sociology and Anthropology* 31 (3): 245–67.

Hoyle, Marcia L. 1995. "A Fitting Remedy": Aboriginal Justice as a Community Healing Strategy. In *Popular Justice and Community Regeneration: Pathways of Indigenous Reform*, ed. Kayleen M. Hazelhurt, 143–64. Westport CT: Praeger.

An Illustrated History of Skagit and Snohomish Counties. 1906. Chicago: Interstate.

Jackson, Michael. 1992. In Search of the Pathways to Justice: Alternative Dispute Resolution in Aboriginal Communities. In Aboriginal Justice. Special issue. UBC *Law Review*, 147–238.

Jacobs, Melville, and Elizabeth Jacobs. N.d. Field Notes. Melville Jacobs Collection, Allen Library, University of Washington.

Jenness, Diamond. 1955. *The Faith of a Coast Salish Indian*. Anthropology in British Columbia Memoir no. 3. Victoria: British Columbia Provincial Museum.

Jilek, Wolfgang. 1982. *Indian Healing: Shamanic Ceremonialism in the Pacific Northwest Today*. Reprint, Vancouver: Hancock House. Original ed., 1974.

Johnson, Ralph W., and Rachael Paschal, eds. 1991. *Tribal Court Handbook for the 26 Federally Recognized Tribes in Washington State*. Olympia: Office of the Administrator for the Courts, Washington State Courts.

Jorgensen, Joseph G. 1978. A Century of Political Economic Effects on American Indian Society, 1880–1980. *Journal of Ethnic Studies* 6 (3):1–82.

Just, Peter. 1992. History, Power, Ideology and Culture: Current Directions in the Anthropology of Law. *Law and Society Review* 26 (2): 373–412.

Kan, Sergei. 1989. *Symbolic Immortality: The Tlingit Potlatch of the Nineteenth Century*. Washington DC: Smithsonian Institution Press.

Keesing, Roger M. 1992. *Custom and Confrontation: The Kwaio Struggle for Cultural Autonomy*. Chicago: University of Chicago Press.

Kew, J. E. Michael. 1976. Salmon Abundance, Technology, and Human Populations on the Fraser River Watershed. Unpublished manuscript, Department of Anthropology and Sociology, University of British Columbia.

———. 1990a. History of Coastal British Columbia since 1849. In The

Handbook of North American Indians, vol. 7, ed. Wayne Suttles, 159–68. Washington DC: Smithsonian Institution Press.

———. 1990b. Central and Southern Coast Salish Ceremonies since 1900. In *The Handbook of North American Indians*, vol. 7, ed. Wayne Suttles, 476–80. Washington DC: Smithsonian Institution Press.

Kew, J. E. Michael, and Bruce G. Miller. 1999. Locating Aboriginal Governments in the Political Landscape. In *Seeking Sustainability in the Lower Fraser Basin*, ed. Michael Healey, 47–63. Vancouver: Institute for Resources and the Environment, Westwater Research.

Kidwell, Clara Sue. 1991. Systems of Knowledge. In *America in 1492: The World of the Indian Peoples before the Arrival of Columbus*, ed. Alvin Josephy Jr., 369–404. New York: Vintage Books.

Knight, Rolf. 1978. *Indians at Work: An Informal History of Native Indian Labour in British Columbia, 1858–1930*. Vancouver: New Star Books.

Krawll, Marcia. 1994. *Understanding the Role of Healing in Aboriginal Communities*. Ottawa: Solicitor General of Canada, Aboriginal Peoples Collection.

Kulchyski, Peter, Don McCaskill, and David Newhouse. 1999. *In the Word of Elders: Aboriginal Cultures in Transition*. Toronto: University of Toronto Press.

Lambert, Justice John Douglas. Address to University of British Columbia School of Law. 29 February 1998.

LaPrairie, Carol. 1992. Exploring the Boundaries of Justice: Aboriginal Justice in the Yukon. Report to the Department of Justice, Yukon Territorial Government, First Nations, Yukon Territory. Ottawa: Department of Justice Canada.

———. 1994. Changing Directions in Criminal Justice. Ottawa: Department of Justice Canada.

———. 1996. The New Justice: Some Implications for Aboriginal Communities. Ottawa: Department of Justice Canada.

LaRocque, Emma. 1997. Re-examining Culturally Appropriate Models in Criminal Justice Applications. In *Aboriginal and Treaty Rights in Canada: Essays on Law, Equality, and Respect for Difference*, ed. Michael Asch, 75–96. Vancouver: University of British Columbia Press.

Lazarus-Black, Mindie. 1994. Slaves, Masters and Magistrates: Law and the Politics of Resistance in the British Caribbean, 1736–1834. In *Contested States: Law, Hegemony and Resistance*, ed. Mindie Lazarus-Black and Susan F. Hirsch, 252–81. New York: Routledge.

Leresche, Diane. 1993. Native American Perspectives on Peacemaking. *Mediation Quarterly* 10 (4): 321–24.

Levin, Michael D., ed. 1993. *Ethnicity and Aboriginality: Case Studies in Ethnonationalism*. Toronto: University of Toronto Press.

Littlefield, Loraine. 1995. Gender, Class and Community: The History of Sne-Nay-Muxw Women's Employment. Ph.D. diss., Department of Anthropology, University of British Columbia.

Llewellyn, Karl, and E. Adamson Hoebel. 1941. *The Cheyenne Way*. Norman: University of Oklahoma Press.

Malinowski, Bronislaw. 1926. *Crime and Custom in Savage Society*. London: Kegan, Paul, Trench, Trubner.

Marino, Cesare. 1990. History of Western Washington since 1846. In *The Handbook of North American Indians*, vol. 7, ed. Wayne Suttles, 169–79. Washington DC: Smithsonian Institution Press.

Mauze, Marie, ed. 1997. *Past Is Present: Some Use of Tradition in Native Society*. Lanham MD: University Press of America.

McDonnell, Roger F. 1992. Contextualizing the Investigation of Customary Law in Contemporary Native Communities. *Canadian Journal of Criminology* 34: 299–316.

———. 1995. Prospects for Accountability in Canadian Aboriginal Justice Systems. In *Accountability for Criminal Justice: Selected Essays*, ed. P. Stenning. Toronto: University of Toronto Press.

McEachern, Chief Justice Allan. 1991. Reasons for Judgement, *Delgamuukw v* R. Smothers Registry. No. 0843.

McHalsie, Sonny. 1999. "That the Business Was Done": Stories of Conflict and Leadership in Stó:lō Oral History. Paper presented at the Stó:lō: People of the River ll Conference, 22 October, Chilliwack BC.

———. N.d. Stó:lō Fishing Law. Manuscript in author's possession.

McMillan, Leslie Jane. 1998. Stó:lō Traditional Justice. Report to UBC-Stó:lō Nation Ethnographic Field School.

McMullan, Cindy. 1998. Bringing the Good Feelings Back: Imagining Stó:lō Justice. Master's thesis, Department of Anthropology and Sociology, University of British Columbia.

Melton, Ada Pecos. 1995. Indigenous Justice Systems and Tribal Society. *Judicature* 75 (3): 126–33.

Merry, Sally Engle. 1988. Legal Pluralism. *Law and Society Review* 22 (5): 869–96.

———. 1990. *Getting Justice and Getting Even: Legal Consciousness among Working-Class Americans*. Chicago: University of Chicago Press.

———. 1991. Law and Colonialism. *Law and Society Review* 25 (4): 890–922.

———. 1999. Pluralizing Paradigms: From Gluckman to Foucault. *Political and Legal Anthropology Review* 22 (1): 115–22.

Miller, Bruce G. 1989a. After the FAP: Tribal Reorganization after Federal Acknowledgment. *Journal of Ethnic Studies* 17 (2):89–100.

———. 1989b. Centrality and Measures of Regional Structure in Aboriginal Western Washington. *Ethnology* 28 (3): 265–76.

———. 1990. An Ethnographic View: Positive Consequences of the War on Poverty. *American Indian and Alaska Native Mental Health: The Journal of the National Center* 4 (2): 55–71.

———. 1992a. Women and Politics: Comparative Evidence from the Northwest Coast. *Ethnology* 31 (4): 367–83.

———, ed. 1992b. Anthropology and the Courts. Special issue. *BC Studies* 95.

———. 1993. The Press, the Boldt Decision, and Indian-White Relations. *American Indian Culture and Research Journal* 17 (2): 75–97.

———. 1994a. Is There a Gender Gap in Tribal Elections? *American Indian Quarterly* 18 (1): 25–44.

———. 1994b. Contemporary Tribal Codes and Gender Issues. *American Indian Culture and Research Journal* 18 (2): 43–74.

———. 1994c. Contemporary Native Women: Role Flexibility and Politics. *Anthropologica* 35 (1): 57–72.

———. 1994d. Who's Looking After the Fish? *Literary Review of Canada* 3 (7): 14–16.

———. 1995. Folk Law and Contemporary Coast Salish Tribal Code. *American Indian Culture and Research Journal* 19 (3): 141–64.

———. 1996–97. The "Really Real" Border and the Divided Salish Community. *BC Studies* 112: 63–79.

———. 1997. The Individual, the Collective and Tribal Code. *American Indian Culture and Research Journal* 21 (1): 107–30.

———. 1998. The Great Race of 1941: A Coast Salish Public Relations Coup. *Pacific Northwest Quarterly* 89 (3): 127–35.

———. 1999. Culture as Cultural Defense: A Sacred Site in Court. *American Indian Quarterly* 22 (1): 83–97.

Miller, Bruce G., and Daniel L. Boxberger. 1994. Creating Chiefdoms: The Puget Sound Case. *Ethnohistory* 41 (2): 267–93.

Miller, Bruce, and Cindy McMullen. 1997. Stó:lō Aboriginal Justice: A Draft Report Submitted to the House of Justice and the House of Elders, Stó:lō Nation, 26 February 1997.

Miller, Bruce G., and Jen Pylypa. 1995. The Dilemma of Mental Health Paraprofessionals at Home. *American Indian and Alaska Native Mental Health: The Journal of the National Center* 6 (2): 13–33.

Miller, Jay. 1991. A Kinship of Spirits. In *America in 1492: The World of the Indian Peoples before the Arrival of Columbus*, ed. Alvin Josephy Jr., 305–38. New York: Vintage Books.

———. 1999. *Lushootseed Culture and the Shamanic Odyssey: An Anchored Radiance*. Lincoln: University of Nebraska Press.

Mills, Antonia. 1994. *Eagle Down Is Our Law: Witsuwit'en Law, Feasts, and Land Claims*. Vancouver: University of British Columbia Press.

Minor, Kevin I., and J. T. Morrison. 1996. A Theoretical Study and Critique of Restorative Justice. In *Restorative Justice: International Perspectives*, ed. Burt Galaway and Joe Hudson, 117–33. Monsey NY: Criminal Justice Press.

Momaday, N. Scott. 1991. The Becoming of the Native: Man in America before Columbus. In *America in 1492: The World of the Indian Peoples before the Arrival of Columbus*, ed. Alvin Josephy Jr., 13–20. New York: Vintage Books.

Monture-Angus, Patricia. 1995. *Thunder in My Soul: A Mohawk Woman Speaks*. Halifax NS: Fernwood.

Moon, Donna. 1999. Stó:lō Alternative Justice Programme: Family Group Conferencing. Paper presented at the Stó:lō: People of the River ll Conference, 23 October, Chilliwack BC.

Mooney, Kathleen. 1976. Social Distance and Exchange: The Coast Salish Case. *Ethnology* 15 (4): 323–46.

Moore, Sally Falk. 1986. *Social Facts and Fabrications: Customary Law on Kilimanjaro, 1880–1980*. New York: Cambridge University Press.

———. 1999. From Lawyer's Law into the Academic Zoo. *Political and Legal Anthropology Review* 22 (1): 101–5.

Morse, Bradford W. 1988. Indigenous Law and State Legal Systems: Conflict and Compatibility. In *Indigenous Law and the State*, ed. Bradford W. Morse and Gordon R. Woodman, 101–20. Providence RI: Foris.

Nader, Laura. 1990. *Harmony Ideology: Justice and Control in a Zapotec Mountain Village*. Stanford: Stanford University Press.

———. 1999. Pushing the Limits: Eclecticism on Purpose. *Political and Legal Anthropology Review* 22 (1): 106–9.

Nader, Laura, and Jay Ou. 1998. Idealization and Power: Legality and Tradition in Native American Law. In New Directions in Native American Law. *Oklahoma City University Law Review* 23 (spring/summer): 1–29.

Nahanee, Theresa. 1993. Dancing with a Gorilla: Aboriginal Women, Justice, and the Charter. In *Aboriginal Peoples and the Justice System: Report of the National Round Table on Aboriginal Justice Issues*, Royal Commission on Aboriginal Peoples, 360–62. Ottawa: Minister of Supply and Services Canada.

Nielsen, Marianne O. 1998. Navajo Courts, Peacemaking, and Restorative Justice Issues. *Commission on Folk Law and Legal Pluralism: Proceedings of the Twelfth International Symposium*, Williamsburg VA, 26 July–1 August, 167–84. Ottawa: Commission on FOlk Law and Legal Pluralism.

Nisga'a Treaty Negotiations: Agreement in Principle. 1996. Government of Canada, Province of British Columbia, and the Nisga'a Tribal Council.

Northwest Intertribal Court System (NICS). 1991a. Traditional and Informal Dispute Resolution Processes in Tribes of the Puget Sound and Olympic Peninsula Region. Edmonds WA: NICS.

———. 1991b. Summary: Traditional and Informal Dispute Resolution Processes in Tribes of the Puget Sound and Olympic Peninsula Region. Edmonds WA: NICS.

———. N.d. Appellate Court Opinions: Northwest Regional Appellate Court. Edmonds WA: NICS.

Norton, Helen. 1985. Women and Resources of the Northwest Coast: Documentation from the 18th and Early 19th Centuries. Ph.D. diss., Department of Anthropology, University of Washington.

O'Brien, Sharon. 1989. *American Indian Tribal Governments*. Norman: University of Oklahoma Press.

O'Donnell, Judge Edward. 1988a. Proceedings at Reasons for Judgement in the Matter of the Family Relations Act and Audrey Thomas and Allan John Jones. No. F-2808. Parkesville BC, 13 July.

———. 1988b. Letter to Chief Judge Josephson. 14 July 1988.

Olsen, Teresa, Gabrielle M. Maxwell, and Allison Morris. 1995. Maori and Youth Justice in New Zealand. In *Popular Justice and Community Regeneration: Pathways of Indigenous Reform*, ed. Kayleen M. Hazelhurt, 45–66. Westport CT: Praeger.

O'Nell, Theresa DeLeane. 1996. *Disciplined Hearts: History, Identity, and Depression in an American Indian Community*. Berkeley: University of California Press.

Pocklington, Tom, and Sarah Pocklington. 1993. Aboriginal Political Ethics. In *Corruption, Character and Conduct: Essays on Canadian Government Ethics*, ed. John W. Langford and Allan Tupper, 42–66. Oxford: Oxford University Press.

Pommerscheim, Frank. 1995. *Braid of Feathers: American Indian Law and Contemporary Tribal Life*. Berkeley: University of California Press.

Povinelli, Elizabeth A. 1993. *Labor's Lot: The Power, History and Culture of Aboriginal Action*. Chicago: University of Chicago Press.

Renteln, Allison D. 1994. Culture and Culpability: A Study of Contrasts. In *Folk Law: Essays in the Theory and Practice of Lex Non Scripta*, ed. Allison D. Renteln and Alan Dundes, 2: 863–79. New York: Garland.

Renteln, Allison D., and Alan Dundes, eds. 1994. *Folk Law: Essays in the Theory and Practice of Lex Non Scripta*. 2 vols. New York: Garland.

Roberts, Natalie Andrea. 1975. A History of the Swinomish Tribal Community. Ph.D. diss., Department of Anthropology, University of Washington.

Ross, Rupert. 1992. *Dancing with a Ghost*. Markham ON: Octopus.

———. 1996. *Returning to the Teachings: Exploring Aboriginal Justice*. Toronto: Penguin Books.

Royal Commission on Aboriginal Peoples. 1996. *Bridging the Cultural Divide: A Report on Aboriginal People and Criminal Justice in Canada*. Ottawa: Minister of Supplies and Services Canada.

Ruby, Robert H., and John A. Brown. 1986. *A Guide to the Indian Tribes of the Pacific Northwest*. Norman: University of Oklahoma Press.

Ryan, Joan. 1995. *Doing Things the Right Way: Dene Traditional Justice in Lac La Martre, N.W.T.* Calgary: University of Calgary Press.

Sampson, Chief Martin H. 1972. *Indians of Skagit County*. Skagit County Historical Society, series no. 2. Mount Vernon WA: Skagit Historical Society.

Sarris, Greg. 1993. *Keeping Slug Woman Alive: A Holistic Approach to American Indian Texts*. Berkeley: University of California Press.

Scott, Colin H. 1993. Customs, Tradition, and the Politics of Culture: Aboriginal Self-government in Canada. In *Anthropology, Public Policy and Native Peoples in Canada*, ed. Noel Dyck and James B. Waldram, 311–33. Montreal: McGill-Queens University Press.

Sharp, John. 1996. Ethnogenesis and Ethnic Mobilization: A Comparative Perspective on a South African Dilemma. In *The Politics of Difference: Ethnic Premises in World of Power*, ed. Edwin N. Wilmsen and Patrick McAllister, 85–103. Chicago: University of Chicago Press.

Sider, Gerald M. 1993. *Lumbee Indian Histories: Race, Ethnicity, and Indian Identity in the Southern United States*. Cambridge: Cambridge University Press.

Sider, Gerald M., and Gavin Smith, eds. 1997. *Between History and Histories: The Making of Silences and Commemorations*. Toronto: University of Toronto Press.

Smith, Marion W. 1940. *The Puyallup-Nisqually*. Columbia University Contributions to Anthropology no. 32. New York: Columbia University Press.

———. 1949. The Indian and Modern Society. In *Indians of the Urban Northwest*, ed. Marion W. Smith. New York: Columbia University Press.

———. 1950. The Nooksack, the Chilliwack, and the Middle Fraser. *Pacific Northwest Quarterly* 41 (4): 330–41.

Snyder, Sally. 1964. Skagit Society and Its Existential Basis: An Ethnofolkloristic Reconstruction. Ph.D. diss., Department of Anthropology, University of Washington.

———. N.d. Field Notes, Melville Jacobs Collection of Manuscripts, Special Collections, and University Archives, Allen Library, University of Washington.

Speck, Dara Culhane. See Culhane, Dara.

Stern, Bernhard J. 1969. *The Lummi Indians of Northwest Washington*. Reprint, New York: AMS Press. Original ed., New York: Columbia University Press, 1934.

Stó:lō Legal Principles and Treaty Presentation and Subsequent Discussion. 1999. Transcription by Kate Blomfield, summer legal researcher for Aboriginal Rights and Title department, Stó:lō Nation, 30 August.

Suttles, Wayne. 1954. Post-Contact Culture Change among the Lummi Indian. *British Columbia Historical Quarterly* 18 (1–2): 29–102.

———. 1963. The Persistance of Intervillage Ties among the Coast Salish. *Ethnology* 2: 512–25.

———. 1987a. *Coast Salish Essays*. Seattle: University of Washington Press.

———. 1987b. Private Knowledge, Morality, and Social Class among the Coast Salish. In *Coast Salish Essays*, ed. Wayne Suttles, 3–14. Seattle: University of Washington Press.

———. 1987c. The Plateau Prophet Dance among the Coast Salish. In *Coast Salish Essays*, ed. Wayne Suttles, 152–98. Seattle: University of Washington Press.

———. 1989. They Recognize No Superior Chief: The Strait of Juan De

Fuca in the 1790s. In *Culturas de la Costa Noroeste de America*, ed. Jose Luis Peset, 251–64. Madrid: Turner.

———. 1990. Southern Coast Salish. In *Handbook of North American Indians*, vol. 7, *Northwest Coast*, ed. Wayne Suttles, 485–502. Washington DC: Smithsonian Institution Press.

Swinomish Tribal Mental Health Project. 1991. *A Gathering of Wisdoms*. LaConner WA: Swinomish Tribal Community.

Tanner, Adrian. 1998. Healing, "Community Wellness" and the Individual. Paper presented to the Canadian Anthropology Society conference, Toronto.

Tennant, Paul. 1992. The South Island Justice Education Project: A Program Review Prepared for the Department of Justice. Manuscript. 30 June.

Thom, Brian David. 1995. The Dead and the Living: Burial Mounds and Cairns and the Development of Social Classes in the Gulf of Georgia Region. Master's thesis, Department of Anthropology and Sociology, University of British Columbia.

Thom, Brian, and Laura Cameron. 1997. Changing Land Use in S'olh Temexw. In *You Are Asked to Witness: The Stó:lō in Canada's Pacific Coast History*, ed. Keith Carlson, 163–80. Chilliwack BC: Stó:lo Heritage Trust.

Thornton, Thomas F. 1997. Anthropological Studies of Native American Place Naming. *American Indian Quarterly* 21 (2): 209–28.

Tso, Tom. 1989. The Process of Decision Making in Tribal Courts. *Arizona Law Review* 31:121–48.

Victor, Wenona. 1999. Traditional Stó:lō Justice: A Comparison and Contrast between Western Concepts of Justice and Stó:lō Concepts of Justice. Paper presented at the Stó:lō: People of the River ll Conference, 22 October, Chilliwack BC.

Vincent, Joan. 1994. *Anthropology and Politics: Visions, Traditions, and Trends*. Tucson: University of Arizona Press.

Vincenti, C. N. 1995. The Reemergence of Tribal Society and Traditional Justice Systems. *Judicature* 79 (3): 131–41.

Warry, Wayne. 1998. *Unfinished Dreams: Community Healing and the Reality of Aboriginal Self-Government*. Toronto: University of Toronto Press.

White, Richard. 1980. *Land Use, Environment and Social Change: The Shaping of Island County, Washington*. Seattle: University of Washington Press.

———. 1991. *The Middle Ground: Indians, Empire, and Republics in the Great Lakes Region, 1650–1815*. Cambridge: Cambridge University Press.

Whitten, Norman. 1996. The Ecuadorian Levantamiento Indigena of 1990 and the Epitomizing Symbol of 1992: Reflections on Nationalism, Ethnic-Bloc Formation and Racialist Ideologies. In *History, Power, and Identity: Ethnogenesis in the Americas, 1492–1992*, ed. Jonathon D. Hill, 193–218. Iowa City: University of Iowa Press.

Wilmsen, Edwin N., and Patrick McAllister, eds. 1996. *The Politics of Difference: Ethnic Premises in a World of Power*. Chicago: University of Chicago Press.

Wolf, Eric. 1982. *Europe and the People without History*. Berkeley: University of California Press.

Worby, Eric, and Blair Rutherford. 1997. Law's Fictions, State-Society Relations and the Anthropological Imagination—Pathways Out of Africa: Introduction. *Anthropologica* 39 (1–2): 65–69.

Wotherspoon, Terry, and Vic Satzewich. 1993. *First Nations: Race, Class, and Gender Relations*. Scarborough ON: Nelson Canada.

Yazzie, Robert, and James W. Zion. 1995. "Slay the Monsters": Peacemaker Court and Violence Control Plans for the Navajo Nation. In *Popular Justice and Community Regeneration: Pathways of Indigenous Reform*, ed. Kayleen M. Hazelhurt, 57–88. Westport CT: Praeger.

———. 1996. Navajo Restorative Justice: The Law of Equality and Justice. In *Restorative Justice: International Perspectives*, ed. Burt Galaway and Joe Hudson, 157–73. Monsey NY: Criminal Justice Press.

Zion, James W. 1988. Searching for Indian Common Law. In *Indigenous Law and the State*, ed. Bradford W. Morse and Gordon R. Woodman, 121–50. Providence RI: Foris.

Zlotkin, Norman. 1984. Judicial Recognition of Aboriginal Customary Law in Canada: Selected Marriage and Adaption Cases. *Canadian Native Law Reporter* 4:11–17.

Zotto, Marco. 1998. A Study of Two Tribal Courts in Washington State. Master's thesis, Department of Anthropology, Western Washington University, Bellingham.

Index

www.ingramcontent.com/pod-product-compliance
Lightning Source LLC
Chambersburg PA
CBHW052124270326
41930CB00012B/2748
9780803282759